BLACK MARKS: MINORITY ETHNIC AUDIENCES AND MEDIA

Black Marks: Minority Ethnic Audiences and Media

Edited by
KAREN ROSS
Coventry University, UK

with
PETER PLAYDON
Coventry University, UK

Ashgate

Aldershot • Burlington USA • Singapore • Sydney

Published by
Ashgate Publishing Limited
Gower House
Croft Road
Aldershot
Hampshire GU11 3HR
England

Ashgate Publishing Company
131 Main Street
Burlington, VT 05401-5600 USA

Ashgate website: http://www.ashgate.com

British Library Cataloguing in Publication Data
Black marks : minority ethnic audiences and media. -
    1. Mass media and minorities 2. Mass media - Audiences
    I. Ross, Karen II. Playdon, Peter
    302.2'3'089

Library of Congress Control Number: 2001088783

ISBN 0 7546 1425 5

Printed in Great Britain by
Antony Rowe Ltd, Chippenham, Wiltshire.

Contents

PART II: NEGOTIATING IDENTITY THROUGH ALTERNATIVE MEDIA USE

Notes on Contributors

S. Elizabeth Bird is Professor of Anthropology at the University of South Florida, Tampa, Florida. She is the author of *For Enquiring Minds: A Cultural Study of Supermarket Tabloids* (1992) and editor of *Dressing in Feathers: The Construction of the Indian in American Popular Culture* (1997), which was named a 1997 Outstanding Book on the Subject of Human Rights in North America by the Gustavus Myers Center for the study of Human Rights in America. She is also the author of numerous articles and book chapters in media and cultural studies.

Stuart Cunningham is Professor and Head, School of Media and Journalism, Queensland University of Technology, Brisbane. He is co-editor of *Floating Lives: The Media and Asian Diasporas*, Queensland University Press, St Lucia, 2000. The book reports research on the media use of communities of Chinese, Fiji Indian, Thai, and Vietnamese origin in Australia. The research was funded under an Australian Research Council Large Grant during 1996-1998. John Sinclair and Stuart Cunningham previously collaborated, together with Elizabeth Jacka,, as co-editors of *New Patterns of Global Television: Peripheral Vision* (1996).

Lynne Edwards is Assistant Professor of Communication Studies and Theatre at Ursinus College in Collegeville, Pennsylvania, USA. She is currently working on a grant to analyse print news coverage of juvenile crime during the last decade.

Alec G. Hargreaves is a Professor in the Institute for Contemporary French and Francophone Studies, Florida State University, USA. His publications include *Voices from the North African Immigrant Community in France: Immigration and Identity in Beur Fiction* (1991; 2nd edition 1997), *Immigration, 'Race' and Ethnicity in Contemporary France* (1995) and, co-edited with Mark McKinney, *Post-Colonial Cultures in France* (1997).

Andrew Jakubowicz is Professor of Sociology at the University of Technology Sydney, Australia, and a member of the Trans/forming Cultures Research Group. His areas of interest link cultural minorities with the media. He is the joint author of *Racism, Ethnicity and the Media* (1994), and *Ethnic Conflict and the Media* (1996). He has also been a consultant to the

Australian Human Rights Commission on racism and the media, and was consultant on New Media and the Cultural Industries to the Commonwealth Government's Creative Nation. He is executive producer of a 3 CDROM multimedia documentary project, 'Making Multicultural Australia - a multimedia documentary' in conjunction with the NSW Board of Studies Interactive Multimedia Group, the NSW EAC and SBS TV/Multimedia (released February 1999).

Marisca Milikowski is formerly an Associate Professor at the Department of Communication and affiliate to the Institute of Migration and Ethnic Studies (IMES) and the Amsterdam School of Communications Research (ASCoR) at the University of Amsterdam, Holland. She began her career as a journalist, and obtained a PhD in the psychology of cognition in 1995. She has published on the subjects of knowledge and thinking, and more recently also on media and multicultural issues.

Elizabeth Poole is a Lecturer in Media Studies at Staffordshire University, UK. She teaches in the areas of media, culture and society and new technologies. Her research interests are ethnicity, representation, news, audiences, diaspora and new media. The research included in this book was completed at the Centre for Mass Communication Research at the University of Leicester, UK.

Dorothy Roome currently teaches Film Studies, Television and Women's Studies at Towson University in Baltimore, USA. Since 1995 she has been working for her PhD at the Centre for Cultural and Media Studies at the University of Natal, South Africa. Her study of multi-cultural female focus groups identifies the connections between gender, race, class and social relations incorporating an ethnographic methodology with a cultural studies perspective. She has published in *Critical Arts*, the *International Journal of Cultural Studies* and the *Journal of Film and Video*.

Karen Ross is Director of the Centre for Communication, Culture and Media Studies at Coventry University, UK. She has published widely in the field of race, gender and representation in popular media and has recently completed a book on women politicians and the media (*Women, Politics, Media: Uneasy Relations in Comparative Perspective*, 2001). Her previous books include *Black and White Media: Black Images in Popular Film and Television* (1996), *Gender and Media* (edited with Deniz Derman and Nevena Dakovic, 1996) and *Managing Equal Opportunities in Higher Education* (co-authored with Diana Woodward, 2000).

John Sinclair is a Professor in the Department of Communication, Language and Cultural Studies, Victoria University of Technology, Melbourne. He is co-editor of *Floating Lives: The Media and Asian Diasporas*, Queensland University Press, St Lucia, 2000. The book reports research on the media use of communities of Chinese, Fiji Indian, Thai, and Vietnamese origin in Australia. The research was funded under an Australian Research Council Large Grant during 1996-1998. John Sinclair and Stuart Cunningham previously collaborated, together with Elizabeth Jacka,, as co-editors of *New Patterns of Global Television: Peripheral Vision* (1996).

Eli Skogerbø is Senior Lecturer in the Department of Media and Communication at the University of Oslo, Norway. She has a PhD in political science on the thesis *Privatising the Public Interest: Conflicts and Compromises in Norwegian Media Politics 1980-1993* (1996), and has published widely on issues related to media politics both in Norway and internationally.

Roza Tsagarousianou is Senior Lecturer at the Centre for Communication and Information Studies of the University of Westminster, UK. She has a PhD in Sociology from the University of Kent at Canterbury. She is the editor of *Cyberdemocracy: Technology, Cities and Civic Networks* (1998) and the author of articles and chapters on electronic democracy, nationalism, ethnic conflict, gender and mass communication, transnationalism, globalisation and diasporic media. She is currently directing a research project focusing on Britain's South Asian and Greek diasporic communities and their media.

Thomas Tufte is Associate Research Professor at the Department of Film and Media Studies, University of Copenhagen. He is the author of *Living with the Rubbish Queen: telenovelas, culture and modernity in Brazil* (2000), and co-editor of the forthcoming book *Global Encounters: Media and Cultural Transformation*. He is an Associate Member of the ORBICOM Network, and a member of the editoral boards for a number of Latin American journals of media and cultural studies. Since 1999 he has been conducting a research project on media and identity among ethnic minorities in Copenhagen.

Acknowledgements

This book has been some years in the making, prompted by my own research for a previous book on minority ethnic images and the media where I found much material on content but very little on audiences. And so the kernel of an idea for this book began to grow. I would like to thank all those who responded to my initial request for interest in providing an essay, all those years ago. I am very grateful to all the contributors whose work appears in this volume, who (mostly) worked wonderfully to the deadlines set and turned around material in excellent time. As with other work with which I have been involved, where essayists write in English although it is not their first language, I am again humbled and fascinated by the wonderful rhythms of the English prose which flows from the minds of those collaborators working from an altogether different linguistic provenance. I would also like to thank the anonymous reviewer of the early outline of this book whose positive take enabled this project to leave the imaginary and enter the realm of the real. I would like to thank all those colleagues and students with whom I have discussed many of the issues which are rehearsed again here, about the nature of 'race' and ethnicity, of the media and of our various reading practices. I would especially like to thank Pete Playdon who has worked diligently with me on shaping this text and whose forbearance in staying with what turned out to be a not inconsiderable editorial project is greatly appreciated. Lastly, my thanks to Barry, as ever.

Karen Ross
Summer 2001

Foreword

As rapid developments in new media technologies have made the world a smaller place, with video conferencing between continents a routine part of transatlantic communication, one of the responses of this push towards globalisation has been a retreat into ethnic nationalism, with conflicts in the Balkans and Israel being only the latest, dreadful casualty of attempts to claim a pristine ethnic identity and territory. Throughout this and all the other momentous events in recent history, the media have been a constant presence, recording, filtering and thus constructing the world in an apparently unproblematic 'as it is' way. Ironically, much of the struggle for territory and 'racial' purity in the 'real' world is predicated on precisely a rejection of the totalising tendencies to talk global instead of local, to talk cultural specificity (but for which read exclusivity/superiority) instead of cultural pluralism and diversity. From the theorising of scholars such as Stuart Hall (for example, 1980, 1988, 1991, 1997) and Paul Gilroy (1987, 1993) to the artefacts produced by 'minority' filmmakers such as Ngozi Unwurah, Julie Dash or Gurinder Chadha, the ambiguities and ambivalences of living through and with difference - and here I am talking specifically about ethnic and 'racial' difference - and claiming multiple identifications, are held in careful balance, sometimes this, sometimes that. The issues which arise as a consequence of living in at least two cultures have provoked fruitful areas for discussion and negotiation within media production and numerous practitioners have thoughtfully explored the intricacies and problematics of their own experiences in their own work, articulating precisely those equivocal and ambivalent themes (Malik, 1994).

'Race' and Media

The implications of a hundred years of minority ethnic communities being represented in the media by white people, constructed out of nothing more informed than the latter's largely prejudiced perspectives, have only recently begun to be addressed. What does it mean that an obviously subordinated minority - the situation of most minority ethnic communities living in Western societies at least - has been consistently portrayed by a white professional elite operating from a position of domination, with the bloodied history of 500 years of colonialism influencing their thinking about 'race' and ethnicity? If we have moved away from the view that the media perform merely a propagandist function and that we, as media consumers, simply sit passively drinking in the message, it is surely not too controversial to suggest that the media, by their framing of *this* event, rather than *that* event, tell us what to think *about* if not *what* to think. If most media products are inscribed with the same set of cultural assumptions (and prejudices) because their producers share the same cultural experiences, then those underlying norms and values which may well be hidden but nonetheless exist, are transmitted as an un-selfconscious truth. When we see a representation of 'blackness', it does not describe the actuality of being black but rather references a particular way of thinking about blackness: it is not about *being* black but being *thought of* as black. Although it is clear that different types of images produce greater or lesser degrees of truthfulness, are differentially close/distant in appearance to optical impressions, no image is other than a social construction viewed from a particular perspective and situated in a particular historical moment.

That most popular of popular media, television, here regarded as the manifestation of a set of discrete structural and institutional practices, plays a significant role in the way in which audiences understand the social world. The way in which programme-makers choose to represent particular communities in particular ways serves to reinforce ideas about cultural 'norms' and behaviours which, over time and with repeated circulation, become seen as simple and incontrovertible 'truths'. In an environment increasingly dominated by visual imagery, where those images themselves are controlled by very few organisations (Ginneken, 1997; Mowlana, 1997; Boyd-Barrett and Tantanen (eds), 1998), what is now at stake is not simply the representational image itself but rather what it connotes in the social world, its meaning and value in both the public imagination and more crucially, in the social order.

'Race' and Audience

The ways in which media researchers think about the collectivity called 'the audience' have changed significantly over the past few decades. An early preoccupation with the propagandist functions of mass media, identified a largely passive audience which indiscriminately consumed whatever messages the media gave them, that is, the one-way flow or hypodermic needle model (Katz and Lazarsfeld, 1955). Media theorists later began to move towards a perception of the audience as more active and individuated, negotiating television meanings in a self-reflexive manner and bringing to their televisual experience all kinds of personal beliefs and values (see, for example, Hall (ed.), 1980; Morley, 1980, 1986). What these theories suggested was that we should stop thinking about a 'mass' audience and instead consider audiences as comprising much smaller, discrete viewing segments: audiences could in fact comprise nothing more than a set of individual viewers all watching the same show but not sharing anything else in common. More recently, theoretical (and indeed empirical) work on 'the audience' has returned to some of the more problematic aspects of audience 'effect' and revisited some of the old orthodoxies around involvement and negotiation (Corner, 1995; Nightingale, 1996; Edelstein, 1997; Webster and Phalen, 1997; Dickinson et. al., (eds), 1998) and considered the new ways in which we can think about the audience in question (Ang, 1996; Alasuutari, (ed.), 1999; Seiter, 1999; Croteau and Hoynes, 2000). In some ways, the reinvention of the 'couch potato', albeit one who is a distinctive and unique entity, would seem to return us to those early theories of viewer passivity, but the crucial difference now is that viewers are assumed to be much more sophisticated in their ability to 'read off' meanings from televisual texts. Not for them an unthinking and uncritical ingestion of mass mediated products but rather a Pandora's Box of possible meanings, meanings moreover which they make, which they choose, depending on their own personal and individual textual reading.

Whilst it may be true that we are all, really, interacting with the television screen in various ways beyond simply exercising choice by the repeated stab of the remote control, it has yet to be proven that our actual behaviour, as viewers and as a collective audience has changed in fundamental ways (Seiter, 1999). And in any case, there remains a belief amongst some communities that the kinds of media representation which are broadcast *do* have effects on individual audience members, so that it *is* possible to talk about 'audience effect' (Ross, 1997). Work that I have undertaken with minority ethnic viewers makes very clear that many people believe that the portrayal of minority ethnic individuals and groups has an impact on the way in which white people deal with minority ethnic communities in real life (see Ross, 1997). In other words, that there is a direct cause and effect between media message and social behaviour.

This book explores the ways in which minority ethnic communities consume media and construct and reconstruct ethnic identity/ies through their negotiations with media texts. As such it provides a useful corrective to the almost complete invisibility of research studies with minority audiences. It brings together contributors from Europe, Africa, North America and Australia who all, in their different ways and with their focus on different ethnic communities, remind us of the diversity of the diaspora experience, the pernicious and stereotypical forms of ethnic address which are often present in mainstream media narratives and the strategies for negotiation and contestation. The book is organised in two principal sections, comprising essays which first look at audience perspectives on and relationships with mainstream media and secondly, which focus on audience resistance through a consideration of media produced by and for minority ethnic viewers, sometimes within the diaspora setting itself and sometimes distributed via satellite.

The book opens with two essays focusing on minority ethnic audiences and mainstream media use and reception in Britain. The essay by Karen Ross argues that minority ethnic audiences in Britain have rarely been asked their views on the way in which 'race' and 'ethnicity' is portrayed on mainstream television, still less how they might change those images, given the opportunity. The paper explores a research study which *did* ask those audiences those questions and provides some interesting insights into what it means to be British and 'Black'[1] in the third millennium. Through the conduct of 35 focus groups with viewers belonging to a variety of minority ethnic backgrounds, taking place across England and Wales, the essay argues that in many ways, minority communities are left out of the television picture and when they do appear, they are often cast in stereotypical roles which are consequent on the uninformed views of the predominantly white television industry. Minority audiences do not want special favours in terms of portrayal but rather would like to see their many and diverse selves and their different lives represented with more balance. For the majority of people who took part in the study, Britain is home and yet they feel dislocated and alienated from the very place which had encouraged their parents and grandparents to think of it as the 'mother country'.

Roza Tsagarousianou's essay draws on research with London's South Asian and Greek-Cypriot communities and their attitudes, evaluations and uses of the media available to them. Her paper examines and discusses the ways in which these communities use the diverse media available to them with particular reference to processes of ethnic community identity building and its positioning in the global/local nexus. Tsagarousianou argues that despite experiences of dislocation, marginalisation and exclusion, ethnic minority audiences display remarkable resilience, resourcefulness and skill in their consumption practices, articulating discourses of cultural rights relating to their ethnic and diasporic specificity but also claiming inclusion in the 'mainstream'. South Asian and Greek-Cypriot audiences' usage of media illustrate their capacity for domesticating, translating and creating meaning that is familiar and intelligible out of the 'foreign', creating a sense of space that is welcoming and inclusive in an institutional and cultural landscape which is often alien and exclusionary.

The next three essays in the collection focus specifically on the experiences of young viewers. For Thomas Tufte, this is in the context of minority ethnic communities in Denmark, while Lynne Edwards focuses on Black teenage girls in North America and Elizabeth Poole on young Muslims in Britain. Thomas Tufte argues that, rather than concentrating on theories of destablisation, the experience of transnational media could be seen to be contributing to a (re)stablising tendency in terms of a more fluid sense of ethnic identity. Migration, media and technology - along with numerous other elements of contemporary globalization - are leading to socio-spatial re-configurations, where the so-called 'national community' becomes just one of many equally important and emerging 'imagined' communities (after Benedict Anderson, 1983). Tufte suggests that members of minority ethnic groups who are also citizens of Denmark belong to diasporic communities which operate within very different socio-spatial and cultural-geographical coordinates and frames compared to their fellow citizens, the 'ethnic majority Danes'. His work draws out the diversity of media consumption amongst young minority audiences, from American sitcoms to Internet chat rooms to 'ethnic' satellite news, arguing that it is this plurality which creates the sense of being both local and global citizens.

Lynne Edwards sets out to answer a number of questions relating to media use by Black[2] teenage girls. Why do they prefer television programmes that feature Black and adolescent characters and what is going on in their lives that may explain these preferences? One explanation could be their need to explore different values at this stage in their lives. According to some psychologists, teenagers experience an 'identity crisis' as they explore different values in search of a value system to commit to. One way for girls to do this, albeit vicariously, is by viewing media content with Black teenage characters who are facing the same issues and concerns as themselves. Findings from Edwards' work show that Black girls do, indeed, prefer television programmes that feature Black and adolescent characters and that their values are reliable predictors of these programme preferences. However, the study also reveals differences in programme preferences according to different value system commitments, suggesting that the relationship between value systems and programme preferences is influenced by the girl's commitment to her values and by the programmes' consistency with those values.

The relationship between young Muslim audiences and the mainstream British press is the focus of Elizabeth Poole's essay. Given current theory on the demonisation of Islam in the British national media, Poole explores how British Muslims make meaning from images they see of Muslims in the national press. Using focus groups and a method of reception analysis, she examines Muslims' responses to a number of newspaper texts, including their immediate responses, their strategies for interpretation, their negotiation of meanings and how these differ in relation to situational factors such as gender. The findings show that young Muslims mostly reject the 'dominant' (being predominantly negative) textual constructions of Islam, even where Muslims are represented from distant ethnic/national groupings and geographical localities. Readers' religious identification with the subjects of news stories often resulted from the story's orientation of negativity in relation to Islam, causing either total rejection of the text or the transferal of negative characteristics onto cultural factors.

The last pair of contributions in this section look at the ways in which minority and majority audiences make different meanings and readings of mainstream texts. Dorothy Roome's essay[2] focuses on South Africa, suggesting that since the democratic elections in 1994, the concept of a nation ready to reconcile differences and homogenise its cultural identity to build prosperity has motivated the Government of National Unity. As part of this movement, the South African Broadcasting Corporation has encouraged the development of television programmes which address changing cultural standards and the negotiation of difference. Roome interviewed English, Zulu and Afrikaans women in a series of focus groups to ascertain their response to the situation comedy *Going Up III*, a programme created by a multi-cultural production team with a multi-cultural cast. In discussions of the text, different discourses emerge which are partially explained by factors such as the levels of education and institutional practices amongst group members. Women audiences explore their own sense of identity in response to the actions of the characters who depict changing circumstances and issues of integration in the new South Africa. Consumerism appears to motivate transformation among some women, who appear to be moving from community-based ethics to the development and valorisation of 'self.'

S. Elizabeth Bird's work looks at the representation of Native Americans, arguing that whilst a significant body of literature documents how American Indians have been represented in popular media, for example, naturalising the image of Indians as 'noble savage', little work has been undertaken on how media audiences, whether Indian or white, actually respond to these representations. Building on her own work in the field with white and Indian viewers, this current study pursues a highly original methodology to access latent beliefs about ethnic specificity. Bird undertakes an ethnographic analysis of the ways in which different viewer groups 'typify' ethnic portraits, asking white and Indian participants to write appealing television programme scenarios via group discussion. White participants tended to replicate conventional genres and created stereotypical Indian characters, while Indian participants explored their ethnic identity in very self-conscious ways. Bird concludes that most white Americans live in a media world that offers a range of pleasurable tools for identity formation, while Indians are permitted only an identity they do not recognise, and which they reject with both humour and anger.

The essays in the second part of the book look at the ways in which audiences specifically resist and challenge the normative renditions of various ethnic 'identities' as represented in mainstream media, either through their use of alternative media sources such as satellite television beamed in from their 'home' countries or locally produced 'minority' media. These essays focus on forms of contestation and negotiation of cultural and ethnic identity/ies, suggesting the dynamic movement of different ethnic identifications at different times in different circumstances, emphasising the fluidity of the concept of 'identity' itself. The first two contributions in this section focus on satellite television, specifically programmes and channels which are produced in 'homelands' and broadcast to widely dispersed diasporic viewing communities. Marisca Milikowski suggests that 'satellite watching' has become one of the most popular pastimes amongst Turkish families in the Netherlands. In order to understand how Turkish satellite television affects the Dutch-Turkish cultural boundary, as perceived by members of migrant Turkish communities themselves, Milikowski conducted a series of interviews and focus group discussions. The interest that migrants take in Turkish television is a complex phenomenon, so that on the affective side, young people and their first generation parents are affirmed in their love of and affinity to Turkish people, Turkish landscapes and Turkish cultural sights and sounds. On the information side, satellite TV has brought some surprises, particularly around changing constructions of what it means to be Turkish. Before the development of commercial satellite TV, younger Turks (that is, the 'second' generation) were caught up in the first generation's defensive definition of Turkishness. But part of the attractions of satellite television to young people today is that it offers a much less traditional picture of Turkishness.

Alec G. Hargreaves' work suggests that the advent of cable, satellite and digital technologies offer major new opportunities to minority ethnic groups and other previously marginalised audiences for alternative forms of ethnic identification. Drawing on fieldwork conducted among Maghrebis in France and Turks in Germany, Hargreaves argues that the impact of cable and satellite TV among minority ethnic audiences is more complex than is often thought. Cultural flows among diasporic groups, he argues, cannot be adequately understood within a simple, bi-polar model constructed around the 'home' countries of migrants on the one hand and the societies in which they have settled on the other. Viewing patterns among minority ethnic audiences need to be seen within a more complex multi-polar framework in which ethnicity, while certainly a factor, is not always the dominant force. Viewing choices are partly determined by other forms of difference traversing ethnic groups, such as age and gender, as well as by the growing diversity of programme sources.

The ways in which media are produced specifically for minority communities in their own locale is the focus of Eli Skogerbø's essay, which explores the little-known Sami community in Scandinavia. Unusually, this chapter looks at a minority ethnic community which is indigenous rather than migrant to a particular territory, here being the northern part of Scandinavia, and discusses the circumstances in which Sami media exist and are consumed. Skogerbø reports the findings from a recent project mapping the content and consumption of Sami media amongst the communities at which they are targeted. The specific focus of the essay is on the role of the media in the processes of identity construction amongst members of Sami society, in particular their concern with language as a marker of Sami culture and ethnic identity. The analysis shows that Sami media have different conceptions of Sami identity and that this leads to the possibilities of different strategies being offered for identification. Further, the analyses also show that significant (potential) audiences for Sami media are unable to access material because of geographical limitations of media distribution.

The last two essays in this collection focus on diaspora communities in Australia and the ways in which cultural diversity and media plurality present alternative identities to those which circulate in mainstream media forms. Stuart Cunningham and John Sinclair's chapter looks at a multiplicity of different 'disaporic' media, including video, television, cinema, music and Internet use, where peoples displaced from homelands by migration, refugee status, or business and economic imperatives, employ media to negotiate new cultural identities. These alternative media offer challenges for how public media and public culture generally can be thought about in our times. This chapter draws on their previous work with Asian diasporas, exploring the industrial dimensions, i.e. the pathways by which media travel to their multifarious destinations. Their analysis is also textual and audience-related, in that their work examines types of diasporic style and practice, where popular culture debates and moral panics are played out in culturally divergent circumstances amongst communities marked by internal difference and external 'othering.' Crucially, Cunningham and Sinclair interrogate further the nature of the public 'sphericules' which are formed around diasporic media.

Andrew Jakubowicz contributes the last essay in this collection, arguing that the Australian mediascape provides a fertile ground for exploring race and ethnic relations in terms of content, involvement in production and audience construction of meaning. His chapter discusses research findings with culturally diverse media audiences in Australia and their patterns of media consumption and use. For many ethnic communities, Australian media provide their main exposure to the 'host' culture and offer guides to what are 'appropriate' social behaviours. But, Jakubowicz asks, what do commercials actually 'teach' Cambodian refugees about child rearing? How does the news inform Serbian Australians about the situation in the Balkans? How have new technologies - the Internet, video, narrowcasting, for example - changed the processes through which meaning-making by audiences takes place? In answer, he suggests that indigenous audiences have sought to create their own communication spaces as they reject 'mainstream' accounts of their lives (or accounts of Australia in which their lives are absent). This multiplicity of audiences with very differing communication needs suggests both a fragmentation of public space, but also a potential realisation of previously excluded communication desires, though the consumption of alternative media forms by diverse diaspora communities.

This book provides a series of snapshots of the ways in which different minority ethnic audiences interact with media texts, sometimes focusing on mainstream media and cultural resistance, sometimes exploring the pleasures derived from consuming media texts produced by and targeted at specific minority ethnic communities. Although the geographical locations are diverse and the 'ethnicities' which form the focus of these chapters are also distinctive and different, there are common themes to be drawn from many of the essays presented here. These threads relate to the ways in which ethnic audiences do not simply 'accept' the renditions of themselves which they find in mainstream media but rather demonstrate that they actively engage and negotiate meaning, contest and refuse the often negative constructions of the migrant 'other' and find pleasure in alternative media texts. Crucially, these essays make clear that forms of ethnic identity and identification are not fixed and immutable but fluid and dynamic, changing within and between communities, generations and genders. At the dawn of the new millennium, these insights into the intricacies of media consumption (and representation) amongst migrant, diaspora and minority ethnic communities show the complex nature of the multicultural, multiethnic and polysemic world in which we all now live and the importance of media in both maintaining and subverting 'old' versions of 'new' realities.

Notes

1   For the purposes of this chapter, 'Black' is taken to mean individuals who are not white and who are regarded as different to 'white' Britons on the basis of their skin colour rather than their nationality, since the majority of non-white Britons were born in Britain.

2   A longer version of this chapter was published in *Critical Arts*, 1997, vol. 11, no. 1-2, pp. 66-94.

References

Alasuutari, P. (ed.) (1999), *Rethinking The Media Audience: The New Agenda*, Sage, London.

Ang, I. (1996), *Living Room Wars. Rethinking Media Audiences For A Postmodern World*, Routledge, London and New York.

Boyd-Barrett, O. and T. Rantanen, (eds) (1998), *The Globalization of News*, Sage, London.

Corner, J. (1995), *Television Form And Public Address*, Edward Arnold, London.

Croteau, D. and Hoynes, W. (2000), *Media/Society: Industries, Images And Audiences* (2nd edition), Pine Forge, London and Thousand Oaks, CA.

Dickinson, R., Harindranath, R. and Linne, O. (eds) (1998), *Approaches To Audiences. A Reader*, Arnold, London.

Edelstein, A. S. (1997), *Total Propaganda: From Mass Culture To Popular Culture*, Lawrence Erlbaum, Mahwah, N.J.

Gilroy, P. (1987), *There Ain't No Black In The Union Jack: The Cultural Politics Of Race And Nation*, Hutchinson, London.

-- (1993), *The Black Atlantic: Modernity And Double Consciousness*, Verso, London.

Ginneken, J. Van (1998), *Understanding Global News· A Critical Introduction*, Sage, London.

Hall, S. (ed.) (1980), *Culture, Media, Language. Working Papers In Cultural Studies, 1972-79*, Hutchinson in association with the Centre For Contemporary Cultural Studies, University Of Birmingham, London.

-- (1988), 'New Ethnicities', in K. Mercer (ed.), *Black Film: British Cinema*, ICA document no. 7, British Film Institute/ICA, London, pp. 27-31.

-- (1991), 'Old and New Identities, Old and New Ethnicities', in A. D. King (ed.), *Culture, Globalization and the World-System*, Macmillan, Basingstoke, pp. 41-68.

-- (ed.) (1997), *Representation: Cultural Representations and Signifying Practices*, Sage, London.

Katz, E. and Lazarsfeld, P. F. (1955), *Personal Influence. The Part Played By People In The Flow Of Mass Communications*, Collier Macmillan, London.

Malik, S. (1994), 'Beyond Identity: British Asian Film', *Black Film Bulletin*, 2(3), pp. 12-13.

McQuail, D. (1997), *Audience Analysis*, Sage, Thousand Oaks, London.

Morley, D. (1980), *The Nationwide Audience: Structure and Decoding*, British Film Institute, London.

-- (1986), *Family Television*, Routledge and Kegan Paul, London.

PART I
MINORITY AUDIENCES
AND MAJORITY MEDIA

1 White Media, Black Audience: Diversity and Dissonance on British Television

KAREN ROSS

I cannot think of a single TV programme from this country where I have seen the major role taken by a black person and this is a problem. They use television in a racist, stereotypical way to keep our people down and flood us with sad and bad news. (James, London)

Introduction

In Britain, although two of the four principal terrestrial television channels have discrete departments dedicated to producing and/or commissioning programmes for black minority viewers, the attitudes and beliefs of those viewers have never (before) been canvassed in any systematic way. Unlike in America, where concern over the representation of non-white Americans (for example, Dines and Humez (eds), 1995; Gray, 1995; Wilson II & Gutierrez, 1995; hooks, 1996; Gandy Jnr., 1998) has provoked a number of studies into the views of minority communities (Fife, 1987; Gray, 1989, Ziegler and White, 1990; Gray, 1995), private and piecemeal public protest amongst minority ethnic viewers in Britain and a growing body of work which looks at the representation of minority ethnic communities in mass media (for example, Hartmann & Husband, 1976; Young, 1995; Ross, 1997) has not been followed by concerted institutional action.[1]

The research on which this essay is based, therefore, represents an almost unprecedented exploration of a great diversity of black minority voices articulating a variety of views on the ways in which 'race' and ethnicity are represented, but whose views nonetheless cohere in consensus around a number of highly significant and important aspects of minority ethnic representation.

The discussion which follows, then, makes the fundamental assumption that diversity in/and difference exists, both as rhetorical device and, as importantly, lived reality. But I also want to state, categorically, that my position is informed by a belief that there *are* messages and images which, through their repetitive display and unproblematic usage, promote a particular understanding of minority ethnic communities which impact negatively on white viewers and influence their thinking about minority ethnic communities in their own social world. Moreover, that those words and images have the same impact on many members of white mainstream society such that it is possible to talk about their reception by an audience, not just by individual viewers. In other words, media *do* matter.

As I do believe that it is possible to comprehend of an audience segment, at least, if not the homogeneous audience which we used to think existed, I therefore also believe that there is value in working with groups of audiences who share particular characteristics and who also believe that the sharing of a particular characteristic makes it possible to talk of them as an audience sub-set which, for my purposes, is the sub-set of minority ethnic viewers. It is the views of members of this group of media consumers which inform the remainder of this essay, which captures not just the sense of 'we' but also the 'I' voice which all too often gets obscured in the rush to try and give weight to a particular view by discussing the particular issue in aggregate terms. The discussion considers the ways in which minority ethnic viewers interact with television images and explores the perceptions which members of different minority ethnic groups hold towards mainstream televisual output.

Research Methodology

In the mid-1990s, the BBC commissioned the Centre for Mass Communication Research at Leicester University to undertake an audience reception study with minority ethnic audiences in order to identify how such viewers regarded the portrayal of 'race' and ethnicity on television and their views on the way in which minority ethnic communities were portrayed across the spectrum of TV programming, to include both fictional and factual shows. It is notoriously difficult, if not completely invidious, to try and identify 'representatives' of any group, let alone attempt to locate 'typical' black or Asian[2] viewers and indeed, part of the explicit strategy of the baseline study was precisely to explode the notion of a homogenous 'black' community and to speak instead of diverse and multiple identifications.[3] The research team, together with the BBC, therefore decided to advertise for participants, thus ensuring that respondents self-identified as fitting the criteria for inclusion - the advertisements called for 'Black' and 'Asian' viewers to take part in a study about television and 'race.' Using census data, 10 locations[4] were selected which had significant concentrations of Britain's predominant ethnic minority groups and were geographically spread. Approximately 150 community groups and associations were contacted in these areas and an advert was also placed in *The Voice*, Britain's best-selling black newspaper. It should be noted that most of the respondents to *The Voice* advert were based in London, so the capital city was the site of a number of focus groups. As a result of these two publicity strategies, 353 people took part in the study, organised in 35 focus groups. The ethnic mix of participants largely reflected that of the minority populations in Britain as a whole, with slightly more than half the sample coming from Indian, Pakistani or Bangladeshi communities and slightly less than half claiming African, African Caribbean or other 'black' identities.

Once participation had been agreed with focus group organisers - either community workers or *Voice* readers - the groups were set up and run in community centres or in private residences. All community groups who responded positively to the invitation to take part in the study subsequently did so - no selection criteria were used to include or reject groups.[5] Similarly, all individuals who responded to the various advertising strategies took part in the study, largely by attending a local focus group or by completing a questionnaire. All participants were paid to take part in the study: all completed a short questionnaire and most also kept a television diary for seven days prior to the group discussion and this combination of questionnaire, diary and taped interview yielded an abundant and rich data source. The focus groups themselves were facilitated by members of the research team and were tape-recorded.[6] What follows is a discussion of the main findings of this study, together with some thoughts on how the reactions of minority ethnic audiences towards television might be usefully incorporated into broadcasting policy in the future.

Mainstream Programming and Minority Ethnic Characterisations

All the focus groups began by discussing participants' favourite programmes and this general discussion, in nearly every case, proceeded very rapidly to a consideration of the minority ethnic characters in those shows. Sometimes this happened almost immediately, for example if a participant said that s/he liked programmes which featured minority ethnic people or, more usually, when discussions moved to the topic of soap operas. Whatever the circumstance, a desire to talk about the representation of Black and Asian communities in both fiction and non-fiction programmes dominated discussion in all the focus groups and informed the messages that groups had for broadcasters at the end of their deliberations. It is for this reason that the substantive element of this essay concentrates on the very

5

specific race-oriented themes which spontaneously emerged from the group discussion.

'Race' as Stereotype

For most viewers, although the number of Black and Asian people on television had improved over the past few years, there was still dissatisfaction with the range of characterisations and their marginalisation in a so-called multicultural society, particularly in programmes set in geographical locations where minority ethnic communities are highly visible in 'real' life but almost entirely absent in fictional programming.

> There are two issues here. Firstly we're negated by our absence: in a whole range of programming we just don't appear. Then when black people *are* shown, it's all crime and disaster. Things like *EastEnders* try but there are so many things wrong with so many of its black characters. (Josie, London)

A number of specific criticisms about Black and Asian characterisations in mainstream programmes emerged from the study which can be described as follows. Characters are rarely perceived as realistic, are never properly integrated into the community they inhabit and are mostly peripheral to the main action. When the viewer *is* allowed into a Black or Asian character's home, there is no ornament or decoration or picture which suggests the personality or history of its incumbent. Crucially, there is nothing culturally distinctive in their homes, no signs of a provenance outside *white* mainstream culture. What often irritated viewers was a lack of cultural authenticity, where Muslim characters had Hindu names or where a Caribbean elder was seen eating the 'wrong' food or where individuals are shown doing something completely against what viewers believed to be the 'acceptable' cultural norms.

Characters in Two-Dimensions

As a matter of routine, Black and Asian characters are rarely shown associating with other members of their family, so they are never allowed to develop as fully-rounded characters with mothers and fathers, partners, sisters, children. They are destined to act out stereotypical roles which do not reflect the broad diversity of 'real' experiences. Where are the Asian doctors, Black lawyers and accountants in small screen visions of 'multicultural' Britain? Where is *that* reality represented? The exception to this kind of isolation is when an entire family is introduced into a programme's storyline, but even here they are never allowed to be an

6

ordinary family, but must always be the Black or Asian family. There is always something distinctive about them, something deviant and they are never allowed to stay in the cast for too long.

For Asian audiences especially, there were considerable and strong differences of opinion over 'Asian' characters in soaps in ways which were not replicated in discussions with Black viewers. Broadly, the divisions were between older Asian viewers who believe that characters are often too westernised, whereas younger people feel that they represent more realistic portraits and show clearly the synergies between different cultural communities. Gillespie's work with young Punjabis in London found exactly the same contradictions in operation between her interviewees and their parents (Gillespie, 1992, 1995).

It is interesting to note that many of the older South Asian respondents liked Australian soap imports such as *Neighbours* and *Home and Away* in preference to their more 'realistic' British counterparts precisely because they perceived them to be 'safe' and 'nice' with 'no sex or bad language.' But of course, this is the safety of the highly sanitised and considerably distanced 'other': *Neighbours* no more represents an authentic Australian reality than *Cosby* reflects actual American society and the abiding power of racist colonial discourse is subtly encoded to insinuate itself as cultural norm. Where are the stories of 'ordinary' Aboriginal peoples or Torres Straits Islanders in the rosy world of Ramsey Street? Where are the storylines of Anglo-Asian relationships which are so troubling Prime Minister John Howard's administration in real-time Australia? Many of the younger South Asian viewers in the study, on the other hand, liked watching British soaps for precisely the reason that they could be used to rehearse possible strategies in their own lives, looking to soap narratives to gauge the bounds of 'acceptable' behaviour. Some mentioned wanting their parents to watch soaps with them so that they could understand some of the complexities of their own lives without their having to raise issues more explicitly themselves.

I don't like those attitudes because programmes have very negative effects. We are Asian and our culture is very different and those stories go against our culture. In *EastEnders*, something happened to the Asian family which doesn't happen in all families and this might be an encouragement to teenagers. Television shouldn't show that because it is a medium which should be giving us good programmes with moral values. (Shireen, Birmingham)

With Gita and Sanjay, they are very westernised and we're nothing like that. They are trying to change us into westerners which we're not. They shouldn't do that. They should leave us to be ourselves. In that way, the message gets across to people that they have their ways and we have ours. (Sourayya, Leicester)

I think Gita and Sanjay are quite realistic. Their stories really describe what it's like. But Gita can be a bit dull sometimes. (Farida, Birmingham)

Where's the Caribbean food, the rice and peas? They've got Jules Tavernier, the grandfather, eating beans on toast. They don't eat that in Trinidad. (Anne, London)

The Ubiquity of 'Racism' in Storylines

As well as criticisms around specific characters and character types, there was also concern over the storylines in which Black and Asian characters feature. Racism is regularly rehearsed as a suitable topic in soaps, driven as they are by controversy and melodrama. While many viewers are quite satisfied with the use of themes such as racism and discrimination within narratives, believing that the introduction of such themes in storylines enables the issues to be played out in ways which are 'safe' for the majority audience, there are resentments about the way in which minority ethnic characters are then made to deal with situations.

You remember when they [*EastEnders*] had that problem with the skinheads and all they did was to have Alan, Steve and Sanjay getting drunk. That's not very positive. It really irritated me. Waiting around until midnight with a baseball bat. That was a very negative portrayal of how black people handle racism, getting out a bottle of Cinzano Bianco and knocking it back. It was really bad. (Janet, London)

Amongst African Caribbean viewers, there were very strong criticisms that in popular police series like *The Bill*, the minority ethnic characters are nearly always criminals of some kind. When minority ethnic police officers *do* figure prominently, it is usually because 'race' is a theme in a particular episode or else they have been drafted in to deal with a problem in a particular minority ethnic community, bringing with them their first-hand knowledge of 'their own' people and having to run the usual gamut of abuse from the 'black' criminal fraternity.

On-Screen Relationships - Black-on-Black as Taboo

In most shows, particularly soaps, minority ethnic characters are usually shown with white partners. On the very rare occasions when minority ethnic actors are 'allowed' to have 'black' partners on screen, the woman is considerably paler and is usually so light-skinned and European-featured that she is practically white. While it might seem rather distasteful to interrogate and criticise characterisations to this degree of detail, minority ethnic viewers view such casting strategies as deliberate rather than accidental devices which contribute to their subordination through privileging 'whiteness' as the ultimate goal. There were two main reasons which viewers believe underlie decisions to pair minority ethnic characters with white (or near white) partners. Firstly, because the possible 'threat' of their blackness is neutralised and domesticated by their involvement with a white partner which makes them more acceptable to white viewers. In addition, there is a belief that most (white) scriptwriters have no idea about black-on-black relationships, so they script stories based on what they do know and write storylines for white couples and hope that they will fit.

Although such black-white relations were generally regarded negatively, this was not the only reading as the following dialogue sequence shows, generated during one of the London-based discussion groups. The two speakers are both women and there are a number of important issues which come out of the exchange. The point about putting white audiences off by seeing a minority ethnic couple is not borne out by the evidence but is clearly something that the speaker feels is important.

> I think they've got Alan and the white woman in *EastEnders* because if you look at the East End, there are a lot of mixed relationships and that's what they're trying to show. (Sarah)

> They can show mixed relationships, OK, but they should also have black on black relationships as well. (Lola)

> But that could put people off watching. I mix with a lot of real East Enders. Some are all right but a lot are racist. (Sarah)

Although Alan's character was rather weak and negative and he never had a permanent job, his role as father and stepfather is a very positive aspect of his character and he takes his paternal duties seriously by being around his children, looking after them and treating them all as his own in an extremely caring and nurturing way. It is troubling, therefore, that even this element of his character is roundly dismissed as fantasy, 'a black guy just wouldn't stay around for those kids', or worse.

> Alan's character is probably credible for a white audience, but it's very painful for young black children to see this man, a black man, acting as stepfather to white children when they know that there's no one acting like a caring father to them, as black children. (Claudine, London)

9

Much of the criticism around minority ethnic characters relates to what viewers believe to be the lack of fit between the ethnicity of characters and that of writers, producers, editors and other members of programme production teams, as well as a more vaguely articulated view which could be loosely described as institutional racism. Crucially, if most people working in television are white, then there are necessarily going to be problems in developing credible minority ethnic characters because productions will be shaped and informed by the cultural baggage of a colonial history.

> I think it's a bit sinister. People know how powerful the media are. They know how to send out subliminal messages, even through the simplest scenes on the telly. They know exactly what they're doing. (Shirley, London)

> I cannot think of a single TV programme from this country where I have seen the major role taken by a black person and this is a problem. They use television in a racist, stereotypical way to keep our people down and flood us with sad and bad news. (Joe, London)

There was a strong belief amongst participants in nearly all groups, that writers simply have no idea of the real lives of minority ethnic communities and have even less interest in finding out. It was often the case for these viewers, that attention to detail was missing, for example, developing a specifically Hindu character and then showing her or him on their way to a mosque. Although it seems a small inaccuracy, and highly unlikely to be picked up by a white viewer, it signals among minority ethnic audiences a disregard and disrespect for cultural veracity which in turn reflects the low value attached to the portrayal of authentic and credible minority ethnic characters. Even minority ethnic writers will not necessarily write more authentic characterisations, either because they are removed, for reasons of class, education, lifestyle and so on, from the particular community about which they are writing or because they will not be 'allowed' to deliver more diverse portraits because broadcasters prefer to retain their prejudices for themselves and their audiences. For some, though, being 'black' was not essential to writing an authentic 'black' character because what was more important was their ability to write *well*.

The Mainstream (White) Audience and Images of 'Race'

Viewers in all the focus groups believe that white people are greatly influenced by the types of black minority images they see on television because they have very limited knowledge of African, Caribbean, South

10

Asian and other minority ethnic communities. This perception is, to some extent, borne out by a number of studies which have looked at white audiences and 'black' images (see for example Broadcasting Standards Council, 1992; Ross, 1992). For minority ethnic viewers in this study, the largely stereotypical portraits which emerge from both fictional and factual programmes, from soaps to news, serve to reinforce the prejudices that pervade the white consciousness already and impact on viewers who are often a little too ready to believe the worst.

> Television reinforces their prejudices. They have been socialised into thinking that black people are inferior, less intelligent. They shouldn't bias the white majority against us, but that's what they do. (Steve, London)

> When something terrible comes on the news, a mugging or a rape, I'm only listening for what colour the assailant is. If he's black I think, "oh no." If he's white I breathe a sigh of relief. I think we all do. (Carol, Nottingham)

One of the issues which most concerned Black and Asian viewers was the way in which television has a tendency to slide into a homogenising 'blackness'. If distinctions are made between different minority ethnic groups, they are generally made between the crude categories of 'Black' and 'Asian'.[7] Hindu and Sikh groups were especially keen to define their own specific cultural context and were highly critical of the way in which the boundaries between different South Asian cultures were constantly blurred. For them, the crucial issue was that they did not want to be associated with Islam and what they considered to be extremist and fundamentalist views. Similarly, the African groups were depressed with the way in which 'black' was increasingly taken to mean Caribbean and that Africa was only ever invoked in the context of disaster or killing. They did not want to be associated with Jamaica and 'yardie' culture and were dismissive of 'Caribbean' comics who constantly poke fun at Africans.

Many viewers believe that the way in which minority ethnic groups are portrayed on television not only has a negative effect on white viewers, but also affects their own communities in very unhelpful ways too. The lack of positive role models and the way in which minority ethnic characters are routinely stereotyped contribute to feelings of low self-esteem and failure. Almost without exception, Black and Asian viewers did not feel that they were valued as a specific viewing public; they did not feel that their viewing needs were being met; and they did not feel that they were getting value for money from the licence fee.

Because most Black and Asian children are now born in Britain (Modood et. al., 1997), their knowledge of 'home' is very limited, gleaned from what their relatives tell them and, of course, what they see on television. Viewers reported sadness at the reaction of their children to their homelands of Africa, India or Pakistan which, because the media's particular slant on the developing world tends to be negative, making young people feel ashamed of the 'backwardness' of their countries.

> My children were born in this country and don't know anything directly of Africa. What they see of black people on TV forms a bad picture in their head about the country where I was born. (Sula, Manchester)

Where Next for TV2000?

Viewers commented that disparate Black and Asian communities are nearly always homogenised into a totalising and indiscriminate 'blackness'. African Caribbean viewers believe that their communities are constantly pathologised as criminal and feckless, abounding with street robbers, dope-dealers and welfare-scrounging single mothers. Indian, Pakistani and Bangladeshi viewers criticise the disaster-orientation of much of the programming which focuses on the developing world and the preoccupation with exploring attachments to cultural traditions, such as arranged marriages and the dowry system which are deemed inappropriate in a Western context. For all these viewers, 'multicultural' has come to mean cultural homogeneity, a proliferation of uni-cultures into which all their disparate and diverse voices, interests, views, identifications and practices dissolve into a formless mass of stereotypical essences - this is what *Caribbean* people are like; this is what *Asian* people do. What participants in this study want, then, is a recognition of their difference to each other, to mark out their own distinctiveness from all the others who might be squashed in under the generic terms 'Black' or 'Asian'.

Minority ethnic communities are visible in television spaces in two discrete ways. Firstly in mainstream programmes where stereotyping and caricature are the main criticisms. Second, in multicultural programming strands where they are effectively denied access to the public mainstream space by having to speak from the more private and marginal space of the 'multicultural'. If television is a public space for us, the viewers, then public space-changing strategies must be instigated to make that space a more representative and accessible one for television's many and diverse publics.

The crucial point is that there is more to life for minority ethnic groups than their engagement with a black-as-victim or black-as problem discourse. What *they* want from television is a fair reflection of all their complex diversity, not simply exchanging negative with positive frames but replacing both with a framework of *reality*. There is an aching desire for minority ethnic characters to be created and given storylines which recognise their humanity, not simply their 'blackness' and difference to white people (Daniels, 1990). It is precisely because there are so few minority ethnic characters in mainstream programming that each one must be subject to an unbearable scrutiny by audiences who criticise each one for what it is not, each one forced to stand as emblem of a generalisable 'blackness' for white audiences who are without any counter-intuition to combat the stereotypes.

While Black and Asian viewers were, on the whole, pleased to be given the opportunity to express their views about television, they were sceptical that broadcasters would actually do anything concrete as a result of their reactions and suggestions. But if broadcasters are serious in their commitment to represent the full plurality of the audience, to respond to the viewing needs of all their diverse constituents, then the voice of the viewer must be attended to. As Simmonds argues forcefully when discussing African Caribbean and African American women in film narratives, debates around 'black' representation must locate 'black' voices at their centre, they must include black people themselves in those discussions (Simmonds, 1992). One of the most significant issues to arise from this study was the question of balance, whether it was minority ethnic characterisations in mainstream popular programming or the focus and orientation of documentary series allegedly catering for minority ethnic viewers or treating with 'black' issues/problems. If we accept the primary role of the media, and particularly television, in meeting our demands for entertainment and information,[8] then we must also acknowledge the significance of the media's combined power in selecting products for our consumption. Moreover, if, as Kellner (1990) suggests, television stands at the centre of our symbolic universe, providing repetitive and mythical celebrations of dominant ideologies, then ways must be found to rupture, subvert and challenge that hegemonic orthodoxy in order to let in the sweet sounds of other singers and other songs.

Implications for a Global Research Agenda

Although the focus of this essay has been on minority ethnic viewers in Britain, the broad issues around minority representation which have emerged are, arguably, generalisable to wider contexts. Of crucial concern is the question of who has control over the image and in whose likeness is that image constructed. It is everywhere the complaint that images of one 'category', say, Pakistani women or gay men or older people are *imagined* from the second-hand experience of an entirely other 'category', say English men or straight women or young people. Don't just imagine, ask the folks concerned!

The rise of various minority ethnic media around the world[9] demonstrates a clear supply-side response by ethnic communities to see alternative images (of themselves) to those currently provided by mainstream, majority media (see also Cottle, (ed.), 2000). However, what is of equal importance is the value placed by *all* writers/producers/directors on cultural authenticity and diversity. It is not feasible for characters to be written only by individuals who share identical characteristics, but it is possible to ensure that basic details are correct.

Perhaps the conventions of documentary and news genres mean that it is mostly 'bad' events and situations which reach our TV screens, but a balance can nonetheless be maintained by working a bit harder to discover more positive/diverse developments taking place in the world and at the very least canvassing views amongst local people who *live* the (West's) news every day. Where are the reports from indigenous news crews reporting on what is happening on their own ground, in their own backyard and about which they have more than a passing interest?

The agenda that audiences want the media to consider, and the discussion summarised above comprises a set of issues which are not impossible to tackle: what is required is commitment and motivation and, in the words of many respondents, a *respect* for a significant segment of the viewing public who are part of the public, like everyone else and, in the context of Britain's media financing policy, whose payment of the licence fee surely entitles them not just to have their voices heard but actively *listened* to.

Most of the dissatisfactions expressed by minority ethnic viewers in this study have an application in many other multi-ethnic societies: they are not merely British complaints but the cries of diaspora communities around the globe whose lives are routinely constructed by the mainstream majority media out of nothing more concrete than their own imaginings. If the media do not tell us *what* to think, they set the agenda on what we should think *about*. If the media, and television in particular, think of themselves as presenting a window on the world and reflecting reality, we have to ask, whose world? Whose reality? Whose truth?

Notes

1   An earlier version of this chapter was published in J. Dacyl and C. Westin (2000), pp. 228-250. I undertook this work while working with Annabelle Sreberny at the Centre for Mass Communication Research, University of Leicester and I would like to thank her for her support.

2   For the purposes of brevity and the particularities of discussing 'race' and ethnicity in a British context, the remainder of this essay will use the terms 'black' and 'Asian' to provide a crude but pragmatic description of the two principal minority ethnic communities living in Britain, where 'Black' refers to individuals of African, African Caribbean descent and 'Asian' refers to individuals primarily of Indian, Pakistani or Bangladeshi descent: all names have been changed.

3   In Britain, approximately 5.5 per cent (3 million) of the population are deemed to be from minority ethnic backgrounds: South Asian groups are the largest minority (2.6 per cent), followed by the broad category 'black' which includes Black-Caribbean and Black-African peoples (1.6 per cent).

4   Bedford, Birmingham, Bradford, Coventry, Glasgow, Lancashire, Leeds, Leicester, Manchester and Nottingham.

5   Most of the focus groups took place in England, although one group of Chinese women were interviewed in Scotland.

6   Most of the focus groups lasted approximately two hours, although some were shorter and a few were much longer.

7   And of course I am acutely aware of my own culpability in using this crude shorthand, although it is hard to be culturally specific when the variety of ethnic and racial descriptors which individuals apply to themselves run into more than 20 categories.

8   I would argue that it is rather less successful when it comes to fulfilling Lord Reith's third stated objective for television – education.

9   See for example Riggins (ed.), 1992; Dowmunt (ed.), 1993; Husband (ed.), 1994.

References

Broadcasting Standards Council (1992), *The portrayal of ethnic minorities on television*, BSC Research Working Paper 7, London.

Cottle, S. (ed.) (2000) *Ethnic Minorities and the Media: Changing Cultural Boundaires*, Open University Press, Buckingham.

Dacyl, J. and Westin, C. (eds) (2000), *Governance of Cultural Diversity*, Centre for Research in International Migration and Ethnic Relations, Stockholm University, Stockholm.

Daniels, T. (1990), 'Beyond negative or positive images', in: J. Willis and T. Wollen (eds), *The Neglected Audience*, British Film Institute, London, pp. 66-71.

Dines, G. and J.M. Humez, (eds) (1995), *Gender, Race and Class in Media: a Text Reader*, Sage, Thousand Oaks, Calif., and London.

Dowmunt, T. (ed.) (1993), *Channels of Resistance: Global Tensions and Local Empowerment*, British Film Institute, London.

Fife, M. (1987), 'Promoting Racial Diversity in US Broadcasting: Federal Policies Versus Social Realities', *Media, Culture and Society*, (9), pp. 481-505.

Gandy Jnr., O.H. (1998), *Communication and Race: a Structural Perspective*, Arnold, London.

Gillespie, M. (1992), *The role of television in the negotiation of cultural identities and differences among Punjabi Londoners*, PhD Thesis, Brunel University, London.

-- (1995), *Television, Ethnicity and Cultural Change*, Routledge, London and New York.

Gray, H. (1989), 'Television, Black Americans and the American Dream', *Critical Studies in Mass Communication* (6), pp. 376-386.

-- (1995), *Watching Race: Television and the Struggle for 'Blackness'*, University of Minnesota Press, Minneapolis and London.

Hartmann, P. and Husband, C. (1976), *Racism and the mass media: a study of the role of the mass media in the formation of white beliefs and attitudes in Britain*, Davis Poynter, London.

hooks, b. (1996), *Reel to Real: Race, Sex and Class at the Movies*, Routledge, London.

Husband, C. (ed.) (1994), *A Richer Vision: the Development of Ethnic Minority Media in Western Democracies*, UNESCO/John Libbey, Paris.

Jakubowicz, A. (ed.). (1994), *Racism, Ethnicity and the Media*, Allen & Unwin, St Leonards, NSW.

Kellner, D. (1990), 'Advertising and Consumer Culture', in J. Downing, A. Mohammadi and A. Sreberny-Mohammadi (eds), *Questioning the Media*, Sage Publications, Newbury Park, Calif., pp. 242-254.

Modood, T., Berthoud, R., Lakey, J., Nazroo, J., Smith, P., Virdee, S., and Beishon, S. (1997), *Ethnic Minorities in Britain: Diversity and Disadvantage*, Policy Studies Institute, London.

Riggins, S. (ed.) (1992), *Ethnic Minority Media: An International Perspective*, Sage, Newbury Park, London, Delhi.

Ross, K. (1992), *Television in black and white: ethnic stereotypes and popular television*, Research Paper in Ethnic Relations no.19, Centre for Research in Ethnic Relations, University of Warwick, Coventry.

-- (1996), *Black and White Media: black images in popular film and television*, Polity Press, Cambridge.

-- (1997),'Two-tone telly. Black minority audiences and British TV', *Communications: the European Journal of Communication Research*, 22(1), pp. 93-108

-- (2000), 'Viewing 'race': minority ethnic audiences talk popular television', in J. Dacyl and C. Westin (eds) *Governance of Cultural Diversity*, Centre for Research in International Migration and Ethnic Relations, Stockholm University, Stockholm., pp. 228-250.

Simmonds, F. N. (1992), '*She's Gotta Have It:* the representation of black female sexuality on film', in F. Bonner, L. Goodman, R. Allen, L. James and C. King (eds), *Imagining Women. Cultural Representations and Gender*, Polity Press in association with the Open University, Cambridge, pp. 210-220.

Wilson II, C.C. and Gutierrez, F. (1995) *Race, multiculturalism and the Media: from Mass to Class Communication* (2nd edition), Sage, Thousand Oaks, Calif., London.

Young, L (1995) *Fear of the Dark: Race, Gender and Sexuality in the Cinema*, Routledge, London.

Ziegler, D. and White, A. (1990), 'Women and Minorities on Network Television News: An Examination of Correspondents and Newsmakers', *Journal of Broadcasting and Electronic Media* (34), pp. 215-223.

2 Ethnic Minority Media Audiences, Community and Identity: the Case of London's South Asian and Greek-Cypriot Communities

ROZA TSAGAROUSIANOU

Introduction

Recent literature on globalisation and diasporas has tended to be rather enthusiastic regarding the rootlessness and mobility of diasporas, and by extension, their transnational experiential horizons. In their otherwise stimulating book *Nations Unbound* (1994), Linda Basch and her co-authors talk about certain diasporas' ability to live 'transnationally', to 'transfer themselves from one place to another' (1994, pp. 4-7) but do not consistently focus on the experiences of marginalisation, exclusion and *aporia* that go hand in hand with the often traumatic process of dislocation that migration entails. This rather optimistic and selective perspective is not uncommon in discussions of diasporic and migrant cultures and communications (cf. Bhabha, 1994; Appadurai, 1996).

This chapter attempts to contribute to the re-examination of such assumptions by focusing on diasporic/migrant community cultural consumption. Drawing upon research with London's South Asian and Greek-Cypriot ethnic communities and their attitudes, evaluations and uses of the media available to them, it examines and discusses the ways in which these communities use the diverse media available to them with particular reference to processes of ethnic community identity building and its positioning in the global/local nexus.[1]

The majority of the empirical material upon which this paper is premised has been collected in the course of a research project on diasporic media focusing on London's South Asian and Greek-Cypriot communities, the diasporic media that they have at their disposal and the way they use the media (diasporic and 'mainstream') available to them. The material drawn upon here is from open audience interviews: 24 focus group sessions have been conducted between June 1998 and February 2000.[2] Recognising and acknowledging the possibility of a common experience of migrancy as well as of the not negligible differences in cultural and socio-economic terms, my analysis pools together the information collected from both communities and seeks to identify commonalities as well as differences in experience and practice between and within these.

Tracing the Emergence of Ethnic Community Media in the United Kingdom

Post-World War II immigration to the United Kingdom, especially, although not exclusively from Commonwealth countries culminated in the formation of significant ethnic communities in Britain and has considerably contributed to the multiethnic and multicultural character of British society. According to the 1991 Census, out of a population of just over 55 million, over 3 million people declared they considered themselves 'non-white'[3] while members of ethnic minorities that could be categorised as 'white' could either describe themselves as such or use the 'other ethnic group' category as a solution to the non-availability of more appropriate identification categories. Although as a result of these limitations the Census might not reflect adequately the diversity and heterogeneity of the British population it is difficult to overlook the fact that migrants and their descendants are now an integral feature of the British political, cultural and economic landscape.

The integration of migrant or formerly migrant groups into British society during the post-cold war period has not been easy. Although by the 1970s significant ethnic communities had been formed in most major urban centres of the UK and played a central role in the multiethnic and multicultural transformation of British society, their members had to cope with numerous challenges. Official policy and discourse, as well as popular reactions to the transformation of British society, have varied considerably, from racist and exclusive official and popular practices to different 'multicultural' experiments that promoted 'ethnic' community representation and institutionalised 'ethnic' presence in various levels of local government and public authorities.[4]

The politicisation of questions about race and immigration from the 1960s onwards has given rise to discourses of exclusion of the migrant populations from most aspects of 'mainstream' society but has also prompted the formulation of a particular version of multicultural policy

18

frameworks, mainly by local authorities. Often marked by a mixture of paternalistic and democratic political culture, this variant of British multiculturalism often involved the co-option of migrant personalities and associations, not always reflecting the communities concerned, to committees related to service provision. Although this is not the place to assess the impact of these policy frameworks, it suffices to say that it has had mixed results as it entailed consideration of ethnic community needs in determining policy and allocation of resources on the one hand, but reified communities and their 'representation' on the other.

As far as the British broadcast media are concerned, they proved slow to respond to the changing composition of the British population and the social, political, economic and cultural changes that immigration to the United Kingdom entailed. Reflecting its Reithian educational ethos, the BBC initially perceived its role as one of facilitating the adaptation and, possibly, integration of migrant communities to British society. Thus its philosophy of addressing the needs of Britain's ethnic minorities was initially geared towards 'education' and 'acculturation'. This ethos, often underpinned by specific assumptions regarding the aptitudes, capabilities and cultural competence of ethnic community members and the 'civilising mission' of public media, informed policies that could be characterised as paternalistic. Alongside the BBC, the independent broadcasting sector (ITV) and later independent radio, were equally oblivious and unresponsive to the changing composition, needs and tastes of Britain's audiences that immigration had brought about. Faced with such persistent institutional attitudes towards them, Black, Asian and other ethnic communities felt increasingly alienated as a result of their perceived marginalisation in the media.

This situation often prompted members of these communities to retreat into apathy and resignation but also led to the emergence of ethnic community cultural politics. This soon culminated in what one could term a 'guerrilla' war against the exclusive public and independent media sectors: in the main metropolitan conurbations of Britain, community-based experiments with pirate radio were in earnest throughout the late 1970s and early 1980s. In London, the Greater London Council (GLC) embraced this movement as part of its policy of supporting the trend towards more localised and often community-specific radio. From 1982 onwards, the GLC leadership funded a variety of groups in the field of arts and community politics and developed its Community Radio Development Unit which enabled Afro-Caribbean, Asian and other minority ethnic groups to set up several ethnic community radio projects and organise a vigorous campaign for ethnic community media (Lewis and Booth, 1989; Tsagarousianou, forthcoming).

The establishment of Channel 4 in 1982 added a new dimension to this media landscape, as it was statutorily required to appeal to minority (including ethnic community) tastes and interests and to encourage innovation and experiment. Channel 4 not only encouraged the creation of numerous independent production companies specialising in catering for minorities of 'taste' and 'interest' but also prompted its established competitors (mainly BBC2) to embrace innovation and consider alternative ways of addressing Britain's ethnic minority communities (Harvey, 1994).

A decade later, the 1990 Broadcasting Act brought further changes as it introduced the liberalisation of the airwaves and substantial deregulation of the media sector. In this new context licence bids by Black, Asian, Greek and Turkish radio projects (and pirates) and a number of television projects targeting ethnic communities were made, with considerable degrees of success, while satellite and cable broadcasters targeting Britain's ethnic communities were granted licences to operate. South Asian and Greek Cypriot activists and entrepreneurs played an important role in both the experimental/'pirate' and commercial stages in the development of British ethnic media and have since established their presence in the ethnic media sector, especially though not exclusively in the greater London area where substantial parts of these communities live and work.

As far as the South Asian media sector, catering for London's South Asian diaspora, is concerned, at the time of writing there is one London-wide FM radio station (Sunrise Radio) and a number of Asian television broadcasters, notably Zee TV Europe (a satellite company formerly operating as TV Asia), Asianet (cable), Sony Entertainment Television Asia (satellite and cable), Namaste TV (satellite) and more recently Bangla-TV, a broadcaster targeting exclusively Bangladeshi viewers in the UK. At the time of writing a licence for a limited terrestrial Asian television service in Northern England has been approved by the ITC whereas digital broadcasting has provided more space for further Asian television services such as the Asian film channel, B4U launched by Sony Entertainment Television Asia. Finally, Spectrum International, a London-wide AM radio station broadcasts South Asian language programmes and music as part of its overall multicultural programme, while a limited local licence has been given in the past few years to Ramadan Radio, an East London based station, to broadcast to the local Muslim – largely Bangladeshi - community during the month of Ramadan (Tsagarousianou, forthcoming).

The Greek-Cypriot community, on the other hand, can tune in to London Greek Radio, a North London-based FM radio station and Hellenic TV, a cable television programme provider in the London area, while satellite dish owners can receive the programmes of an array of public and, increasingly, private broadcasters from the Republic of Cyprus and Greece.[5] It is important to note that the Greek-Cypriot community appears to have more limited options as far as the diasporic media choices available to its members are concerned, largely because of its relatively small size when compared to the South Asian community of London. On the other hand, one should not underestimate the fact that Greek-Cypriots are one of a very few other minority ethnic groups in Britain who have access to 'ethnic' or 'diasporic' media, although other groups are rapidly catching up.

As a result of this process of transformation of the media landscape, London's South Asian and Greek-Cypriot communities in Britain now have access to a considerable array of media. These range from mainstream public service and commercial broadcasting to local and transnational radio and television that claims to be addressing them as ethnic communities and not as part of the 'mainstream' audience.

Research with Ethnic Minority Audiences: Some Prolegomena

Before entering a discussion of ethnic minority audiences' views, attitudes and consumption it is imperative that some unavoidably brief remarks are made regarding the ways in which ethnic minority communities and audiences are understood in this chapter. It is important to note that the term 'ethnic community' carries with it a number of connotations that might often *reify* and reduce the complexity of the complex social phenomena to which it refers.

'Ethnic communities' are neither static aggregates of people sharing a common ethnic origin or culture as some simplistic definitions would have them, nor monolithic and homogeneous entities. Ethnic communities in general and ethnic audiences in particular, are highly heterogeneous and diversified, and their patterns of media and cultural consumption extremely complex. What is more, their 'ethnic' character should not be viewed as a *property* or *essence* but as a *process*, unfolding continuously and intersecting with other experiences and identifications.

Behind the term 'community' - often taken to denote unity and a degree of homogeneity - one can discern various and distinct experiences relating to class, gender and age that are constantly in flux. In addition, the experiences of displacement and mobility that are central to the processes of formation of private and public narratives within migrant ethnic communities are also marked by substantial diversity: the different ways in which migration and integration to the 'society of settlement' have been experienced and lived have often affected life perceptions, aspirations, tastes and preferences. What is more, the divergence of life experiences between different generations, a not uncommon societal phenomenon, acquires an additional dimension as far as ethnic communities are concerned; generational experiences may vary markedly as emotional and material links with a more or less remote place of 'origin', a 'homeland left behind' tend to decrease in second and third generation members of migrant communities.[6]

Indeed, some critics of research into minority or ethnic communities and audiences have argued that the identification of ethnic communities to be studied is largely the product of the emphasis on the *ethnic*, or *minority* factor by researchers and their research agendas (Machin & Carrithers, 1996). As a matter of fact, they tend to argue, the ethnic dimension is merely one in a multitude of factors that may relate to audience preferences, attitudes and practices. Thus the study of ethnic and minority audiences has, not entirely unjustifiably, been the object of criticism as, it has been argued, 'describing the responses of such "interpretative communities" artificially isolates individuals into categories that may have little reality in the flux and flow of social life.' (Machin and Carrithers, 1996, p. 343) Nevertheless, I would argue that although, when premised on qualitative methods, audience research should be informed by such concerns and strive to avoid such pitfalls, it is also best placed to test the fundamental assumptions upon which a research hypothesis is predicated. In other words qualitative audience research has the capacity of being self-reflective and, as a result, the researcher is in a position to determine whether, and the extent to which, the ethnic or minority factor plays a role in audience practices.

Ethnic Minority Audiences and the Media

Mainstream Media: Attitudes and Consumption

When asked to evaluate the different media available to and accessible by them, the majority of the respondents of all ages have been overwhelmingly critical of what they perceive as a lack of public provision (encompassing both public service and mainstream commercial broadcasting). The belief that ethnic minorities and their cultures were not finding a space in mainstream broadcasting is widespread in audience responses as is an overwhelming resignation to what they consider as their non-incorporation into national/public and commercial broadcasting policy and discourse. Audience discourses, however inarticulate, tend to display both bitterness and pragmatism when confronted with what is widely perceived as the inability and, for many, the unwillingness of mainstream institutions to

22

adjust what audiences perceive as essentially monocultural perceptions of British society.

> They do not have adequate provision of programmes for people like us although we are licence payers. We are living in this country and we are contributing too. (Christalla, 56yrs, Greek Cypriot origin)

> I do not think that we will ever reach the point where they will be giving us 5% of their air time although we are contributing 5% of the country's revenue from TV licence. (Sukhdeep, 27yrs, Punjabi origin)

Such discourses characteristically raise the issues of membership and inclusion to British society and, to an extent, attempt to point out that the latter should be redefined in a more inclusive way. 'Living in the country' and 'contributing' to the national funds that maintain its main national broadcasting institution are seen by most respondents as evidence of full participation in national life and introduce questions of public responsibility as far as the national broadcasting institutions are concerned.

A feeling of non-representation or, at best, under-representation and exclusion, was prevalent in audience responses as the overwhelming majority perceive that membership of British society is effectively denied to them, as minority audiences are denied representation in broadcasting. Even on occasions in which some provision is made, respondents compared the ways in which they and 'mainstream' audiences are being treated. According to audience evaluations, even on such occasions tokenism and ghettoisation appear to be the main effects of such attempts of limited provision by national broadcasters.

> It's like that *Goodness Gracious Me* sketch. You can have a 10-minute slot on Sunday morning. At 7:00am in the morning, who the hell's going to be watching? It's at 11:00am now but still marginalised. (Suresh, 26yrs, Gujerati Hindu origin)

Another, quite significant, dimension of audience evaluations of 'mainstream' broadcasting is related to the ways into which, through these discourses which are marked by a broadly shared pessimism, respondents articulate demands and expectations. Generally, audience discourses expectations of a recognition of the particular contribution to 'Britishness' that their diasporic condition brings about are prevalent and, quite often, unequivocal. Such expectations often take the form of what one could identify as demands for cultural rights.

The widespread feeling of alienation from mainstream broadcasting does not mean that audiences of South Asian and Greek Cypriot origins do not engage in the consumption of 'mainstream' media products. Among female respondents from both communities over the age of 50, soap operas and natural history programmes appear to be most popular, while men of the same age group tend to favour the latter, together with what they often called 'social' movies. Soaps appear to be widely popular among audiences in all other age groups, although in the case of younger audiences with fewer or no linguistic and cultural competence problems, the patterns of mainstream broadcasting viewing and listening are more diverse and rich. Music programmes are at the top of 16 to 24 year olds' preferences of both sexes from both communities, and it is worth noting that over half of the respondents in this age group expressed preferences for pirate or less 'mainstream' music radio. Although this is not the place to elaborate on such preferences, a cursory evaluation of the relevant responses would seem to indicate that trends in hip hop and other non 'mainstream' music seem to attract a substantial number of young people with a minority ethnic background. Indeed respondents confirmed that they shared such pastimes mainly with friends from different ethnic minority backgrounds precisely because the sub-cultural character of these music styles appears to provide a common denominator of their experiences of difference and marginalisation. Clearly, these remarks are rather speculative but the questions they raise indicate that this is an area in need of further extensive research.

Returning to older audiences, it is highly probable that their preferences for soap operas and natural history programmes are partly, though not exclusively, related to attempts to overcome problems of cultural and linguistic competence. As respondents from older age groups are more likely to have been born and, possibly, to have grown up in a country other than the United Kingdom, their ability to speak and understand English and to adjust to 'mainstream' British society might have been limited at the time of their settlement to Britain. In response to the limited provision of programmes for new migrants by national broadcasters, older ethnic minority audience members seem to have developed selective patterns of viewing and listening premised on the accessibility of specific programmes conducive to cultural 'translation'.

Although it mainly focuses on the success of imported soap operas, the literature on the cross-cultural reception of this genre is of relevance in the context of this paper. There is no doubt that the consumption of mainstream television serials by migrant viewers is in effect a process of cross-cultural reception, as mainstream soap operas are effectively *imported* into the culture of migrant viewers and are premised on processes of *translation* - both linguistic and cultural. Soap is a genre that can lend itself to translation from one cultural milieu to another (Baldwin, 1995; Gillespie,

1995a; Miller 1995) due to the often familiar, yet polyvalent and open character of soap narratives (cf. Liebes and Katz, 1990).[7] As the research of Marie Gillespie has demonstrated, young viewers of the Australian soap *Neighbours* used the soap opera as a vehicle for making sense of their own everyday life in Southall and their South Asian community, as the narrative of the television serial allowed them to 'recognise' real-life relationships in it (Gillespie, 1995b, pp. 142-174). Similarly, South Asian and Greek-Cypriot audience responses appear to confirm such findings, as they indicate that the reasons for watching mainstream soaps are that they are 'easy to follow' (Katharine, 53yrs, Greek-Cypriot origin), 'about family' (Fatima, 36yrs, Pakistani origin), 'the stories are so real', or 'one has no difficulty to understand what the heroine goes through' (Sasha, 58yrs, Greek-Cypriot origin).

Despite the considerable differences between the genres, analogies can be drawn between soap opera (and the 'social movies' for which some expressed a preference) and the natural history documentaries South Asian and Greek Cypriot older interviewees talked about. The latter are equally accessible in terms of the linguistic and cultural skills required and their content is familiar to most of their viewers. Although empathising or linking the narrative to everyday life might not be that relevant in this case, natural history documentaries appear to often evoke memories of the rural settings from which a substantial part of these ethnic minority communities originates: 'they remind you of things back home' (Rajeev, 59yrs, Bangladeshi origin).

Clearly, delving into the mainstream television viewing practices of older members of the two communities one can discern strategies of cross-cultural transfer of meaning and of creative appropriation and domestication of 'mainstream' programmes especially when other forms of entertainment/media products are unavailable and/or inaccessible to them. Older audiences display considerable resourcefulness and flexibility by importing such programmes into their everyday life and translating them in ways that they become meaningful and relevant even when they have limited ability to speak and understand English and to appreciate the values and norms of 'mainstream' British society.

Uses of Ethnic Minority Media

Members of both the South Asian and the Greek-Cypriot communities, especially, though not exclusively, those born outside the UK, stressed the importance of media catering specifically for their ethnic community for a variety of reasons, ranging from their usefulness in maintaining some kind of contact with the country of origin or its culture and traditions, to more complex accounts of their centrality in community building and identity formation processes.

Interviewees often pointed out that such media are best placed to provide links with their country of origin or with their South Asian or Greek culture. It was often argued that ethnic minority media fill a gap that exists within mainstream broadcasting as they offer a more or less objective and balanced picture of their countries of origin as well as their cultures and politics.

> They [mainstream media] always show you the shanty towns of Bangladesh... They never show anything nice. (Sima, 39yrs, Bangladeshi origin)

> It is always disasters, floods and the like. As if nothing good comes from there. (Jamal, 48yrs, Pakistani origin)

> It [Cyprus] is rarely in the news. We hear about it only when something terrible happens. We want, however, to know the news from Cyprus, and Greece too. (Dimitris, 56yrs, Greek-Cypriot origin)

This contact, according to most older respondents, is vital for them as it reduces the sense of distance from their country of origin. It is this reduction of distance, physical as well as emotional, that most respondents have stressed in their responses. Bangladeshi respondents have stressed how important the daily Bangladeshi news slot on Spectrum radio is to them, and have described the almost ritualistic preparation for this unique moment in their families' daily routine. For many Bangladeshis, especially those with no access to the recently established Bangla-TV, this remains their only means of daily contact with their country of 'origin'.

Not surprisingly, members of the South Asian and Greek Cypriot communities also saw in ethnic minority media an important ally or tool for the maintenance and inculcation of 'their' culture. Again, evaluations of this sort were more prevalent among older interviewees, who expressed their concern about the need to keep the younger generations attracted to their parents' culture, religion and language. The intense debates within focus groups on whether the language used in ethnic radio and television should give way to English in an attempt to attract younger audiences, or whether culture and language should be seen as inseparable are indicative of the importance attributed to the acculturation function of ethnic minority media.

However, the relationship between audiences and ethnic community media is not exhausted in processes of linking diasporic communities with countries of origin or their cultures. As a matter of fact, they are used as resources for processes of identification and for the construction of life

26

worlds which are intelligible and manageable to audiences that are often traumatised by the experience of dislocation and uprooting that migration entails.

> For many years after we arrived [in Britain] you could rarely hear your language being spoken. I knew some English, but this was not important. We were lost. I was like a crazy woman. We did not have these things [Greek radio and TV] then. (Gheorgia, 60yrs, Greek Cypriot origin)

> For me Sunrise is a daily companion....It gives me the music I enjoy and up-to-date accurate news. All in a way that makes sense. (Priya, 50yrs, Indian origin)

Comments such as 'it's a daily companion', 'I no longer feel lonely,' 'it is like having someone keeping you company' were common in interviews and focus groups. Apart from being familiar, and making sense, or precisely because of these attributes, these media provide a structure or support to the daily activities of people who would otherwise be or feel physically or psychologically isolated because of disability, linguistic constraints or even cultural distance from other contexts and frameworks of daily life. As I argue elsewhere, passionate expressions such as 'I was like a crazy woman' very dramatically, but also very starkly, illustrate the *aporia* and the intensely felt *subaltern position* which members of diasporic communities, especially 'recent immigrants' to Britain have experienced (Tsagarousianou, in press).[8] For older people who may lack the cultural, linguistic or emotional competence to adapt to an essentially alien environment that makes little sense to them, ethnic community media may be instrumental in the transformation of an 'empty place' of settlement into a 'lived space' that makes sense to them and allows them to structure their everyday practices.[9]

Linked to this aspect is the strategy whereby audiences integrate certain ethnic community media into the 'intimate realm', which I have discussed more extensively elsewhere (Tsagarousianou, in press). This sense of intimacy was evident in the responses of several members of the audience of mainly local ethnic minority media such as Ramadan Radio, a local limited licence station, which operates every year during Ramadan in the Borough of Tower Hamlets, and London Greek Radio. Interviewees consistently talked about these radio stations in affectionate and intimate ways, referred to persons involved in their operation (not only DJs and presenters but also managers and editors) by using their first names or even with affectionate nicknames, both on air (during 'talk in' shows) and during interviews and focus groups sessions. The discourse of these respondents was one of membership, or even ownership, reflecting an attempt to

27

emotionally appropriate these media and to use them as a resource in the process of identity formation of the audience as members of a community. Following Herzfeld's discussion of what he calls 'cultural intimacy' (Herzfeld, 1997, pp. 74-88), I would argue that this audience strategy provides the infrastructure for collective self-representation. Ethnic community media are thus incorporated into the vernacular and everyday culture of the communities in question and occupy an important role in the processes of the communities' collective self-representation. Through incorporation to the domain of intimacy, these media become a crucial, local element of what audience members identify as 'home'.

Ethnic Community Specificity

Audience responses regarding the availability and usefulness of ethnic community media are not, however, as straightforward and appreciative as one might think. In contrast to the assumed clear cut distinction between more 'cosmopolitan', and therefore more critical, younger audiences and the more culturally introverted, and therefore appreciative, older audiences (Gillespie, 1995; Karim, 1998), older and younger audiences alike appear to be critical of what they perceive as significant shortcomings of ethnic community media.

Backwardness, lack of professionalism and bad quality as well as the inability or unwillingness of ethnic media to address the different needs of the second generation audiences appear to be the most prevalent reasons for disapproval among younger interviewees:

> One of the major problems with Sunrise is the quality of sound. There is no point in listening to it for Indian music that you can buy on tapes with a 100% better quality of sound. The tapes are dirt cheap anyway. (Jag , 26yrs, Gujerati Hindu origin)

> Sunrise is irrelevant. They have so much advertising in their programmes and they do not care about community. And in any case, I as a Muslim and Bangladeshi cannot relate to Sunrise. It is so anti-Muslim [approving nods from all group members]. (Razia, 24yrs, Muslim Bangladeshi origin)

Older respondents, although overall more appreciative, appear also to be in a position to adopt a critical attitude towards diasporic media and indeed they do so. Their arguments often echo younger audiences' complaints about low quality.

The quality of the image is not at all good. And these movies are so old - we have seen them again and again....If one is to pay a lot of money in order to have Hellenic TV, one expects more. (Maria, 62yrs, Greek Cypriot origin)

Many arguments also target the increasing commercialisation of diasporic media, especially, though not exclusively radio, perceiving it as betrayal of community.

I am not happy with Sunrise at all. I think there is far too much advertising [all focus group members nod with approval] There are not enough quality programmes available. (Ravinder, 62yrs, Indian origin)

They [the station management] have turned their back on the community that nurtured them and supported them. They do not want to know us any more; it is profits now that they are interested in. (Stelios, 64yrs, Greek Cypriot origin)

Another important cause of disquiet has to do with the cultural specificity of the diaspora as opposed to the 'country of origin'. Diasporic media (satellite television as well as local cable TV and radio), in their effort to address the largest audiences possible or due to financial constraints, often treat their audiences as a mere extension of the 'homeland' or as undifferentiated audiences that just happen to live in different countries or as just members of an undifferentiated diaspora. In contrast to this, a desire for emphasis on and respect of the local dimension of the diasporic community and its needs seem to be present in many audience responses. Even among older audiences who are at first sight complacent and offer a positive evaluation of diasporic media, a complex interpretation of the transnational character of their diasporic condition is present or discernible in their narratives.

They [Hellenic TV] keeps on showing us political discussions, talk, talk, talk. We are not interested in the parliament, we are not living in Cyprus or in Greece anymore. They do not see that we have other needs here. (Eleni, 60yrs, Greek Cypriot origin)

Why don't they show us something more interesting? Always the same old movies. There is that much of it that one can see. They think we do not need more? We have different interests too. We live here, we have our families here but they do not understand this. (Vanita, 56yrs, Gujarati origin)

Such responses are very common and indicate the complexity of the processes of identification unfolding among both South Asian and Greek-Cypriot audiences. Interviewees from both communities, while they often stress their 'ethnic' minority origins or identity, appear to be in no doubt as far as the specificity of their diasporic identity is concerned. Contrary to the quite widespread assumption, especially by satellite media strategists but also by government and local authorities in Britain as well as in the Indian subcontinent, Cyprus and Greece, diasporic audiences express their dismay at being treated as appendages of a 'home audience' and express demands for more locally specific programming that addresses their needs, interests and distinct identity. Interviewees are effectively attempting to navigate through the different claims and assumptions of policy makers and media organisations and to negotiate modalities of belonging in different cultures and societies while retaining their particularity. Their responses are clearly demonstrating that they expect to be treated in a way that acknowledges and accepts the fact that they are living in a different place (physically and socially) and are attempting to negotiate their inclusion to the national community of their country of origin in ways that assert their difference, at the same time affirming their common elements with fellow nationals living in their home countries or in other diasporas (Tsagarousianou, in press).

Conclusion

This paper has examined London's South Asian and Greek-Cypriot communities' attitudes and evaluation of the media available to them and focussed on a number of consumption-related practices that ethnic community audiences are engaged in. Audience responses indicate the existence of shared, though not identical, evaluations of, and attitudes towards the media, mainstream as well as ethnic, among the two communities.

Despite the experiences of dislocation, marginalisation and exclusion so common among ethnic minorities, audiences display remarkable resilience, resourcefulness and skill in their consumption practices, articulating discourses of cultural rights relating to their ethnic and diasporic specificity but also claiming inclusion in the 'mainstream'. South Asian and Greek-Cypriot audiences' usage of the media available to them illustrate their capacity for domesticating, translating, and creating meaning that is familiar and intelligible out of the 'foreign', creating a sense of space that is welcoming and inclusive in an institutional and cultural landscape that is often alien and exclusive. Ethnic communities often find themselves in conditions of other-determination, whereby assumptions and decisions regarding their identities, loyalties and rights are made by external cultural and political centres, situated in the so-called 'countries of origin' or in the 'countries of settlement'. Such perceptions have clearly been reflected in audience interviews and focus group sessions as also have strategies of self-determination and differentiation from both audiences (and communities) 'back home' and in the mainstream of the country of settlement. Consumption of media and cultural products in this context is a creative process which, within the limits of what is accessible and available attempts to articulate discourses of difference and particularity, integration and membership not so much in transnational cultural milieux as it is often suggested but on fairly well grounded local contexts of meaning and interaction.

Notes

1   The empirical research upon which this paper is premised has been funded by the Centre for Communication and Information Studies of the University of Westminster.

2   These have been conducted by the author (Greek Cypriot audiences) and the author and Hasmita Ramji (South Asian audiences).

3   In the 1991 Census 'ethnic group' question, respondents were invited to describe themselves as: *White, Black Caribbean, Black African, Black other, Indian, Pakistani, Bangladeshi, Chinese, any other ethnic group*. Obviously this classification restricts the range of possible responses and does not allow for 'white' ethnic minorities to be recorded.

4   For a discussion of some of these responses see J. Solomos and L. Back, 1995, pp. 50-66.

5   A more detailed discussion of the ethnic community media sector can be found in Tsagarousianou, 1999.

6   Indeed, it can be argued that, although they often share experiences of marginalisation and exclusion with their parents, the usage of the term 'migrant' when referring to second and third generation members of migrant communities might not be appropriate.

7   This argument has been subjected to criticism for what has been seen as its one-dimensionality as well as the oversimplifying assumptions contained in it. Nevertheless, it provides a useful start for considering the success of cross-cultural reception of serial television drama: for an interesting critique of Liebes and Katz see Cunningham and Jacka (1994).

8   For an extensive discussion of issues relating to the concepts of *aporia* and *subaltern position* see Spivak (1988, pp. 271-313).

9   For the definitions of 'place' *(lieu)* and 'space' *(espace)* that I am adopting in my analysis, see De Certeau (1984, pp. 117-118). In short, space is a practised, lived place, produced by flows, operations and practices which situate it and temporalise it, give a meaning or meanings to it.

References

Appadurai, A. (1996), *Modernity at Large*, University of Minnesota Press, Minneapolis.

Baldwin, (1995), 'Montezuma's Revenge', in R. C. Allen (ed.) *To Be Continued: Soap Operas Around the World*, Routledge, London, pp. 285-300.

Basch,L., Glick Schiller, N. and Szanton Blanc, C. (1994), *Nations Unbound: Transnational Projects, Postcolonial Predicaments and Deterritorialised Nation States*, Gordon and Breach, Amsterdam.

Bhabha, H. K. (1994), *The Location of Culture*, Routledge, London.

Cunningham, S. and Jacka, E. (1994), 'Neighbourly Relations? Cross-Cultural Reception Analysis and Australian Soaps in Britain', *Cultural Studies*, 8 (3), pp. 509-526.

De Certeau, M. (1984), *The Practice of Everyday Life*, University of California Press, Berkeley.

Gillespie, M. (1995a), 'Sacred Serials, Devotional Viewing and Domestic Worship', in R. C. Allen (ed.) *To Be Continued: Soap Operas Around the World*, Routledge, London, pp. 354-380.

- - (1995b), *Television, Ethnicity and Cultural Change*, Routledge, London.

Harvey, S. (1994), 'Channel 4 Television: From Annan to Grade', in S. Hood (ed.) *Behind the Screens: The Structure of British Television in the Nineties*, Lawrence and Wishart, London, pp. 42-59.

Herzfeld, M. (1997), *Cultural Intimacy; Social Poetics in the Nation-State,* Routledge, London and New York.

Karim, H. K. (1998), 'From Ethnic Media to Global Media: Transnational Communication Networks Among Diasporic Communities', Working Paper Transnational Communities Series, WPTC-99-02, June 1998.

Lewis, P. and Booth, J. (1989), *The Invisible Medium: Public, Commercial and Community Radio*, Macmillan, Basingstoke.

Liebes, T. and Katz, E. (1990), *The Export of Meaning: Cross-Cultural Readings of Dallas*, Oxford University Press, New York.

Machin, D. and D. Carrithers (1996), 'From "interpretative communities" to "communities of improvisation" ', *Media, Culture & Society*, Vol.18, pp. 343-352.

Miller, D. (1995), 'The Consumption of Soap Opera: The Young and the Restless and Mass Consumption in Trinidad', in R. C. Allen (ed.) *To Be Continued: Soap Operas Around the World*, Routledge, London, pp. 213-233.

Solomos, J. and L. Back (1995), *Race, Politics and Social Change*, Routledge, London.

Spivak, G. C. (1988), 'Can the Subaltern Speak?' in G. Nelson and L. Grossberg (eds) *Marxism and the Interpretation of Culture*, Macmillan, London, pp. 271-313.

Tsagarousianou, R. (1999), 'Gone to the Market? The Development of Asian and Greek-Cypriot Community Media in Britain', *Javnost/The Public,* VI (1), pp. 55-70.

-- (forthcoming) 'Ethnic community media, community identity and citizenship in contemporary Britain', in N. Jankowski and O. Prehn (eds) *Community Media in the Information Age: Perspectives, Findings and Policy*, Hampton Press, New Jersey.

-- (in press), '"A space where one feels at home"; Media consumption practices among London's South Asian and Greek Cypriot communities', in R. King and N. Wood (eds), *Media and Migration*, Routledge, London.

3 Minority Youth, Media Uses and Identity Struggle: the Role of the Media in the Production of Locality

THOMAS TUFTE

Introduction

In November 1999 there was a serious clash between police and youngsters in Nørrebro, an old working class neighbourhood in central Copenhagen. What began as rioting developed into a serious incident of social unrest and violence between citizens and authorities. Some of the youngsters involved were ethnic minorities. Some months later I asked 14-year old Kalicia from Nørrebro about her opinion on the discussion that had followed in the media, which had focused heavily on the 'problems' related to the presence of ethnic minorities in Denmark:

> Kalicia: I just feel they [the media] stir up the whole thing. I can understand why old people are racists, because they are influenced by television, so you cannot become anything else than a racist.

> TT: When one stays at home all the time?

> Kalicia: Yes. I go out, I go to school, I am among people, I know how it is. But if I just sat at home and watched television I think I would also be angry at them. Because the television really turns them into villains.

> TT: Are you saying that the problem lies in the media?

> Kalicia: Yes, because the media don't ever say anything good [about ethnic minorities] and they don't say 'now you'll hear about this good family that does this, and the dad works in a good job'. No, you don't hear about them. You only hear about the bad ones.

> TT: So you are actually arguing that the media should tell some positive stories?

Kalicia: Yes. Or people should stop listening to the media. But that's not possible.

Othering and Belonging

When describing the media's way of reporting on ethnic minorities, Kalicia refers to the process of 'othering', whereby identity boundaries are drawn between oneself and others. The process of othering here refers to the problem-focused and often negative categorisation of ethnic minorities vis-à-vis ethnic Danes, and as such it can be see as a continuation of the problematic raised by Edward Said regarding the relation between the West and the Orient (Said, 1979). My thesis is that the general representation of non-Western ethnic minorities in the Danish media reinforces a discourse of ethnic minorities as 'other', constrasting them with the human and social values upon which Danish identity understands and qualifies itself.

The media's coverage of the incident mentioned above - an incident which I present more fully below - has in Kalicia's view reinforced the boundaries between older Danes and the 'others', here understood as ethnic minorities in general. The characteristics of this reporting about ethnic minorities are substantially documented in several analyses (Togeby & Gaasholt, 1995; Hussein et. al., 1997; Hervik, 1999; Togeby & Moeller, 1999; Hussein, 2000; Jensen, 2000). They generally confirm the problem-focused media representation of ethnic minorities, focusing on issues such as criminal incidents, conflicts around women wearing scarves, Halal-slaughtering and forced marriages. The general conclusion is clear: the process of othering between, on one side, ethnic Danes, and on the other, ethnic minorities as a whole, is clearly reinforced by the media.

However, the question remains of how these processes of othering, articulated and reinforced in the media, are *experienced* by ethnic minorities? How does it affect their understanding of themselves, and thus their process of identity formation? The approach here is deliberately multi-ethnic, exploring how different ethnic minorities living in Nørrebro have *shared experiences* of othering within the Danish society. There are more than 40 different ethnic minorities living in Nørrebro (Indre Nørrebro Bydelsrapport, 1999), obviously representing a rich variety of cultures, life styles, languages and beliefs. But is there uniformity in their experience of othering, transcending their diversity of origin? My fieldwork, conducted among ethnic minority youth in Inner Nørrebro between October 1999 and May 2000 shows that many of them have similar experiences of feeling socially marginalised vis-à-vis ethnic majority Danes.[1] In this chapter I analyse the dynamics of othering and of social marginalisation among these youngsters and especially how these feelings were articulated around the November 1999 incident.

Exploring how ethnic minority youth experience the process of othering will lead me directly on to the question of *belonging*. What sort of belonging do the ethnic minority youth in Nørrebro feel to the neighbourhood and the country they live in and are citizens of? Using Arjun Appadurai's notion of 'locality' my question is: how do these local citizens - minority youth in Nørrebro - 'produce locality'? And what locality is this? Producing locality here refers to the process of social agency whereby people produce a sense of belonging (Appaduari, 1996).

Appadurai's focus is on what locality might mean in a situation where the nation-state faces particular sorts of *transnational destabilisation* (Appadurai, 1996). The situation of conflict in Denmark, not least in the neighbourhood of Nørrebro, reveals exactly this: a process of transnational destabilisation. It is composed of different parallel movements that have been underway for some time. On the one hand there is the physical presence of ethnic minorities, migrants and refugees. Despite the fact that immigrants having been living and working in Denmark since the mid-late 1960s, it is only in recent years that their presence has evoked serious and substantial political debate and challenged the self-understanding of ethnic Danes about what it is to be Danish.

On the other hand there is the transnationalisation of the media. This process is demonstrated by the fact that the dramatic events in Nørrebro were immediately exposed to international audiences via CNN, BBC, etc. It is also more strongly manifested in the range of media increasingly accessible from homes in Nørrebro: Indian, Bosnian, Kurdish and Turkish satellite TV channels, Jasmineli websites, Macedonian and Arab radio stations are all broadcast in Copenhagen. Some scholars argue that this increased accessibility of ethnic programming reinforces the ethnic identity of their audiences and develops problematics of ethnic and social isolation. However, as Aksoy and Robins (2000) have rightly argued, it is more complex than that. It is a constantly changing scenario which needs to be studied in much more detail in order to uncover the very many multi-vectoral cultural and social dynamics at stake in these homes and in the neighbourhood overall.

With respect to this, my thesis is that what we are experiencing internationally these days is more a transnational *re-stabilisation* rather than a transnational destabilisation. Migration, media and technology - along with numerous other elements of contemporary globalisation - are leading to socio-spatial re-configurations, where Benedict Anderson's national community (Anderson, 1983) becomes just one of many equally important and emerging imagined communities (Morley and Robins, 1995). Ethnic

35

minorities, while citizens of Denmark, also belong to diasporic communities that operate within very different socio-spatial and cultural-geographical coordinates or frames compared to their fellow citizens, the 'ethnic majority Danes.' Analysing their production of locality will show some of the complexities of the on-going *transnational restabilisation.*

Analysing the production of locality in the case of ethnic minorities in Nørrebro has to deal with these movements - the (more or less recent) migration to Denmark, and the transnationalisation of the media, the latter providing numerous new possibilities for maintaining mediated cultural contact to the country of origin, and to the diasporic communities to which many pertain. The relationship between media uses and identity struggles in the lives of ethnic minority youth in Copenhagen is at the core of this chapter.

Nørrebro: Minority Youth and Everyday Life

Nørrebro is a neighbourhood with a tradition of social organisation, including the labour movements of the 19th century, which were born here. The social democrats and the socialists have always had strongholds in this neighbourhood. The focus of this project is the central part of Nørrebro, *Indre Nørrebro* (Inner Nørrebro). This is an area with 30,000 inhabitants, constituting an independent sub-municipality under the municipality of Copenhagen. It has its own administration and democratically elected political board, currently headed by a socialist.

Since the 1970s, Inner Nørrebro has undergone substantial demographic and physical changes, the old workers' flats having been largely torn down and replaced. It has given Inner Nørrebro more room, less inhabitants but also a dramatic change in population. Large parts of the population have been replaced in the course of the last 20 years. Many newcomers have been immigrants and refugees. Today 21.5 per cent of the population are of ethnic origins other than Danish, namely Turkish, Pakistani, Jasmineli, Lebanese, Palestinian, Kurdish and ex-Yugoslavian (Danmarks Statistik, 1999).

13 Youngsters - Housing, Schooling and Family Background

In Kalicia's 8th grade class (the students are between 13 and 15 years old) at a public school in Inner Nørrebro, all 13 students have at least one parent of an ethnic origin other than Danish. For 10 of the 13 who comprise my sample, both parents are of an ethnic minority background. This is quite unusual for any Danish public school, and is also above average for this particular school.[2] However, the class had had more than double the number of students back in 1st grade (28), when a large number were ethnic majority Danes. Some have since moved to other public or private schools in the neighbourhood, some have moved out of the neighbourhood with their families and a small number have been expelled, a gradual process leading to the current situation. Parallel to this, the class has in recent years received 5 new students, all but one being refugees. Thus, today, only 8 are left of the original core group of 28 students. Nevertheless, the students are very united, enjoying a pleasant social climate in the classroom, and extensive social contact in their leisure time, with most of them considering their class mates as best friends: 'Everybody in the class are like best friends...We talk about everything together' (Nadia, 14). Socially, it is a well-functioning class.

The students have origins in Turkey, Turkish Kurdistan, Iranian Kurdistan, Pakistan, Morocco, Bosnia, Italy, Armenia and the Greek, Turkish and Albanian parts of Macedonia. In terms of official religious affiliation, nine are Muslims, one Greek-Orthodox, one Catholic, one Christian and one Jewish. In contrast to this multiplicity of ethnic origins and religious affiliations, their socio-economic situations are similar.

In terms of housing, all 13 live in rather small flats where quite a number share bedrooms with sisters or brothers. About half of them have their own room - most have shared rooms with siblings until recently, but the teenage girls are increasingly obtaining their own rooms, forcing their brothers to share together.

Their parents are predominantly from less educated backgrounds, and only two have elder siblings who are studying at universities or equivalent higher education (Maria and Jamal). According to their class teacher, only a very limited number of these students will qualify to enter higher education. The majority of them will be recommended to seek other educational pathways after completing their schooling.

As for language proficiency, all of them speak and write Danish better than the language of their own or their parent's origin. However, most of them speak a language other than Danish to at least one parent. Generally, the language they communicate with their siblings in is Danish, occasionally mixed with another language. Neelem and Angili both attend state-supported Urdu classes three times a week, this being a way of acquiring an improved proficiency in their mother tongue.

November 1999: A Neighbourhood in Flames?

A number of recent events have fuelled a strong media focus on ethnic minorities, and in particular one event sparked what developed over three or four months into an intense public debate about the role, rights, obligations and problems of ethnic minorities in the Danish society.

Around 10 pm on the night of the 7th November 1999 a large riot began in Nørrebro. A small group of about 20 young people, their faces covered by hoods, began smashing shop windows and setting fire to garbage containers. The group grew to an estimated 100 youngsters, who smashed approximately 300 shop windows, burnt cars and garbage containers, and cut off the electricity in the neighbourhood. The police took one and a half hours from the time of the first unrest until they felt they had gathered a strong enough force to enter the neighbourhood and put an end to the disorder. Their entry, however, resulted in street fights with the rioters for most of the night.

The youngsters were apparently both ethnic minorities and ethnic Danes, and the apparent motivation for the incident was the extradition from Denmark to Turkey of a 23-year old Turkish citizen. He was supposed to complete a 3-year prison sentence in Denmark and then be extradited, despite having being born and lived all his life in Denmark. The rioters supposedly came from many parts of town, the incident being something that, in the absence of the police, quickly attracted youngsters from several suburbs of Copenhagen.

The incident was reported on the BBC, CNN and many other media outlets in neighbouring countries. It was portrayed as the most violent incident of social unrest in Denmark since May 18th 1993 (when Danes protested, in the same neighbourhood, against the result of the Maastricht census). In the Danish media the event was immediately tied up with a rapidly growing discussion about the problems of integration for immigrants and refugees. It became a very emotional discussion, led mostly by ethnic Danes discussing the 'others', the immigrants and refugees, living in Denmark. The issue became a core issue in Social Democrat Prime Minister Rasmussen's Millennium speech, given on January 1st 2000, a speech where he spoke about 'the strangers' in Denmark, referring to immigrants and refugees, some of whom have lived here since the 1960s, having both children and grandchildren here. Without arguing direct causality, the fact is that the extreme right-wing political party Dansk Folkeparti (The Danish People's Party), climbed to new heights in the polls, with more than 15 per cent of the Danish voters supporting them in mid-January 2000.

In the midst of this, Nørrebro was, in the minds of the public, a war-torn battleground, an unpleasant place with social unrest, crime and gang-fights, a dangerous neighbourhood to live or work in. The citizens of Nørrebro, however, were fed up with their neighbourhood once again being represented in such away. As 14-year old Maria said: 'it was made into a huge thing. And I had not heard it. It was not until the next evening that I was told about it by a friend who said: 'Have you heard what happened?', and I hadn't even noticed a thing...' Asked whether they had spoken about it in school the day after, she responded: 'No, no, because nobody had really taken notice of it, well yes, my friend had said that it was very messy in Nørrebro, but she did not really know what had happened...and then we said that it is always messy in Nørrebro, and then we didn't really take it seriously.' Maria didn't discover what had really happened until the evening after the event.

Nadia was also shocked, having heard about it at school, but only discovering the reason for it in the media the night after the event: 'We did not know until we saw it on television...When we drove over here in the morning we thought, because we didn't know at all, we just thought: what has happened here? We saw paint and smashed windows and everything. It was completely crazy.' Another class member, Serap, stated: 'I did not hear anything. I saw it on television.'

Karina, when asked her opinion on the treatment Nørrebro got in the media, said: 'I think it is a pity, because I am here myself, so I am able to see that it is not true. People get the impression, my family for example, they call sometimes and say: 'So - are you still alive? Haven't you been killed by stones?' While it is the treatment of the neighbourhood in the media Karina complains about, Neelem is more direct. She is angry at the media, accusing them of always blaming the immigrants. Asked about the best and the worst about the neighbourhood she states: 'The best is the people that live here, at least those I know...I don't really think there is something which is the worst. Maybe when you watch the news, you become a little afraid [...] I think they always blame the immigrants, and it may also be that they are to blame, but it is always them that things are wrong with.' Neelem's reaction to the media coverage of what happened was: 'I did not become angry, I just thought 'fuck 'em.'

Like most of her schoolmates, Kalicia only found out what had happened afterwards. However, speaking to some of the participants in the riot, she learned that the extradition was just one issue that sparked much deeper social discontent and frustration. As Kalicia states:

I didn't know at all what happened. I only got to know about it afterwards. I don't think they should do it, I think it is wrong, but I have also heard from them who have done it and from others who know then, and I have also heard the reason.

TT: Being the case about the fellow who was extradited?

Kalicia: No, it was not only because of that.

TT: What do they say? How do they explain it?

Kalicia: They explain it by saying they have not been treated well. The police have not treated them and their families well. Because the son has done something, they have threatened the parents. It's those kind of things, but nobody knows about that.

For most of the youngsters in this case study, the riot became a mediated experience. The media reported in dramatic ways, leaving an impression in the general public of an insecure and violent neighbourhood - a representation of Nørrebro which contradicted their own experience of living there.

The portrayal of 'Nørrebro in Flames' (front page of *EkstraBladet*, 8 November 1999) rearticulated the point of view that ethnic minorities (in addition to the so-called 'autonomous', young rebellious Danes) were both the cause (the extradition case) *and* the agents of social unrest. What did not reach the media or what the media did not broadcast were the more nuanced causes behind the riot and the motivations to engage in it: the everyday harassment. The reaction among the ethnic minorities living in the neighbourhood was a reinforcement of their distanciation, their 'othering' in relation to Danish society, the media and the ethnic majority Danes. Neelem's comment captures the atmosphere and feelings when she simply stated: 'Fuck them'.

The media coverage that followed the 'riot' had a significant long-term damaging effect, sparking emotional outpourings from right-wing politicians who articulated opinions and feelings against ethnic minorities in general, thus letting youngsters like those represented in this chapter pay the highest price - an increased social marginalisation and disassociation from the Danish society. However, while the media coverage overwhelmingly contributed to a process of social marginalisation, the everyday uses of the media show many other facets of the diverse and varied ways media enter and influence everyday life.

Media Uses and the Production of Locality

The process of producing locality occurs by articulating and forming relations between 'the sense of social immediacy, the technologies of interactivity, and the relativity of contexts' (Appadurai, 1996, p. 178). The media are central in these processes, not only as a technology. Rephrasing Appadurai's statement as a question, with a particular emphasis on the role of the media, would result in this: What sense of social immediacy do different forms of media use articulate? Which communication technologies are used, and how are they used vis-à-vis producing senses of social immediacy and feelings of social and cultural belonging? While locality on one hand consists of a material expression, locality is also *a structure of feeling*. Everybody wants to belong somewhere, actively doing something to feel at home. The media influences the materiality of locality, in particular in the physical organisation of the home, but more importantly, the media influences the structures of feeling locality consists of.

The purpose of focusing on everyday media use is also to excavate the foundations of an often-recurring statement vis-à-vis media consumption. Many of the youngsters cited watching television or videos, chatting on the Internet or listening to music as recurrent media practices that took place when they didn't really have anything else to do. Neelem had no specific television programmes that she *had* to see: 'It's not that I just have to see it. If I don't have anything to do, then I do like to see it.' Jamal also states, about video: 'When I don't have anything to do then I watch it' and Claudia states 'I don't watch anything anymore...' besides MTV, which, 'when I am at home, then its just turned on.' Liv can sometimes sit and chat and surf on the Net, 'Yes, on Chili-net sometimes, but not really, only sometimes, if I don't have anything to do.'

A lot of media use seems to be something that simply just occurs, for want of better opportunities, or with no real conscious proactive motivation.. What does this lack of explicit choice and priority signify? Does is make the media less important? I don't believe so - and my analysis will show how this 'meaningless' and unconscious media use has significant importance for the youngsters in making sense of the world around them. Two main points will become explicit in the course of this analysis. First, that each technology and each genre provides its own particular opportunity for social relationships. While some contribute more to the symbolic construction of locality and belonging - for example reinforcing a diasporic community - others mostly contribute to the material construction of locality and belonging - for example the reinforcement of a neighbourhood identity. Secondly, that some media use contributes to social integration and social positioning in everyday life. Thus, rather than focusing on the large scale media 'events' or rituals that function more as suspension from everyday life, the focus here is on the ordinary and frequent media uses that have a socially integrating function in everyday life (Larsen & Tufte, 1999).

Media Access

As is the general tendency in Denmark, new technology is rapidly finding its way into the homes of these youngsters (Fridberg, et. al., 1997). Many of them have mobile phones, almost all of them have home computers, and a few have Internet access. Those who don't have their own mobile phones have access through relatives, while those without domestic computers and Internet access have free access at school and public libraries and can pay for access at Internet cafés, of which there are four in the immediate neighbourhood.

These young people belong to a generation of young urban Danes that have been brought up with cable TV as a 'natural' technological infra-structure in their household, along with radio, video and stereos. Satellite TV is also widespread, although more limited than other technologies. Cable TV has provided this generation with access to all the major Danish and Nordic commercial channels, in addition to a variety of other channels, including some from their countries of origin. Obviously, cable networks only serve audiences of significant size, so there are channels for the Turkish and Pakistani communities in Copenhagen, but not for the smaller Bosnian or Armenian communities. However, to improve accessibility to channels from their country of origin, five out of the 13 families have supplemented their cable packages with private satellite dishes (Kalicia, Nadia, Neelem, Peter, Angili and Claudia). Access to the 'homeland' channels are usually the principal motivation for acquiring satellite TV: 'We have had the Selector, right. It was because of the war. That Kosovo war. My father, he followed it, he always had to watch, so we have had Selector.' (Claudia) Angili confirms the same motivation: 'We have the Selector. We watch Urdu, Indian, it is Indian' (Angili).

As this outline of media access suggests, television, often combined with video, is the dominant medium in the lives of these 13 youngsters and their families. Measured in time, it is by far the medium they spend most time with. Compared to television, most of the other traditional media exist marginally in their everyday lives; radio and newspapers in particular are very marginal. Radio, in most cases, seems to have acquired a very marginal position. Many confirm the limited radio usage, while some do use radio for music purposes. There is generally very little access to daily newspapers, which first and foremost reflects the lack of interest in newspapers among their parents. For those who do have newspapers at home, there is very limited usage, usually just the TV guides. Generally, they have a limited understanding of the fact that one could subscribe on a daily basis to newspapers. As for magazines, a few of them mentional occasional buying of the youth magazines *MIX* or *Vi Unge*. Books however, do play a role in individual cases, for example in the case of Serap (see below).

Overall, there are no significant obstacles in terms of access to information and entertainment via communication technologies. However, there are still socio-economic constraints, especially regarding accessing satellite television, mobile phones and the number of TV sets in the home. In addition to the socio-economic factors influencing media access, there are limits on domestic accessibility rooted in belief and opinion. Angili's father, for example, did not want either Internet access or video in his home. As Angili explained, they used to have video: 'We did have it, but now we have given it away. My father doesn't want us to begin watching films and all that. Because as soon as we start watching videos we forget school. So that's why he won't buy a video for us. He has bought Selector for us, but that was on one condition: "If you do your homework and do the things that have to be done, then you may have it. Otherwise, I will have it stopped."' Regarding Internet access, Angili explained: 'Somebody probably convinced him that there are dirty things on the Internet. So he probably believes we go in, clicking on to this and watch it. He is so stupid!' Other parents had similar opinions, but this restriction is limited to the domestic sphere: Angili accesses the Internet at school and at the public library.

Uses of Television

Television, together with video, is instrumental in the process of using media to negotiate identities. This is clearly seen in young people's patterns of use and through analysing what they watch, with whom, when, and where. Of the traditional media, television is for all of them by far the most significant medium in their everyday life. All have TV at home, 11 of them have television in their rooms, and most of them have grown up with domestic cable TV access.

While the principal place of television consumption is in the home, this covers a large variation in the forms of use, including programme choice. What comes across in the analysis of media use among these 13 young people is a multi-layered use, reflecting multiple and very different scales of socio-cultural orientation and reflecting many levels of identity. Their media use is guided by and reflects age, sex, gender, cultural background and life history.

Among the striking absences in their programme choices and preferences are three issues: they watch no Danish television fiction; they watch very little news; they have only a very limited use of the two Danish

Public Service channels, DR1 and TV2, historically the largest and strongest channels among Danish audiences.

Among the striking similarities in their programme choices and preferences can be noted the following: a very high consumption of predominantly American TV series and American talk shows; a preference for the three Danish commercial channels, TV3, TV3+ and TV Danmark; a strong gendered media use; the existence of an 'ethnic' media use, understood as a layer of media consumption focused on channels from either countries of origin, linguistic or cultural regions of origin, or local media in Denmark with a focus on issues related to migrants and refugees.

Regarding this last point, there are some clear generational differences between these youngsters and their parents. Within their ethnic media use, these 13-15 year olds have an orientation towards national or local Danish news programmes dealing with ethnic minority issues in Denmark or in Copenhagen, while their parents have a somewhat stronger orientation towards programs from their country or region of origin. We must however be cautious in drawing clear distinctions between parents' and children's orientation, because some youngsters feel very strongly about their country or region of origin, reflecting this in their music or film preferences as well as their news consumption during the Kosovo war (despite the fact that they generally have a very limited news consumption). Again, in relation to their 'territory of origin' there are multiple conceptual variations inviting the question: what constitutes this territory of origin? What can we rightfully characterise as ethnic orientation and not cultural, religious or something of plain general interest? Neelem, for example, is Pakistani, Pakistan being a country historically in conflict with India. Nevertheless she has a strong orientation towards Indian film, due to her Urdu-language background and also, she argues, due to the quality of Indian films compared to Pakistani films. Neelem also argues that they are more 'modern.' Angili, who is also Pakistani, has a similar interest in Indian films.

Asu Aksoy and Kevin Robins have problematised this issue in a recent article about Turkish transnational media, demonstrating the diversity now present in Turkish media culture and arguing the need for more nuanced thinking about this space (Aksoy and Robins, 2000). The same could be argued about several other regions. Obviously one must be careful to distinguish between the Danish channels, and it is equally simplistic to generalise about 'ethnic' or 'homeland' media. In analysing multi-layered media consumption the variety and diversity of media for each country or ethnic group we speak of must be taken into consideration. At this stage, the main points I wish to emphasise are that this media consumption from 'territories of origin' can be highly diverse and varied, and that the consumption and use of these media does not reflect a cultural isolation or regression towards the country of origin, but reflects the same sort of cultural ambivalence and ongoing identity negotiation generally taking place in each individual.

This invites us to explore further the meanings of this multi-layered-ness in media consumption. In this chapter, without going into substantial detail, I have distinguished the following four categories of media: local media in Denmark; national media in Denmark; international media; homeland media. I have also distinguished four types of content: homeland content; ethnic content (referring to issues about refugees and migrants in Denmark); mainstream Danish content; mainstream international content. This article does not discuss in detail the national media in Denmark or the homeland media. These categories remain very general, but, with the categories of content, can give some general indication of the media flow the audiences expose themselves to.

In the media use of these 13-15 year olds, homeland media consumption is generally concentrated around parent-initiated media consumption in the home - be it TV news turned on by the parents (Maria, Jasmine, Peter, Nadia), films chosen from the parent's video archive (Serap) or radio listened to by parents (Angili, Jamal). However, music is a field where the youngsters themselves have a strong interest in music from their countries and regions of origin. This is demonstrated in their preference within domestic video recordings (of family parties, etc.), in what they like to sing, in rented videos, in their choice of CDs and cassettes, etc. Neelem reconfirms her musical interest in her Internet-surfing, the Bollywood website being one of her favourites. Claudia speaks of Macedonean music and songs from their home videos of parties, etc. David learnt to sing and play Armenian folk songs while at the Red Cross Refugee Centre upon arrival in Denmark. However, this musical interest is cultivated alongside their interest in Techno, Latin and other preferences similar to most Danish youth.

Mainstream media programmes dominate their television consumption. This is manifest and clearly documented in their preferences for American TV series, talk shows and films. As mentioned, there is also a clear gendered difference in what they see - a gendering which also counts for their homeland media consumption. Gendered TV preferences appear in the afternoons, when television consumption begins (apart from MTV in the morning, which several of the girls watch). Most of these youngsters have naps in the afternoons, some do homework, and subsequently very many of them watch different TV series or go over to (same-sex) friends to do homework. Viewing of TV or video is then done within distinct gendered groups.

While the boys prefer *Vore Værste År* (Married with Children), *Jerry Springer*, *Robinson* (AKA *Survivor*), *Drew Harry*, *Rap Fyr i LA* (Fresh Prince of Bel Air), action movies and comedy, the girls prefer *Friends*, *X-Files*, *Ricki Lake* and romantic TV series. One gendered characteristic regarding genre is that many of the girls like thrillers, something confirmed in their reading and film preferences (Serap, Neelem, Karina, Liv).

What this brief overview of mainstream and homeland media use points towards is the combined multiplicity and diversity of their media use on one hand, and the uniformity and similarity of it on the other hand. These 13 individuals each compose their media menus based not only on age and sex, but also on cultural background and life history. Very roughly speaking we see that age and sex articulate uniform interests, linked very much to youth lifestyles, while cultural background and life history determine the very individual and diverse layers of their media consumption. For example, when asked why he likes *Beverly Hills 90210*, contrary to many of the other boys, 14-year old David responded 'because it is such a peaceful place'. This statement may be banal, but it becomes somewhat more meaningful when contextualised into his life history as a refugee, having lived in five countries, and in the last two years in Denmark having been moved to a total of four different refugee centres and five schools.

Conclusion

It is worth noting that the shared cultural references of these young people are to be found in a number of American talk shows, TV series and films, watched primarily on the new commercial networks. As such, they have a shared - albeit gendered - media experience, these reference points being used in their social interaction and peer conversation. It is a media experience very similar to that of most Danish youth their age - they generally don't watch either Danish TV fiction or Danish public service channels. For a country such as Denmark, which until 12 years ago had only one national public service channel (DR1) this is a significant change, which still has to be better understood with regard to cultural changes in Danish society.

In addition to this shared level of media consumption, the individual media menus include programs of homeland content and ethnic content, the first generally being film and music, while the ethnic content mainly refers to the Danish news coverage of migrants and refugees in Denmark.

The media consumption thus provides different opportunities for these youth to work with their identities, cultivate cultural and aesthetic tastes and interests, emotional experiences, etc. They navigate between different cultural universes and produce locality on several levels, in relation to their immediate neighbourhood, in relation to the nation in which they live, in relation to the diasporas some of them belong to, and so on. Having an immigrant or refugee background gives them, compared to most Danish youth, a more complex process of identity work, requiring them to navigate between more layers and worlds of meaning, producing many, not just one, senses of belonging.

The media representation of ethnic minorities, exemplified by the November 1999 event, but confirmed in general statements about everyday media representation, is a strong articulator in the process of social division and boundary marking. It reinforces a boundary between, on one side the ethnic majority Danes, and on the other side the ethnic minorities living in Danish society. This is a clear feeling and experience among the 13 young people. They feel a lack of subtlety in the media's representations, which articulate a shared experience of being 'other' in the society they live in and form part of. A similar boundary is found in the social organisation of everyday life among these 13 youngsters, with a general tendency to have friends from other ethnic minority groups, and not from within the ethnic majority Danes.

Notes

1   My fieldwork focused on the everyday life of 13 youngsters in the 8th grade at a public school in Inner Nørrebro. It is based on participant observation, focus group interviews, individual interviews with key informants and with the 13 youngsters. I also used fotoethnography, written exercises with the youngsters, surveys and literature review. The names of the youngsters have been altered.
2   In this particular school 80.5 per cent of the students are of an ethnic origin other than Danish.

References

Aksoy, A. and Robins, K. (2000), 'Thinking across spaces: transnational television from Turkey', *European Journal of Cultural Studies*, Vol.3, No.3, pp. 343-365.
Anderson, B. (1983), *Imagined Communities: Reflections on the Origin and Spread of Nationalism*, Verso, London.
Appadurai, A. (1996), *Modernity at Large: Cultural Dimensions of Globalization*, University of Minnesota Press, Minnesota.
Danmarks Statistik. (1999), *Yearbook*, København.
Fridberg, T., Allerup, P., Drotner, K., Joergensen, P. S. and Soerensen, A. S. (1997), *Mønstre i mangfoldigheden. 15-18-åriges mediebrug i Danmark*, Borgen/Medier, København.
Gaasholt, D. and Togeby, L. (1995), I syv sind. Danskernes holdninger til flygtninge og indvandrere, Forlaget Politica, pp. 1-18.

Hervik, P. (ed.) (1999), *Den generende forskellighed: Danske svar på den stigende multikulturalisme*, Akademisk Forlag, København.

Hussein, M. (2000), 'The Muslim Family in Europe: Islam, Media and Minorities in Denmark', *Current Sociology*, 48 (04), pp. 195-216.

Hussein, M, Yilmaz, F. and O'Connor, T. (1997), *Medierne, minoriteterne og majoriteten - en undersøgelse af nyhedsmedier og den folkelige diskurs i Danmark*, Akademisk Forlag, København.

Indre Nørrebro Bydel. (1999), *Integrationsrapport og evaluering af helhedsplan*, Nørrebro Bydel, København.

Jensen, I. (forthcoming), 'Journalistik som socialt felt' [Journalism as a social field], *MedieKultur*, 32, special issue on Media and Ethnicity.

Larsen, B. and Tufte, T. (1999), 'Is there a Ritual Going on? Exploring the Social Uses of the Media', in I. Bondebjerg & H. K. Hastrup (eds) *Sekvens: Yearbook 1999, Intertextuality and Visual Media*, Dept. of Film- and Media Studies, University of Copenhagen, Copenhagen.

Morley, D. and Robins, K. (1995), *Spaces of Identity: global media, electronic landscapes and cultural boundaries*, Routledge, London.

Said, E. (1979), *Orientalism: Western Conceptions of the Orient*, Vintage Books, New York.

Togeby, L. and Møller, B. (1999), *Oplevet Diskrimination - en undersøgelse blandt etniske minoriteter, Nævnet for etnisk ligestilling*, København.

4 Black Like Me: Value Commitment and Television Viewing Preferences of US Black Teenage Girls

LYNNE EDWARDS

Introduction

According to a recent article in *The Philadelphia Inquirer*, seven of the ten most-watched programmes by Black people are the seven programmes that come in dead last with white people (Storm, 2000). These programmes, *The Parkers, Moesha,* and *The Steve Harvey Show* to name a few, share one common characteristic: they feature predominantly Black casts. Although Black and white audiences do watch integrated shows like *ER* and *The Practice* in similar numbers, the two groups prefer to watch programmes that reflect their separate worlds. In other words, we watch television the way we live – segregated (Storm, 2000).

From the industry perspective, it pays to have segregated audiences for television programming. According to Larry Gross, advertisers, who prefer a white target audience with disposable income, will pay premium rates for programmes with stories that revolve around characters like this target audience (Storm, 2000). New, up-and-coming networks benefit from targeting the often-ignored Black audience with Black-oriented programming – and then abandoning them for more lucrative white audiences. For example, Fox became the 'fourth network' on the strength of Black audiences brought to the network by programming like the multi-racial *21 Jump Street* and the predominantly Black *In Living Color*; however, these programmes were eventually dropped in favour of predominantly white programmes like *Married...with Children* and *X-Files*.

Media history is repeating itself with the fledgling Warner Bros (WB) network. WB increased its audience in 1998 on the strength of programmes for teens like *Felicity, Buffy the Vampire Slayer* and *Dawson's Creek* – and two of the top-rated programmes for Black audiences, *The Steve Harvey Show* and *The Jamie Foxx Show* (Aucoin, 1999). At a time when other networks are coming under attack from the National Association for the Advancement of Colored People for lack of racial diversity in their programming, WB has remained relatively unscathed, three of the top seven programmes for Black audiences being on the WB line-up.

In response to the NAACP campaign, networks increased the presence of on-screen minorities in shows for the fall 1999 line-up. However, despite the inclusion of minority characters, Black audiences still didn't watch these programmes (Storm, 2000). One possible explanation for this phenomenon is the frequency of a special-to-television stereotype – low-impact roles for Black actors. This 'new' stereotype has a double edge. First, these roles are generally 'high authority' roles, like chief of detectives or head surgeon, but they have very little impact on the outcome of most episodes. Second, these high authority characters are frequently the only minorities in the cast; in other words, as the status of Black characters has increased, the number of Black characters has not (Storm, 2000).

Despite fickle networks and the prevalence of old and new stereotypes in television programming, Black people continue to be heavy television viewers – and they continue to prefer Black-oriented television programmes. This chapter argues that the motive for this viewing behaviour rests in the values held by Black viewers and the extent to which they are committed to these values. Values are examined as the primary motivation for viewing selections because of their function as behavioural guides; individuals often act in accordance with their values, from consumer purchases to voting decisions. Value commitment is examined, in particular, because 'commitment' is believed to function as a further behavioural constraint. Being committed to one's values should strengthen the association between values and their related behaviours.

Uses and Gratifications

Uses and gratifications researchers suggest that audiences actively select among media options to satisfy unmet psychological needs: determining their motives for making these choices is the focus of most uses and gratifications research. To this end, several uses and gratifications researchers have posited models of viewer programme choice that examine leisure, social, and psychological factors as possible predictors of choice behaviour (Katz, et. al., 1974; McGuire, 1974; Rosengren, 1974; Rubin, 1977; Frank & Greenberg, 1980; Lee and Browne, 1980; Perse, 1990). According to Webster and Wakshlag (1983), there are several assumptions concerning the relationship between viewers' programme choices and programme content in uses and gratifications research. First, this perspective assumes that the viewer's programme choices consistently demonstrate some preference for those content types that best gratify certain needs. The second assumption is that viewers have programme preferences that are systematically related to types of content. A third assumption is that viewers will demonstrate their preferences through their programme choices.

In addition to psychological and other motivations for viewing particular programmes, there are also environmental constraints that must be considered. For example, while Darmon (1976) hypothesises that programme type preference explains viewing preferences, Webster and Wakshlag (1983) argue that patterns of programme choice based on programme type preference may be random since programme choices are constrained by the types of programmes available. Due to the structure of programme options made available to the viewer by the industry, there are a limited number of programme 'types' available at a given time for viewers to choose from. The authors and others (Heeter, 1985; Barwise and Ehrenberg, 1988) also argue that audience availability and awareness adds 'considerable variation' to choice behaviour that is unrelated to specific television content.

These differing models suggest that programme choices are not simply content-driven, rather, they are constrained by what programmes are available to view, by audience availability to view, and by audience awareness of what is available to watch. That programme choices are not content-driven, however, is contradicted by the viewing preferences of Black audiences: Black audiences prefer Black-oriented programmes. Given the constraints of programming and personal availability, Black audiences are driven to view those programmes that seem to reflect their lives and their realities.

Black Audiences

Researchers who study Black subjects argue that being a member of a minority 'race' in America carries with it certain psychological burdens that may impact on behaviour (Clark, 1989; Gibbs, 1989; Jones (ed.), 1989; Taylor, 1989). The realities of racial discrimination and violence, occupational and educational inequities and shorter anticipated life expectancies may adversely affect the world view of Black community members: being young, Black and female may further impact this view. As teen drug use continues to plague the Black community and images of Black teen mothers on welfare continue to fill the media, the outlook for today's

Black youth is increasingly bleak. Despite their environmental conditions, however, Black teens continue to thrive, as Gibbs (1989, p. 179) suggests:

> As a result of generations of discrimination and deprivation, Black adolescents have developed high rates of psychological and behavioural disorders, as well as certain problematic psychosocial behaviours. However, in spite of the high incidence of these problem behaviours, many Black youth have also managed to become competent, well-functioning young adults.

Black adolescents may have developed a unique coping mechanism that enables them to live in this troubled environment and to still thrive. One way of coping may be through escaping into media narratives or by learning coping strategies from these media narratives. Early research has demonstrated that young Blacks prefer Black-oriented programming (Carey, 1966; Liss, 1981). Several studies have linked motivations for television viewing with negative psychological states in Black viewers such as low self-esteem (Tan and Tan, 1979) and depression and alienation from self (Kubey, 1986). Stroman (1986), however, found that viewing habits of Black children were not related to low self-concepts.

Other research has suggested that young Black people watch television primarily for learning and entertainment purposes (Carey, 1966; Greenberg and Dominick, 1968; Comstock and Cobbey, 1979; Frank and Greenberg, 1980; Lee and Browne, 1981; Albarran and Umphrey, 1993). Anderson and Williams (1983) examined the impact of Black television programmes on a group of 78 Black children in North Carolina. Children identified their five favourite programmes as *Good Times* (71 per cent), *What's Happening* (38 per cent), *The Jeffersons* (23 per cent), *Happy Days* (19 per cent), and *The Six Million Dollar Man* (14 per cent). The children then identified their favourite Black programmes: *Good Times* (58 per cent), *What's Happening* (11 per cent), *The Jeffersons* (7.6 per cent) and 'Other' (23.4 per cent). Their reasons for liking these shows included liking shows about Black people (93 per cent), racial pride and identification (40 per cent), appreciation for their entertaining qualities (24 per cent), and a source of information and instruction about Black life (5 per cent). Those who claimed not to like Black programmes (7 per cent) cited shame, embarrassment, and the desire for disassociation from negative stereotypes.

An individual's personal value system may be another factor influencing viewing preferences for Black people. In his study of Black college student viewing preferences, Gandy (1984) sought to determine the association between values and television programme preference. He found that female students were more likely to report using television for companionship and that they placed a somewhat higher value on self-respect than men. Gandy (1984, p.219) concluded that Rokeach's Terminal and Instrumental Values are 'reliable predictors' of the ratings that individuals assign the programmes they watch which, he claims, suggests that audiences 'differ in their valuation of programmes in a manner consistent with their different value structures.' Gandy in fact questions whether individuals 'watch those programmes that reinforce their values or if their values arise from viewing programmes that espouse those values' (1984, p.217).

Values

Within the uses and gratifications framework, television viewing may function to fulfil particular value needs or to provide value-congruent programming. Rokeach (1973, p.5) defines a value as an 'enduring belief that a specific mode of conduct or end-state of existence is personally or socially preferable to an opposite or converse mode of conduct or end-state of existence.' These beliefs have cognitive, affective and behavioural dimensions that guide one's actions and determine what one thinks and feels about those actions. Once a value is learned and adopted, it is integrated into one's value system, a hierarchical structure of the individual's values.

Through their function as behavioural and attitudinal standards, values act as constraints upon the individual's actions and decisions. Values aid the individual in deciding between alternative behavioural choices, guiding the individual's choices among alternatives to the option that is least costly in terms of compromising her value system. The individual's values, then, can be said to constrain her behavioural and ideological choices to those alternatives that are most closely related to those values she holds.

Values aid the individual in deciding between alternative behavioural choices, guiding the individual's choices among alternatives to the option that is least costly in terms of compromising her value system. Rokeach further suggests that those values that are most 'substantively and logically' related to a given behaviour should be the ones that will best predict it, i.e., religious values predict religious behaviour, political values predict political behaviour, and so on. Converse (1964) refers to this ability to predict future behaviours and attitudes based on those currently held by the individual as 'constraint'. The individual's values, then, can be said to constrain her behavioural and ideological choices to those alternatives that are most closely related to those values she holds.

Rokeach and others (Kluckhohn and Strodtbeck, 1961; Pugh, 1977) claim that individuals only hold a limited number of values to facilitate the decision-making processes. An individual is faced with an unlimited number of values-related choices throughout her lifetime: such choices would be impossible to make if the individual had to 'sift through' an infinite number of values in order to make a decision. Rokeach estimates that there are approximately thirty-six values which represent the full spectrum of human goals and beliefs. He divides these values into two groups, terminal and instrumental values. Terminal values refers to ideal 'end-states of existence' - where and how the individual sees herself in the future. Instrumental values refer to the ideal actions necessary for functioning successfully in society and for achieving desired end-states of existence.[1]

Commitment

This conception of values and how they function suggests that holding particular values makes an individual more likely to perform certain behaviours. Actually performing these behaviours, in accordance with one's values, suggests a certain level of commitment to those values by the individual. Commitment is defined as 'the pledging or binding of the individual to behavioural acts' (Keisler, 1971, p. 30) and personal dedication to her beliefs (Trigg, 1973). The degree of the individual's commitment is an indication of how closely the behaviour is tied to the individual's sense of self, i.e. how strongly she identifies with the belief or action in question. The greater the degree of commitment, the more the individual is resistant to changing her behaviour. Janis and Mann (1977) suggest the reason for this resistance lies within the public and personal nature of commitment. The threat of publicly losing face before one's peers may serve as to prohibit commitment change or motivation to withstand an attack against commitment. Additionally, the amount of physical and psychological time that an individual invests in making a commitment may also make them more resistant to change.

Value Commitment and Identity Development

During adolescence, the most important question the teen must ask and answer is 'Who am I?' (Erikson, 1959). Erikson suggests that the formation of and commitment to a personal value system is one of the critical elements of adolescent development. For the teen, this period of growth is often characterised by an ever-changing sphere of influence. Time spent with family and the influence that family wields over the adolescent begin to decrease in importance as the teen spends more time away from home with peers (Havighurst, 1987; Kelly and Hansen, 1987; Larson, et. al., 1989). As the teen's sphere of influence begins to change, she begins to explore different values to which she is now exposed through interactions with peers and others.

Erikson (1959) identifies eight stages of development in the human life cycle with each stage characterised by a specific developmental task or crisis to be resolved during that phase.[2] Successful resolution of each phase's task prepares the individual for resolving crises in later phases. The primary objective in the adolescent phase is for the teen to resolve her identity crisis, to decide who she is and how she relates to the world around her; the identity crisis is the task to be resolved. The internal conflict that adolescents experience as they struggle to determine which occupational, religious and political values to adopt as their own is the crux of what Erikson terms the 'identity crisis'.

Determining which values to commit to is a crucial element of the process of identity development. Those who are able to commit to a set of values after seriously exploring the alternatives are considered successful in the development process; those who cannot commit are considered unsuccessful. For the adolescent, this process often involves reconsidering parental values concerning occupation and religious and political ideology and exploring other values and value systems.

Erikson defines identity as the individual's ability to 'synthesise the experience gained from previous developmental stages, thereby contributing to the continuity of self over time' (1959, p. 92). It is a mechanism used to organise and to understand previous experiences in order to progress through subsequent stages. Identity also allows the individual to develop and maintain a connection between self and society. The identity serves as a constant reminder to the individual of her role in society and how it relates to the way she views herself. It provides a yardstick of values by which individuals judge themselves and others, a 'stable, consistent, and reliable sense of who one is and what one stands for in the world' (Josselson, 1987, p.10).

Erikson identifies identity achievement and identity diffusion as the two possible resolutions of the identity crisis. Identity diffusion indicates the individual's inability to explore or commit to any particular value system. Identity achievement represents the successful integration of previous experiences; the teen has explored a variety of values and has committed herself to a particular value system.

Erikson's theoretical model was expanded by James E. Marcia (1964), who identified two additional statuses, moratorium and foreclosure, along the continuum from identity diffused to identity achieved. The adolescent in moratorium actively struggles to choose among alternative values, but is unable to commit to any one particular value system. The foreclosed adolescent, on the other hand, is definitely committed to a value system; this commitment, however, tends to be parentally defined and involves very little value exploration.

Identity Development Research

As with most early research, identity development studies focused primarily on white male college students without exploring the possibility that identity development may differ for women or minorities. Erikson (1959) acknowledges that minority adolescents may differ in their approach to the identity crisis due to different life experiences in earlier stages of development. Unlike the universal physiological experience of puberty-related changes, identity development can be affected by other factors like gender, economic status and racial status, causing it to vary for different adolescents (Murray et. al., 1989, p. 50). For example, minority children may not experience their first developmental crisis until parents and teachers (and the mass media) attempt to socialise them into the dominant culture, creating the desire of the minority child to disavow his culture in favour of 'a more American personality' (1989, p. 90).

Researchers who examine identity development in Black adolescents have found that this group tends to be in the committed identity statuses and that ethnicity plays a role in their developmental process. Watson and Protinsky (1991) sought to determine the identity status of a group of Black adolescents and to observe the effects of age and sex on these statuses. Aries and Moorehead (1989) specifically examined the influence of ethnicity in the identity development of Black adolescents. Finally, Rotheram-Borus (1989) examined differences in identity status and related behaviour problems by ethnicity.

Watson and Protinsky (1991) obtained a sample of 237 Black adolescents from the 9th, 10th, 11th, and 12th grades from a predominantly low-income community in Philadelphia. The authors found that less than 7 per cent were in the foreclosure status, and that the moratorium group represented about 21 per cent of the sample. Approximately 21 per cent of the sample comprised the two committed statuses, foreclosure and achievement. Watson and Protinsky found that the young women in their sample, in general, were in the committed statuses, foreclosure and achievement; they accounted for 78.8 per cent of the achievement status group.

Aries and Moorehead (1989) examined ethnicity in the identity status breakdown of a Black sample. They found that, overall, 63 per cent of the subjects were located in the achieved status and 13 per cent were in foreclosure. In the area of ethnicity, a considerable portion of the sample, 92 per cent, was located in the two committed statuses; ethnicity was also found to have the highest concordance (82 per cent) with overall identity status.

Rotheram-Borus (1989) examined how ethnicity affected the relationship of a teen's identity status to behaviour problems, social competence and self-esteem. The sample for this study (N=330) was comprised of white (23 per cent), Black (30 per cent), Puerto Rican (28 per cent), and Filipino (19 per cent) teenagers from an integrated high school: 62 per cent were young women. Results showed that minority students reported identity achieved scores similar to white students' scores but 'significantly lower ethnic achieved scale scores than white students' (p. 371). Rotheram-Borus suggests from this finding that resolving one's ethnic identity is a longer process for minority youth because it is more complex than for white youth.

Methodology

In my study, participants were administered three surveys: Rokeach's Instrumental and Terminal Value Survey, the Objective Measure of Ego Identity Status (OMEIS), and a frequency of viewing survey. Demographic information about the participants' race, age, grade in school and television viewing habits was also collected at this time.

Rokeach's Instrumental and Terminal Value Survey (1973), presented the 18 terminal and 18 instrumental values and required girls to indicate how important, on a scale of 0 to 10, each value was to her independently of the other values. These values were later reduced to values indices based on the girls' ratings of them. The programme preference survey consisted of a list of 34 programmes that participants were instructed to indicate how frequently they viewed during the past year (from 0 = 'never' to 5 = 'every day'). The list of television programmes was originally derived from the Arbitron Television Ethnic Report for November 1993. This report provides audience estimates for Black households in the Philadelphia metro rating area for the period November 3, 1993 to November 30, 1993. The thirty-four highest rated programmes for Black teens, ages 12 through 17, were selected for analysis.[3] These programmes were also reduced to programme indices based on the girls' ratings of them.

The Objective Measure of Ego Identity Status (OMEIS) (Adams, et. al., 1979) is a twenty-four-item Likert scale questionnaire with six items forming a subscale for each of the four identity statuses (diffused, moratorium, foreclosed, and achieved). Subjects were asked to indicate the degree to which they agree or disagree with the each of the items and their responses were scored according to the manual developed by Adams et. al. (1989).[4]

Sample

The sample for this study, 209 Black adolescent girls, was obtained from three test sites: a senior high school (grades 10 through 12) and a junior high school (grades 7 through 9) in Atco, New Jersey, and an all-girl high school (grades 9 through 12) in Philadelphia, Pennsylvania.

Discussion

There were several significant findings in this study. First, there are significantly identifiable patterns of programme preference for teenage Black girls. Black girls prefer Black-oriented programming and sitcoms, particularly sitcoms about non-traditional families.

The strength of the Black Urban Comedy index factors suggests that these girls enjoy sitcoms that are situated in urban contexts with characters who enjoy successful careers in law, business and publishing, to name a few. Programmes in this index also feature performers who cross-over from the music industry. The presence of rap stars, The Fresh Prince and Queen Latifah, may provide their respective programmes with a sense of urban legitimacy for young Black viewers.

The girls' pattern of preference for programmes featuring non-traditional families, as seen in the Diverse Family Comedy index, is also significant. Programmes in this index feature adopted twin sisters, step-families, and extended families – family structures that may reflect the girls' actual living conditions. According to national census data from 1998, over 6 million Black teens under the age of 18 live in single-parent households, compared to 4 million living in two-parent homes. Just as the Black urban setting in the previous index may reflect the girls' immediate surroundings, the diversity of family structures found in the programmes that constitute this index may more accurately reflect the essence of their familial support group. It is perhaps these programmes that offer 'lessons' for the girls in this sample: how to get along with siblings, how to handle dating rejection and trouble at school are some examples.

Finally, the girls' preference for the programmes in the Black Patriarchal Comedy index may serve a dual purpose. For girls living in two-parent or father-headed households, these programmes may reflect their realities; for girls in mother-headed households, these preferences may hint at an escapist or fantasy motivation. The highly visible role played by the father figures in these sitcoms may meet un-addressed needs for a positive, active father-figure.

Another significant finding was the pattern of values deemed important by these girls. The value patterns or indices, and their related ratios, seemed to split naturally into a self versus other dichotomy. Both ratios suggest a value system that privileges neither the self nor the other, but rather alternates between concern for others and self. This may be a reflection of the adolescent's living situation. As minors, these girls are dependent upon others for their basic food and shelter needs; if something happens to the family, the girls are powerless to fend for themselves. However, as minors these girls are also at a very self-involved and self-concerned stage of development: they are spending more time with friends outside the home and demanding more independence for themselves from their parents.

Interestingly, only the 'self' and 'other' indices were significantly related to the girls' programme preferences. The strongest relationships were with the programmes in the Diverse Family Comedy index, which suggests that the family context in these programmes is strongly related to values preferences, particularly 'other directed' values; however, the 'self-directed' values index was inversely related. This inverse relationship would suggest that those girls who are particularly self-concerned may not relate to these programmes. This same pattern held true for the Black Patriarchal Comedy programme index.

The relationship, or lack thereof, between the girls' values and the Black Urban Comedy index was an unexpected finding, given how strongly these programmes factored with this group. This finding could suggest that Rokeach's values don't predict Black girls' preferences for programmes like these. Such programmes may tap into more racially-based or gender-based value orientations than do other more mainstream programmes.

The presence of commitment did improve the relationship of values to programme preferences for this group, especially for the Black Patriarchal Comedy index. This finding could suggest that there is stronger resolve to view these programmes or that viewing these programmes has aided in value commitment for these girls. The greater increase in strength for the Black Patriarchal Comedy index is intriguing. It would appear that for girls who are committed to their values, their values serve as a more reliable predictor for viewing programmes that feature dominant father figures. Since commitment to values signals the resolution of the adolescent crisis, these girls may be moving onto the next stage of development where relationships and marriage form the primary crises.

Conclusion

This study sought to determine Black girls' television viewing preferences within the dynamic context of adolescence. Adolescent girls are in psychological flux as social, cultural, and biological pressures force them to make choices that will have life-long impacts. At this stage in their lives, these girls are exploring careers, exploring relationships and exploring themselves. For Black girls, in particular, this search for an identity is further complicated by issues of race and the realities of social and cultural limitations faced by minorities in the United States.

Black girls are an oft-ignored group whose television viewing habits are rarely studied by communications scholars and when they are studied, it is often from a pathological perspective. This current study, however, found that television viewing meets some positive psychological needs for this group. First, these girls demonstrate an overwhelming preference for Black programming and for diverse, family-based programming. Similar to Anderson and Williams'(1983) findings, these girls appear to enjoy programmes that feature characters who look like them and whose lifestyles they admire. Second, there is a significant relationship between their values and these programme preferences. The girls in this study appear to share a dichotomous value system that is equally concerned with the 'self' and with the 'other'. These values held a particularly strong relationship with the programmes in the Diverse Family Comedy index and the Black Patriarchy index. Finally, the relationship between values and programme viewing preferences is stronger for those girls in the study who have a stronger commitment to their values.

What makes this study particularly interesting, however, are the unexpected findings and the questions they raise. First, the lack of relationship between these values and the Black Urban Comedy index is intriguing. Programmes in this index, like *Fresh Prince of Bel Air* and *Martin*, seemed to target this audience in particular with their urban settings. Despite the fact that the girls in this study all reside in urban neighbourhoods, there was no relationship between their value systems and these urban programmes. One explanation could be that the casts of these programmes are primarily Black adults and therefore the narratives may revolve more around adult issues and not issues related to teens. Although the girls in this group may be in the process of searching for an identity that will prepare them for the future, perhaps they don't wish to model themselves after the characters in these programmes. As such, viewing programmes in the Black Urban Comedy may serve more of an escapist function than an instructional one for this group.

The inverse relationship between the 'self' value index and these programmes is especially curious. This relationship suggests that Black girls who place more emphasis on values related to 'other' enjoy these programmes more than girls who place more emphasis on values related to the 'self .' This pattern suggests two radically different conclusions. One possible conclusion is that the emphasis on family and family-centred issues taps into the concerns for 'other' in these girls' value systems. The importance of family is a central tenet in most Black families and for most young women; it seems logical that girls whose value systems privilege 'other' over 'self' would prefer these programmes that do the same.

A second possible conclusion is that the 'other' value system index refers to a foreign 'other' who doesn't belong to the girls' family or cultural group. An emphasis on values that privilege the 'other' may represent a deference to the expectations of the dominant culture. The positive relationship between the 'other' value index and Diverse Family Comedy index suggests that these girls enjoy these programmes because they fulfil their curiosity about the 'other'; although the programmes are fiction, they provide a glimpse into the 'other' world.

At a time when Black girls are struggling to define themselves vis-à-vis their parents, their racial-cultural group, and their social context, their media choices should reflect this confusion, as should their value commitments. The 'self/other' dichotomous nature of their value system is indicative of the separation angst these girls are facing as they begin to assert their independence from their parents. It may also represent an attempt by the girls to separate themselves from their cultural group to learn about the 'other'. The findings of this study suggest the need for further research into the patterns of programme preferences for Black teenage girls and the viability of values (and value commitment) in predicting these preferences. Understanding why young Black girls prefer programmes that feature Black characters and diverse families may have significant implications for their future viewing habits and for future industry programming decisions.

Notes

1   Rokeach's terminal values are: Accomplishment, Comfortable life, Equality, Exciting life, Family security, Freedom, Happiness, Inner harmony, Mature love, National security, Pleasure, Salvation, Self-respect, Social recognition, True friendship, Wisdom, World of beauty, and World at peace. Rokeach's instrumental values are: Ambitious, Broadminded, Capable, Cheerful, Clean, Courageous, Forgiving, Imaginative, Independent, Intellectual, Logical, Loving, Obedient, Polite,

Helpful, Honest, Responsible, and Self-control. For further discussion, see M. Rokeach (1973), *The Nature of Human Values*, The Free Press, New York.

2   Erikson's eight stages of development, with related crises in parentheses are: Infancy (trust vs. mistrust), Early childhood (autonomy vs. shame and doubt), Play age (initiative vs. guilt), School age (industry vs. inferiority), Adolescence (identity achievement vs. diffusion), Young adult (intimacy vs. isolation), Adulthood (generativity vs. self-absorption), and Mature age (integrity vs. disgust and despair). For further discussion of these terms, see E. Erikson (1959), 'Identity and the life cycle: Selected papers by Erik Erikson', *Psychological Issues*, 1 (1).

3   The thirty-four programmes used in this analysis were: *Amen, Beverly Hills 90210, Blossom, Cartoons, The Commish, COPSs, The Cosby Show, Entertainment Tonight, Family Matters, The Fresh Prince of Bel Air, Full House, Home Improvement, The Jeffersons, Living Single, Local News, Married With Children, Martin, Matlock, Melrose Place, Music Videos, Oprah, The Real World, Roc, Roseanne, The Simpsons, Sinbad, Sister/Sister, Soul Train, South Central, Star Trek Next Generation, Step by Step, Wheel of Fortune*, and *The X-Files*.

4   For more information, refer to G. Adams, L. Bennion, and K. Huh (1989) *Objective Measure of Ego Identity Status: A Reference Manual*.

Notes on Statistical Analysis

The average age of the group was 14, with 25.8 per cent of the sample in the 7th grade and 27.3 per cent in the 8th grade. The girls reported that they watched television, on average, approximately 5 hours each school day; 54 per cent reported that they considered television 'somewhat important' in their lives at the time of the survey.

The 34 television programmes were first reduced to three programme indices using factor analysis, Varimax rotation. Those programmes that attained a weight above .5 on a factor were included in that index and all indices were found to be reliable. The three indices were labelled 'Black Urban Comedy' (Alpha=.7781), 'Black Patriarchal Comedy' (Alpha=.7144), and 'Diverse Family Comedy' (Alpha=.7430).

The index labels reflect the context and setting of the programmes that were most significant in the index, as demonstrated by the 'Alpha if removed' statistic. This is an indication of how much reliability an item contributes to an index. An item is considered to be reliable if the Alpha statistic decreases when the item is removed. The Alpha statistic, known as Cronbach's Alpha, is a measure of the internal reliability of the items in an index. Black Urban Comedy, for example, included the programmes *Living Single, Martin, Roc, Sinbad, South Central, and The Fresh Prince of Bel Air*. With the exception of *The Fresh Prince of Bel Air*, these programmes are all sitcoms set in urban areas like New York, Baltimore and Los Angeles. These programmes are also similar in that their casts are all Black: however, they differ in family-orientation. *Roc, Sinbad, South Central* and *The Fresh Prince of Bel Air* are all family-based sitcoms, while *Living Single* and *Martin* focus on the exploits of single young Black men and women. Another interesting similarity is that both *The Fresh Prince* and *Living Single* feature rap artists, The Fresh Prince and Queen Latifah, respectively.

The Black Patriarchal Comedy index includes the programmes *Amen, The Jeffersons*, and *The Cosby Show*, programmes that feature a Black father as the central figure. The majority of the plot lines revolve around the father's ability to cause trouble and to solve their children's problems. In contrast, the Diverse Family Comedy index consisted primarily of programmes with extended families (*Family Matters*), stepchildren (*Step by Step*), adopted children (*Sister/Sister*), and single parents (*Blossom, Full House*). The only exception in this index is *Home Improvement*, a programme about a white 'nuclear' family. This index was also characterised by racial diversity. Both *Family Matters* and *Sister/Sister* have predominantly Black casts, while the remaining programmes feature predominantly White casts.

The 18 terminal and 18 instrumental values were also reduced using factor analysis, Varimax rotation, resulting in two indices each for a total of four values indices. Only those values achieving a factor weight of .5 or better were included in the indices; all four indices were found to be reliable. The two terminal values indices were labelled 'Group Security' (Alpha=.8195) and 'Personal Security' (Alpha = .7200). The Group Security index included the values 'family security', 'national security', 'self-respect', 'wisdom', 'world of beauty', and 'world at peace'. This index was labelled 'group security' because these particular values suggest a concern for the safety and well-being of society or the world at large. The Personal Security index included 'comfortable life', 'exciting life', 'freedom', and 'inner harmony'. These values suggest a more self-centred concern about comfort and safety.

The two instrumental value indices were labelled 'Self-directed' (Alpha=.7585) and 'Other-directed' (Alpha=.6946). The values 'ambitious', 'broadminded', 'capable', and 'independent' make up the 'Self-directed' index; the values 'helpful', 'loving', 'responsible', and 'self-control' make up the 'Other-directed' index. Similar to the two terminal value indices, these instrumental value indices appear to split along a 'self' versus 'other' focus of concern for the individual.

These four indices were then combined into two ratios, one for the terminal values indices (Personal/Group ratio) and the other for the instrumental values indices (Self/Other ratio). The purpose of this procedure was to better capture the concept of a value system, with competing and congruent values at work for the individual. Multiple regression analysis was then used to determine the explanatory power of values for subjects' programme preferences. This is a method for predicting changes in a dependent variable using information about several independent variables. In this study, values and value commitment were the independent variables; programme viewing preference indices were the dependent variables. The Beta score, or regression coefficient, is a number that represents the relationship between independent variable values and dependent variable values. This procedure also allows for the observation of changes in Beta scores and significance at each step and for each television programme index. Using the Enter method, the values indices and ratios were entered for each programme preference index. The only values found to explain variance in programme preferences were the 'Self' index, the 'Other' index and the 'Self/Other' ratio, with the 'Self' index inversely related.

For the Diverse Family Comedy index, the values indices 'Self' and 'Other' and the value ratio 'Self/Other', explained approximately 9 per cent (sig. $F=.06$) of the variance in viewing for this group. For the Black Patriarchal Comedy index, these values measures explained 4 per cent of the variance, but not significantly (sig. $F=.3$); the same was true for the Black Urban Comedy index, with only 1 per cent of the variance explained (sig. $F=.5$).

When the commitment measure was entered into the analysis, the explanatory power of the values measures increased for the programme indices. For the Diverse Family Comedy index, the variance explained increased to 11 per cent (sig. $F=.04$), while variance explained increased to 10 per cent for Black Patriarchal Comedy index and rose to 3 per cent for the Black Urban Comedy index; however, the Black Urban Comedy index remained statistically insignificant (sig. $F=.22$).

When looking at values indices, it is evident that 'other directed', 'self directed', and 'other/self ratio' are particularly powerful in explaining variance in viewing these programmes. In addition, when controlling for commitment, their ability to explain variance increases, especially the 'self directed' values group.

References

Adams, G.R., et. al. (1985), 'Ego identity status, conformity behavior, and personality in late adolescence', *Journal of Personality and Social Psychology*, 47 (5), pp. 1091-1104.

Adams, G., Bennion, L. & Huh, K. (1989) *Objective Measure of Ego Identity Status: A Reference Manual*. University of Guelph, Ontario.

Adams, G.R., Shea, J. and Fitch, S.A. (1979), 'Toward the development of an objective assessment of ego-identity status', *Journal of Youth and Adolescence*, 8 (2), pp. 223-237.

Albarran, A.B. and Umphrey, D. (1993), 'An examination of television motivations and programme preferences by Hispanics, Blacks, and Whites', *Journal of Broadcasting and Electronic Media*, Winter, pp. 95-103.

Anderson, W.H. & Williams, B.M. (1983), 'TV and the Black Child: What Black Children Say about the Shows they watch', *Journal of Black Psychology*, (9-10), pp. 27–42.

Aries, E. and Moorehead, K. (1989), 'The importance of ethnicity in the development of identity in Black adolescents', *Psychological Reports*, 65, pp. 75-82.

Aucoin, D. (1999), 'WB on a Growth Spurt', *The Boston Globe*, Jan. 8, D1, D13.

Barwise, P. & Erehnberg, A. (1988), *Television and its audience*, Sage, London.

Carey, J. W. (1966), 'Variations in Negro/White television preferences', *Journal of Broadcasting*, 10, pp. 199-212.

Carter, E. (ed.) (1978), *How Blacks Use Television for Entertainment and Information*, Washington, D.C., Booker T. Washington Foundation Cable Communications Resource Center-West.

Clark, M.L. (1989), 'Friendship and Peer Relations' in R. Jones (ed.), *Black Adolescents*, Cobbs and Henry Publishers, Berkeley, CA., pp. 175-201.

Comstock, G. and Cobbey, R.E. (1979), 'Television and the children of ethnic minorities', *Journal of Communication*, Winter, pp. 104-115.

Converse, P.E. (1964), 'The nature of belief systems in mass publics' in D.E. Apter, (ed.) *Ideology and Discontent*, Free Press, New York, pp. 206-261.

Darmon, R.Y. (1976), 'Determinants of TV viewing', *Journal of Advertising Research*, 16 (6), December, pp. 17-20.

Erikson, E. (1959), 'Identity and the life cycle: Selected papers by Erik Erikson', *Psychological Issues*, 1 (1).

Fletcher, A. D. (1969), 'Negro and White children's television programme preferences', *Journal of Broadcasting*, 13 (4), pp. 359-367.

Frank, R. & Greenberg, M. (1980), *The public's use of television*, Sage, Beverly Hills.

Gandy, O. (1984), 'Is that all there is to love?: Value and programme preference', in S. Thomas (ed.), *Studies in communication, vol. 1.: Studies in mass communication and technology*, Ablex Publishing, Norwood, NJ, pp. 207-219.

Gibbs, J.T. (1989), 'Black American Adolescents' in J.T.Gibbs et.al. (eds) *Children of color: Psychological interventions with minority youth*, Jossey Bass Publishers, San Francisco, pp. 179-223.

Greenberg, B. and Dominick, J. (1969), 'Racial and social class differences in teenagers' use of television', *Journal of Broadcasting*, 13, pp. 331-344.

Havighurst, R. (1987), 'Adolescent culture and subculture' in *The Handbook of Adolescent Psychology*, Pergamon Books, Inc., New York, pp. 401-412.

Heeter, C. (1985), 'Programme Selection with Abundance of Choice: A Process Model', *Human Communication Research*, 12 (1), Fall, pp. 126-152.

Janis, I.L. and Mann, L. (1977), *Decision Making:A Psychological Analysis of Conflict, Choice, and Commitment*, The Free Press, New York.

Jones, F. (1990), 'The Black audience and the BET channel', *Journal of Broadcasting and Electronic Media*, 34 (4), pp. 477-486.

Jones, R. (ed.) (1989), *Black Adolescents*, Cobbs and Henry, Berkeley, CA.

Josselson, R. (1987), *Finding herself: Pathways to identity development in women*, Jossey-Bass Publishers, San Francisco.

Katz, E., Blumler, J.G. and Gurevitch, M. (1974), 'Utilization of mass communication by the individual', in J. G. Blumler and E. Katz (eds.), *The uses of mass communications: current perspectives on gratifications research*, Sage, Beverly Hills, pp. 19-32.

Kelly, J. and Hansen, D. (1987), 'Social interactions and adjustment', in *The Handbook of Adolescent Psychology*, Pergamon Books, Inc., New York, pp. 131-146.

Kiesler, C. A. (1971), *The psychology of commitment: Experiments linking behavior to belief*, Academic Press, New York.

Kluckhohn, F. and Strodtbeck, F.L. (1961), *Variations in Value Orientations*, Greenwood Press, Westport, CN.

Kubey, R. W. (1986), 'Television Use In Everyday Life: Coping With Unstructured Time', *Journal of Communication*, pp. 109-123.

Larson, R., Kubey, R. and Colletti, J. (1989), 'Changing channels: Early adolescent media choices and shifting investments in family and friends', *Journal of Youth and Adolescence*, 18 (6), pp. 583-599.

Lee, E.B. and Browne, L.A. (1981), 'Television uses and gratifications among Black children, teenagers, and adults', *Journal of Broadcasting*, 25, pp. 203-208.

Liss, M.B. (1981), 'Children's television selections: A study of indicators of same-race preferences', *Journal of Cross-Cultural Psychology*, 12 (1), pp. 103-110.

Marcia, J. E. (1964), 'Determination and Construct Validity of Ego Identity Status', unpublished dissertation, Ohio State University.

McGuire, W.J. (1974), 'Psychological motives and communication gratification', in J. G. Blumler and E. Katz (eds), *The uses of mass communications: Current perspectives on gratifications research*, Sage, Beverly Hills, pp. 167-196.

McQuail, D. and Gurevitch, M. (1974), 'Explaining audience behavior: Three approaches considered'., in J. G. Blumler and E. Katz (eds), *The uses of mass communications: Current perspectives on gratifications research*, Sage, Beverly Hills, pp. 287-301.

Munro, G. and Adams, G.R. (1977), 'Adolescent values: Measuring instrumental and expressive orientations', *Adolescence*, 12(47), pp. 329-337.

Murray, C., Smith, S.N. and West, E.H. (1989), 'Comparative personality development', in Jones, R. (ed.), *Black Adolescents*, pp. 49-62.

Orlofsky, J., Marcia, J.E. and Lesser, I. (1973), 'Ego identity status and the intimacy versus isolation crisis of young adulthood', *Journal of Personality and Social Psychology*, 27 (2), pp. 211-219.

Perse, E.M. (1990), 'Involvement with local television news: Cognitive and emotional dimensions', *Human Communication Research*, 16 (4), pp. 556-581.

Pugh, G. E. (1977), *The biological origins of human values*, Basic Books, New York.

Rokeach, M. (1973), *The Nature of Human Values*, The Free Press, New York.

Rosengren, K.E. (1974), 'Uses and gratifications: A paradigm outlined', in J. G. Blumler and E. Katz (eds), *The uses of mass communications. Current perspectives on gratifications research*, Sage, Beverly Hills, pp. 269-286.

Rotheram-Borus, M.J. (1989), 'Ethnic differences in adolescents' identity status and associated behavior problems', *Journal of Adolescence*, Vol. 12, pp. 361-374.

65

Rubin, A. (1977), 'Television usage, attitudes, and viewing behaviours of children and adolescents', *Journal of Broadcasting*, 21, pp.355-369.

Storm, J. (2000), 'Black and White TV', *The Philadelphia Inquirer*, April 20, pp 11, 16.

Stroman, C.A. (1986), 'Television viewing and self-concept among Black children', *Journal of Broadcasting and Electronic Media*, 30 (1), pp. 87-93.

Tan, A.S. and Tan, G. (1979), 'Television Use and Self-Esteem of Blacks', *Journal of Communication*, 29 (1), pp. 129-135.

Taylor, R.L. (1989), 'Black youth, role models and the social construction of identity', in R. Jones (ed.), *Black Adolescents*, pp. 155-174.

Trigg, R. (1973), *Reason and commitment*, Cambridge University Press, London.

Vogt, W.P. (1993), *Dictionary of statistics and methodology*, Sage Publications, London.

Watson, M.F. and Protinsky, H. (1991), 'Identity Status of Black Adolescents: An Empirical Investigation'. *Adolescence*, 26 (104), pp. 963-966.

Webster, J. and Wakshlag, J.J. (1983), 'A theory of television programme choice' *Communication Research*, 10 (4), pp. 430-446.

5 Interpreting Islam: British Muslims and the British Press

ELIZABETH POOLE

Introduction

This chapter explores the responses of young British Muslims to their representation in the British press. The research is part of a larger project which has examined media representations of British Muslims both quantitatively and qualitatively. The theoretical rationale for this project is based on a particular historical, political and social context which, it is argued, has led to a particular image of Islam in the Western media (Ahmed, 1992). Current theory posits that a shift in the global-power equation, due to the collapse of Communism, has led to anxieties and attempts by 'the West' to maintain its hegemony (Hippler & Lueg, 1995). In this New World Order, Islam has been constructed as the new enemy (a global force which represents an ideological and physical threat). This threat is attributed to the rise of 'political' Islam, the Iranian Revolution of 1979 being the initial signifier. According to Esposito (1992) and Halliday (1996) the rise of Islamism, in actuality, comprises heterogeneous movements defined and determined by national state and rival political factions and Islam, therefore, cannot be an explanatory factor for all Muslim behaviour.

In this context, the media, as an instrument of public ideology, reproduces, and sustains the ideology necessary to subjugate Muslims both internationally and domestically. The portrayal of extremist images within a framework which advances an historical 'myth of confrontation', Halliday (1996) suggests, absolves 'the West' of any need to justify their hostility. Rather than see the relationship between Islam and the West as having a unilinear history, I would prefer to see it as constructed in historical moments where crises have led to popular discourses reflecting the needs of the time. The current resurgence in the demonisation of Islam then, is due to a specific political context. As Said has already identified, an Orientalist discourse is a product of certain 'cultural, professional, national, political, and economic requirements of the epoch' (1978, p. 273). The current epoch is one whereby opposing sides use an essentialist discourse and historical relation of confrontation to justify specific actions, to 'legitimise, mislead, silence and mobilise' (Halliday, 1996, p. 7).

Thus, what results is often an equally unsatisfactory position, a homogenised 'West' and 'Western media'. The media is located within different social systems which have different political circumstances and motivations. These media systems are not homogenous and incorporate a range of communication modes, genres, affiliations, and constraints. I am suggesting that the image of 'Islam' will differ according to these and cannot be a unified global image as imagined. I chose, then, to examine a specific genre within a specific context: the British press, using a systematic empirical approach (see Poole, 1999).[1]

Recent events in Britain can be identified as bringing the presence of Muslims into public awareness and have led to the growth of a Muslim consciousness. Ahmed (1992) suggests that the 'Rushdie Affair' was a catalyst for the British demonisation of Muslims, exposing the vast gaps in understandings of each other. This, and some Muslim support for Saddam Hussein in the Gulf War, led to a questioning of their loyalty to Britain (Werbner, 1994). The response for Ahmed (1992, p. 113) was based on an undervalued powerless community's 'cry of identity', which in turn sharpened the sense of a Muslim identity(ies) and led to the politicisation of Muslims.

These processes have led to Muslim communities in Britain being constituted as separatist and therefore a 'threat within' by the wider public (Halliday, 1996).[2] The contemporary manifestation of this Orientalist discourse has been defined as 'Islamophobia' (The Runnymede Trust, 1997). In Britain then, as elsewhere, Islam has come to be represented as a homogenous threat despite representing differing sects, ethnicities, and language groups which have been further fragmented through emigration. The ideology of a fundamentalist threat allows the British government to suppress the activities of Muslims at home. This has been seen recently in the suppression of 'terrorist' dissidents in London, amid fears of US embassy attacks following the American air strikes on Afghanistan, aimed at Osma bin Laden (August 1998). However, despite this largely negative imagining of Islam, the political necessity of maintaining harmonious social relations has meant, especially in recent times, that in the UK minorities are allowed space in the public sphere to avoid dislocation and extremism. Hence the image of British Islam (in the UK), to some extent, is both less extreme and more diverse than that of its global 'Other'.

The audience part of the research was based on the assumption that whilst there may be a 'preferred reading' embedded in a text, i.e. a dominant message, that the reading of the message will depend on a number of variables. The aim was thus to examine the variety of socio-cultural factors important in the decoding of mediated information about Muslims, paying particular attention to the variable of cultural proximity in interpreting and understanding the texts, that is knowledge, experiences and familiarity with Muslims and Islam.[3] Differentially situated reader groups were organised on this basis, keeping other variables within the group as homogenous as possible, to include non-Muslim groups with both regular experience and contact with Muslims and those without. It was also felt vital to examine British Muslims' responses to these images on the premise that they would be most likely to be able to formulate independent and differential understandings, in relation to largely negative press discourse, given their closeness to the subject. Here, I intend only to examine the Muslim responses, to examine what meanings are produced in the interaction of text and audience and what frameworks are used to decode these constructions of Islam. What are the implications for Muslims who may be drawn into a dialectical negotiation of identity? Reception analysis was considered the most appropriate approach for this purpose.

The form of reception analysis utilised was based on the encoding/decoding model of Hall (1980) who argued that audiences are positioned by dominant meanings, the 'preferred meaning' of a text, but are able to oppose or negotiate with these on the basis of socio-cultural factors. The model has been criticised for its limited range and 'overtly political' decoding positions; the 'premature closure of the text' with its 'preferred reading' (Wren-Lewis, 1983, p.187); and its lack of context. Morley recognised these limitations in the postscript to his *Nationwide* study (1981). However, I considered it a useful starting point from which a range of variant interpretations can be examined. Taking account of some of these criticisms in the implementation of the research I, however, take the position that texts, as discursive formations embedded within social systems, both limit and structure our understanding and knowledge of the social world. Whilst ideology does then attempt to fix meaning in order to maintain hegemony, meaning is never finally fixed, even after the meeting of text and audience.

This societal model was supported by cognitive models drawn from social-psychology deployed to examine the 'determinations of meaning' (van Dijk, 1988; Corner, 1991; Höijer, 1998). The usefulness of these models in their use of textual analysis allows the researcher to examine the extent to which these determinants are inscribed within or external to the text, and which variables are important to understandings of 'Muslim', paying particular attention, in this case, to cultural proximity on which the hypothesis is based.

Methodology

Focus groups were used as a socially orientated research procedure (important in examining socially constructed meanings). Six groups were organised, with the gender differential evenly split. I intended to construct as similar groups as was feasible, firstly to limit the number of variables at play (and focus on cultural proximity) and secondly to construct an atmosphere where individuals felt happy disclosing their opinions, i.e. with like-minded people. One age group was selected, of the same level of education: sixth form pupils in Leicester (aged 16-18). The setting selected was culturally diverse, so a 'snowballing' sampling technique was used whereby interested participants assisted in finding other people within their own networks (Preston et. al., 1995). This can lead to consensus building within the group, what Paulis (1989) calls the 'false consensus effect' and it is important that this is challenged.[4] By challenging the consensus view, not only are new avenues of discussion opened up but the researcher is able to experience how strongly beliefs are held.

Youth groups were chosen because of recent arguments surrounding the revival of religious identities and political activism in young Muslims, due to their increasing alienation (see below for an extended discussion of this). I also considered that these young people are the adults of tomorrow, the future of British Islam.[5] Single sex groups were convened, following discussions with female Muslims who insisted that this would have to be the case, based on the norms monitoring mixing between genders in their culture. The nature of the groups, therefore, reflected established social networks.

Being part of a larger project, the emphasis on depth rather than representativeness meant that this research was relatively small scale. The aim was to research the collective and comparative nature of local experiences (the 'local-public domain', Burgess et. al., 1991) which cannot be considered as representative of the national context. It is important then to provide details of this local context.

Muslims in Leicester

At the time of writing, there was no exact information available about the numbers of Muslims living in Leicester as statistics are based on ethnic categories compiled from the last Census, 1991. Leicester ranked fifth in terms of absolute numbers of ethnic minorities of all local authorities in 1991. It had the second (to Birmingham) highest number of Asians and the most Indians of any local authority in the UK. It was, however, only 35th for black citizens. The Asian population in Leicester then accounted for

23.7 per cent of its total population (270,493). Seventy-eight per cent of Asians were Indian (60,297). In 1991, there were 2,644 Pakistanis and 1,053 Bangladeshis, a total of 3697, 1.4 per cent of the total population. Research by Leicester City Council showed a rise in the non-white population over the period from 1983-1991 corresponding with a fall in the white population. It is likely that this trend has continued and that the number of Asians and Muslims in Leicester has grown compared to white people since 1991. Census information shows the majority of Asian citizens are in the 0-30 years age range (10 years younger than the average white person) with an equal number of men and women. The Asian population appears to be relatively affluent and has a high level of participation in the community with the highest rates of owner-occupation and access to cars, and a similar degree of economic activity to their white counterparts, with slightly more being self-employed. The unemployed tend to be retired, sick or students.[6] However, this data disguises the differences between Asian groups, making it difficult to differentiate the Muslim experience. It does not reveal the number of Asian workers in manual jobs and less skilled occupations and their lower earnings (compared to white workers and by national comparison) found by Duffy and Lincoln (1990). These Muslim participants were, for example, mainly from an economically disadvantaged inner city area of Leicester, although well educated. Updated information with religious identifiers, to be provided by the next Census, is therefore sorely needed.

The groups were asked to participate on the basis that the research was about finding out opinions of and reactions to newspaper articles. I thought that to reveal the full research purpose would affect the results, although this became somewhat clearer to the participants when the texts were exposed and discussion commenced.

Participants were initially asked to complete a questionnaire to identify variables at play. This revealed that the majority of participants taking part were Gujerati speaking, 83 per cent. Seventy per cent of these originated from India, the remaining Gujerati speakers were of African, Malawi, and mixed descent (African/Indian). The non-Gujerati speakers were of African descent. They gave their first languages as Katchi and English. The majority of the sample reported reading a newspaper daily or regularly, 66 per cent, with young men (self)reporting a greater interest in the news. The participants were most likely to read their local paper, 42 per cent, or *The Times*, 17 per cent, or *The Sun*, 17 per cent. This indicates the importance of examining Muslims' understandings of dominant constructions of 'themselves'. However, as we shall find, the Muslims' opinions (expressed here) seem to be less informed by this sort of allegiance and more by religious belief.

I then asked the participants to firstly respond to the texts chosen, individually, in a written form. The written response forces participants to commit themselves to an answer before entering the group, allowing an assessment of how groups dynamics and conformity to group norms impinge on the individual (Wimmer & Dominick, 1997). The participants were then asked to recount the subject matter of the story and give their reactions to it.

The texts selected for discussion were informed by the content analysis. The topics found to most frequently associated with Islam by the quantitative analysis were then used as a basis for the qualitative analysis. From these, texts that were deemed to be fairly representative of each story were selected. However, I also felt that there should be an opportunity for the participants to comment on the differences between newspapers through exposure to a range. A *Guardian* article was therefore included for its more positive stance.

For the topic of *relationships* an article from *The Daily Mail*, (11 July 1997, p. 17) was used. This article reported on the end of the marriage of Sarah Cook, a 13 year old from Essex and Musa Komeagac, an 18 year old Turkish waiter. This had been a continuing story in the press following their marriage, the birth of their child, and subsequent break-up. The story had been constructed as an example of sexual Orientalism (the corruption of a vulnerable pubescent girl), and had focused on the 'primitive' and 'restrictive' life she was subject to in Turkey (as a result of his Muslim identity). The marriage breakdown was celebrated as an inevitable return to 'normality', based on cultural incompatibility.

For the theme of *Rushdie/blasphemy*, an article from *The Daily Mail*, (30 June 1997, p. 13) was used. This article, although reporting on proposals for the introduction of laws on religious discrimination, interpreted these as laws on blasphemy and reformulated the story, resurrecting old debates on freedom of speech and the unworkability of such laws. It used the example of the 'Rushdie Affair' to present a preferred meaning in opposition to the introduction of any new laws that would upset current power relations.

For the theme of *education,* an article from *The Guardian* (10 January 1998, p. 7) was used. This article was more positive, in accordance with *The Guardian's* liberal stance. It supported the decision to fund these schools with a discourse of equality, inclusivity, rights, and identity. However, it also introduced an element of doubt by quoting ex-headteacher Ray Honeyford's fears on racial segregation.

For the theme of *fundamentalism,* an article from *The Times* (24 November 1997, p. 12) was used. This story posed an ideological dilemma for the paper in terms of national interests. Attacks on Britain's integrity (by foreign governments) are to be defended, but the presence of terrorists within its borders also poses a threat to national security. As a result, the paper was cautious in its acceptance of any charges made against the UK, whilst at the same time condemning the activities and presence of extremists. The resulting formulation of Muslims in the UK is still negative: militant. In the next section I examine the participants responses to these texts – all the participants' names have been changed.

Responses by Young Muslim Men

Young Muslim men fit more neatly into an oppositional position than their female counterparts. They are more likely to have a political conscience, are media literate and read texts as ideological, rejecting them on this basis. However, there are still slight differences between them, reflected in the papers they read which indicate a more critical perspective. The broadsheet readers are less likely to be positioned by the texts in any way. Due to their specific identities as *British* Muslims, these groups do not automatically or always remain in oppositional mode. When the values in the text match their own, they are more likely to accept dominant meanings. This can be seen in response to the article on Sarah Cook where the participants argue that she is too young to be married (see below).

It is fair to say that the young men took an almost entirely oppositional position to the blasphemy article. However, the text's macro-structural organisation works to position the subjects into discussing blasphemy rather than religious discrimination. It has an agenda setting effect, even with this group, who reject the dominant meanings. The male Muslims are much more vocal and emotionally opposed to Rushdie and focus their discussion on this aspect of the article. They resist the text's meanings, arguing that Rushdie committed the ultimate sin in betraying his religion, that the book should be banned, that Christians are hypocritical in allowing him to criticise Islam but would not allow the same treatment of their religion, that Islamophobia does exist, that the laws should exist as a point of equality, that minorities have the right to their religion and other rights despite being a minority, and reject the representation of Muslims and their reaction to Rushdie's book, (although they articulated disapproval about the way the book was protested against, it was felt recourse to these methods was inevitable because Muslims have no other way of voicing their objections in this country). They objected to the sole focus on Islam in relation to blasphemy and argued that there should be limits to freedom of speech when it is offensive to others.

An initial response to the article as being fairly balanced by some of the less media literate of the group was based on the presence of some positive quotes. They were also positioned by the text to identify government support for the laws but responded positively in opposition to the intended response. They also accepted arguments regarding the unworkability of the law but this was mainly based on their experiences of the race laws rather than textual references, although Northern Ireland was selected as an example from the text. However, because of their opposition to the text, they are more likely to use experience as a resource for resistance.

More elements of the message are accepted from the Cook article due to cultural distance (from Turkey) and symmetrical values (to the UK). They are positioned by the article's representation of the parents' irresponsibility (in accepting money for the story), and by the framing of the relationship as a holiday romance:

> ...oh come on, if a 12 year old girl goes on holiday and falls in love with the waiter, it is just a crush if you think about it at the end of the day, a 12 year old girl and her parents taking her seriously about her parents wanting to marry him and with there being such a distance. (Akbar)

However, they remain cynical, believing the article to be culturally biased and concentrate on discussing this, attending very little to any details within it. In opposition to the text, they were more likely to believe it was the Cooks at fault rather than the Turkish waiter and reacted positively to their conversions to Islam (whilst recognising that the article represents hers as forced). They were able to show quite easily how the structure revealed its ideological bias. Their awareness of and experience of cultural bias provided them with situation models which made them much more dismissive of both articles.

Responses by Young Muslim Women

The young women were much more conformist than their male counterparts. They therefore focused more on responding to questions than pursuing their own agenda. Their desire to portray a reasonable face of Islam was reflected in cautious answers to questions, careful wording and by showing awareness of alternative perspectives. They also showed less awareness of news and political issues in general, less media literacy and were therefore more likely to accept messages within the texts than the young men.

Although mainly positioned oppositionally to texts due to their awareness of bias towards Muslims and through Muslim identification, they did, however, slip in and out of preferred, oppositional and negotiated positions on the basis of similarly held values or cultural proximity.

In particular, their gender positioned them in opposition to the Cook article. It was its representation of Islam's treatment of women which was most fervently objected to. They also resisted the preferred meanings by attributing the responsibility to Sarah, responding positively to her conversion, suggesting that Musa's point of view was excluded and objecting to the use of the term 'Moslem' throughout.

Similarly to the young men, they articulated oppositional responses to the blasphemy article. However, their reading of this article illustrates their less political identities. They interpreted the article as positive (i.e. supporting the laws) in response to the event, even though they disagreed with views expressed in it. They were much more cautious in their responses, speaking in neutral tones and in the third party to avoid controversy. They did not linger on political issues for long, preferring to focus on faith.

> ...all I know is that he, [Rushdie] that a lot of people hate him but equally right, a lot of people do follow him and he's been in the news quite a lot. (Amina)

> Well, if you are looking at it from Western eyes you could say that it was his opinion and that he did have the freedom of speech but if you see it from a religious perspective, and that is any religion right, you would probably say like he should not have slandered it writing contradictory things about Islam. (Shabana)

Although their memories of the 'Rushdie Affair' correlate closely with media images such as marches and book burning, they objected to this representation. Responses illustrate how reality is viewed from one's own perspective. Here, a participant articulates a belief that the majority of people objected to Rushdie's book.

> If 10 per cent of the people don't like it then that's all right but if 90 per cent of the population don't like it then there has got to be something done about it. (Aisha)

These responses illustrate the importance of religious identification in framing interpretations for Muslims. However, differential points of identification result in preferred readings. Their symmetrical values (with the text) led them to agree that Sarah Cook was too young for a marriage that was also rushed into. Equally, they stressed the importance of parental responsibility. They were also positioned by the Cook text into discussing the actors, as they had been categorised by the article, in terms of age, nationality, and vocation (waiter), and by the blasphemy article, interpreting the law as being exclusive to Islam (also possibly due to the focus on their own collectivities).

Cultural distance was also a factor in accepting dominant meanings. Although they rejected the meanings in the text which implicated Islam, in the Cook article, their ignorance of Turkish culture meant they accepted the events but suggested they were a result of cultural practices thus making a 'religion-ethnic culture distinction.' (Jacobson, 1997, p.240) This negotiation with the text shows how cultural distance applies to British Muslims, that Islam alone cannot be taken as a means to opposing representations of it, and that knowledge is an important factor in resisting meanings.

The importance of cultural proximity is especially apparent by the Muslims' responses to *The Times* text on fundamentalism. In this article the meanings are multi-faceted, the paper's position shifting in response to various aspects of the event. The Muslims too, have to negotiate with the little knowledge they have, objecting to aspects of the text and anchored by others, due to their conflicting points of identity (Hall, 1992) as *British* Muslims. They voice dissent in relation to the stereotypes of Islam and violence, interpret the funding of Middle Eastern groups as suggesting the Middle East is poor and disagree with this, and reject the idea that these groups are a threat to the UK. However, they agree with the Egyptian President in his accusations that 'killers' should not be allowed to reside in Britain but suggest that these charges are not supported by evidence. They disapprove of the killings but disassociate them from Islam.

This illustrates how Muslims are predisposed to oppose dominant meanings on Islam due to religious knowledge and experience of cultural bias but often lack the specific cultural knowledge to do so. However, this lack of knowledge forces them to engage in a different interpretive strategy. They re-focus attention in the article away from the Islamic militants to the theme of *foreign interference*. This is evidence that people, no matter what material they are given, will at least attempt to formulate meanings that are symmetrical to their own ideologies, even if these appear unsatisfactory and unstable. They use the textual information provided to construct their own meanings as with attempts to shift the blame for funding militant groups to non-Muslim organisations. The responses to this article illustrate the tensions between local and global identifications for Muslims as with Werbner's (1994) study of Pakistanis' responses to the Gulf War. The global sympathetic identification tends to outweigh local interests as 'an all encompassing frame of reference' in recognition of world- wide inequalities (Jacobson, 1997, p. 239).

A further illustration of the complexity of meaning production is in the responses to the *Guardian* text on the funding of Muslim schools. This text negotiates with dominant meanings by supporting the schools and equality for Muslims but introduces an element of doubt through the idea of segregation in accordance with its liberal ideology. Texts, then, as well as audiences, are sites of contradictions and tension. The groups view the text as balanced or positive but not ideological. For them, ideology or bias is associated only with negative representations of Islam. Thus, the responses are oppositional in relation to dominant meanings but in this case correlate with the preferred meanings of the text, supporting funded Muslim schools. The responses to this text illustrate the activity of cultural proximity to the full. Representation is based solely on British Muslims and this allows a straightforward interpretation based on first hand knowledge and experience. The point of view represented in the article is naturalised to the Muslims as it represents their own common-sense perspective. The reaction to this article by the groups has revealed how ideology is naturalised and only becomes apparent when it is in opposition to the readers' ideologies. This is also illustrated by the selection of Ray Honeyford's quote on increased segregation as an example of bias. References in the text to the school's adherence to the National Curriculum, to avert fears over the standard of teaching, are interpreted as an area of concern by those Muslims who suggest this may lead to the compromising of Islamic values, illustrating their more extreme position in relation to dominant values compared to that of the paper.

Assessing the Decoding of Newspaper Texts: Interpretive Strategies and Significant Variables

Frameworks of interpretation are based on 'scripts' which include direct experience and knowledge, media and cultural norms (van Dijk, 1988). Here, I examine the variables important in decoding these texts for Muslims.

It was evident that Muslims are generally concerned with media bias, in particular, towards Muslims, but also show an awareness of the processes of selectivity and the journalistic practices, norms and ignorance that lead to bias. They were generally cynical regarding the intentions of the press and were more than likely to characterise the articles as completely untrue. They were especially critical of the misuse of Islamic terminology which promotes ignorance.[7]

...it's just a clever editing trick that's what it is. I see it on television all the time, when you see things about Muslims, it was about Salman Rushdie again, it was about some guy asking him, a scholar, a guy asking him what he thought about Salman Rushdie and he was saying about Islam and what should happen and after he finishes talking, he says something like, 'Muslims are living in peace and harmony' and straight after he finished there is a picture of Khomeini and then back to the conversation again so it's like 'yes, yes, yes' but on the other hand it is like Khomeini wants to kill everyone. (Mohammed)

This was a negative *expectation* (part of their news schema) which they brought to the texts, affecting their interpretations of articles.

I wouldn't read it at all. I would just look at that word 'Moslems' and just think stereotyped Muslims and think it was probably something about war and leave it. (Humera)

Young men here certainly showed greater media literacy and awareness of political issues in general. According to van Dijk (1988), having a news schema aids comprehension of news texts. This may be one factor in the lack of recognition of the preferred meanings in texts by young women.

Having analysed the surface structure according to their own frameworks of understanding, the participants used aspects of the text to both illustrate textual bias and to provide evidence for their claims. This is further evidence of their asymmetrical position in relation to the texts. Most of these references are attributable to young men which again shows their greater media literacy compared to young women. The male groups showed particular distaste for Rushdie by drawing on his face and writing abusive comments by it. They did use textual references within the preferred meaning, however, if they were symmetrical to their views, for example, quotes that supported the blasphemy laws.

I mean, the person mentioned in here, Dr Hammed, he thinks it's positive as well and all the evidence given here suggests it is positive. (Sadia)

The evidence here supports other research which shows that semantic processing often takes place on very little contact with the text (van Dijk, 1988). A glance at the headline may be all it takes for a person to decide whether it is of interest or relevance to them, which affects the decision whether to carry on reading. If there is some ambiguity, a glance at the picture or highlighted text qualifies this.

Sadia: I'd just usually read the headline and then turn the pages.
Shabana: It's just the title and the way it is set out and the picture, it's like...
Amina: Oh, it's a Muslim there, I'll read it...
Saiema: Yeah, the first thing you see if you see an Asian on the newspaper or the news you always get interested and read it or listen to it you know.

As an example of the cognitive processing of media texts, there is evidence in all groups of 'misreading' the article. This further indicates that people skim for the information they need for a general impression and then fill in the blanks with what is most appropriate to their view of the event. These details tend to be in line with the participants 'preferred meaning'.

Did this notion of bias apply to other religions? Generally, and consistent with previous research with minority groups (Sreberny-Mohammadi and Ross, 1995), Muslims felt that their religion was the most poorly represented but it was likely that all religions were badly portrayed (due to a secular press).

When Rushdie wrote about the Muslims and Islam, like it took centre stage again, all the press were covering it. Recently he wrote about Hindus and his book was banned in India but nobody heard about that. (Abdullah)

They did, however, express some antagonistic attitudes to other religions but were reticent to do so in this context. They were therefore generally evasive but more willing to criticise Christianity as to them it represents the central starting point of their persecution in the West and was seen as hypocritical in its judgements against them.

...yes, there has always been a kind of a feud between Muslims and Jews but I don't think he should just talk about killing just like that [words stilted]. (Farzana)

The article would make me think about.....how many leaders of great religions [Christianity] are backing certain people and allow discrimination against other religions. (Ahmed)

I don't think they would allow a Muslim guy to write about Christianity in the way he [Rushdie] wrote about Islam anyway. (Mohammed)

These Muslims believed that although society is becoming more multicultural, it is dominated by Christian norms. However, the average Briton does not take their religion seriously and this is at the heart of many problems in society. To them, this is why the strength and growth of Islam is perceived to be a threat.

In the context of strongly held beliefs about media bias, I felt it important to gather information about familiarity with coverage of Islam in the media. Actual familiarity with the news stories presented to them in these groups was poor. In common with previous research on minorities and their perceptions of media representation, despite having clear theories on the hostility of the media, they could only provide general examples of this. The Rushdie Affair was, however, particular salient, an indication of the notoriety of the story in the UK. Some *had* seen coverage of the funding of Muslim schools but not the Cook story. Research on news recall suggests that people have difficulty remembering news items but are more likely to remember what is consistent with their own views (Dahlgren, 1988). Knowledge of events reflects the groups' general levels of cultural and political awareness in this area with the Muslims having a greater knowledge (above non-Muslim groups). An illustration of the agenda setting effects of news was their discussions on the British nurses accused of murder in Saudi Arabia in 1997. They were positioned to attend to the issue of Saudi *punishments* but as with other issues, rejected the dominant conceptualisations, mitigating for the Saudi authorities.

It is also of note that the variable 'interest in the news' did not seem to have any bearing on familiarity. Those who claim to be disinterested were just as likely to be familiar with events as those who are interested. However, this variable was measured only by self-identification. Contexts of both over-estimation and underestimation, therefore, are influential factors. Also analysed were statements of interest and disinterest towards the stories discussed in the groups. The lack of engagement by Muslims, despite their interest in their representation, was partly based on their age and distaste for these stories but also the lack of relevance in the foreign element of stories. This would account for the level of recall. The articles solely about British Muslims were, therefore, found to be most interesting, with a gender differential. The young women preferred the education article on the basis of faith and the young men the section on Rushdie based on politics, although they expressed a desire to see the story dropped given its age. It was evident that the intentional formatting which causes people to feel distanced from the main actors (Muslims) and therefore unsympathetic towards them also had some effect on these Muslim groups.

Having established that the media was biased, what was the perceived influence of the media according to these groups? The participants overwhelmingly believed that non-Muslims are influenced by negative media coverage of Muslims, that media coverage is partly responsible for negative attitudes towards them and that, once formed, these attitudes are difficult to change. The young women also showed concern about the impact of this sort of coverage on believers, leading to a loss of faith. This influence, they suggested, was due to a lack of understanding of Islam, the amount of coverage and size of tabloid readerships but they also acknowledged the likelihood of a lack of interest by non-Muslims in Islam. None of them considered that the media may influence *them* in any way.

The importance of religious identification amongst the Muslims in these groups appears to have overridden differing ethnic and language groups, holding as they did a virtually singular perspective in relation to these texts (although only a small number outside the majority ethnic grouping participated due to the intention of encouraging homogeneity, and one could argue that they have similar reference points being all 'British Muslims' at the same age and level of education). This was not the result of a consensus effect but was clearly illustrated by strongly held views. Even those who reported their first language as English argued just as strongly (in contrast to previous research findings, for example Halloran et. al., 1995). Religious identification was not a particularly important variable for other religious groups. All Muslims, however, reported their religion as being extremely important to them. An illustration of this is that initially, the first male group did not take the activity seriously. However, the participants became very serious when the discussion turned to Islam. In relation to these articles, it was the 'Muslim' identification that was most important in resisting the preferred meaning. Increasingly, researchers are finding religion to be a more significant source of identity than ethnicity for young Muslims (Knott and Khoker, 1993; Jacobson, 1997; Modood et. al., 1997).

This research provides some evidence supporting postmodern theories relating to a diasporic experience which facilitates hybridity, but more so for the reassertion of local identities (particularism) in resistance to dominant narratives (Robins, 1991; Ahmed, 1992; Hall, 1992). It is argued that processes of globalisation, including the migration and displacement of peoples across borders, has allowed for the formulation and reformulation of new identities (with multiple subject positions) through the interaction of differences as traditions and boundaries are destabilised in the post-modern world (Hall, 1988; Cohen, 1997; Gilroy, 1997). This is seen as a solution to the problems of an uncertain existence (Hall, 1992). Whilst this syncretic identification (Cohen, 1997) appeared to be at work for the non-Muslim ethnic subjects of this research, for Muslims there was more evidence that their real lived experience of an intercultural existence, disadvantage and marginalisation alongside cultural rejection has resulted in a disaffection for which the solution is a reassertion of religious identity. Processes of media globalisation have increased the religious identification as the inequalities Muslims suffer internationally are recognised (Ahmed & Donnan, 1994). This 'mediated consciousness' (Gilroy, 1997) has resulted in 'imagined communities' where global religious identifications override local national interests (Anderson, 1983; Ahmed & Donnan, 1994; Werbner, 1994; Cohen, 1997).

Alongside these processes, the uncertainties of the global village where Muslims are 'an ever-present ubiquitous reality' (Ahmed & Donnan, 1994) has resulted in a defensive construction of nationality, a discursive strategy to exclude Muslims by host countries (Gellner, 1983; Woodward, 1997). In this historical trajectory, fixed, essentialist, pure identities, have been manufactured to provide ethnic certainties (Gilroy, 1997). The negative expectations and meanings projected onto texts by Muslims which results in resistance is a result of this exclusion and the reality of their position in Britain in their encounters with discrimination. They pay less attention to the textual content, being immediately dismissive (particularly the young men), as they experience 'cognitive dissonance' over what it means to be a Muslim (Höijer, 1998, p. 178). Harmony was achieved by the young women through selectivity, paying attention to discourses that decrease dissonance. This 'discursive discomfiture' (Dahlgren, 1988, p. 297) has led to a counter-identification with religion which has restored self-confidence and strength to young Muslim communities (Werbner, 1994; Jacobson, 1997). Although it is evident that they are not totally at one with their global counterparts, the identification based on a recognition of inequalities across the world further reduces alienation and anxieties.

Whilst it is recognised that all identities are multi-layered, particularly through processes of translation, identity shifts according to the way subjects are addressed (Hall, 1992). News contributes to the way we understand our relations with others and the power of the media is its ability to define and locate people into certain subject positions, mobilising identities, excluding and including groups of people. The emphasis on differences, constructed within a framework of conflict and a 'culture clash', whilst invoking 'Muslim' as a discursive, social category practised in these news articles, encouraged the subjects to respond as collectives, exacerbating predispositions (Turner, 1985). The newspapers manufacture and then exploit bounded impermeable differences which make the polarisation normative; 'Identities are produced, consumed and regulated within culture-creating meanings through symbolic systems of representation about the identity positions we might adopt' (Woodward, 1997, p. 2).

The unfortunate consequences of these reductive processes are evident from this audience research. Issues are presented in black and white rather than allowing identification and resolution. By concentrating attention on conflicts that seem insoluble, it allows the real issues to be hidden and less likely to be acted upon. This is evident in the macro-structural organisation of the blasphemy article, its attention to the Rushdie

Affair raises accusations of incitement by the Muslims (for employing these examples when others could be used) however, they rise to this provocation.

Social distance is enhanced as the groups take oppositional sides based on those identities mobilised. Muslims' commitment to their religious identities is reinforced and expressed through social practices and markers of difference which confirm, through experience, the media images to the non-Muslims (Jacobson, 1997). Furthermore, it increases the antagonism between different disadvantaged groups. This consolidates and naturalises both the differences and boundaries further. Hence, we witness the circularity of power: 'This cycle between reality and representations makes the ideological fictions of racism empirically "true"' (Mercer and Julien, 1994, pp.137-138). Such media coverage therefore invokes social solidarity, accounting for the ethnic consensus apparent here (Anderson, 1983). This works to maintain power relations and cultural hegemony (Gellner, 1983) and the 'myth of confrontation' is sustained (Halliday, 1996).

These interpretations illustrate the problems with using the encoding/ decoding model as the production of meaning is more complex than the positions it offers. Young Muslim women reconstructed their own meanings in relation to the text on blasphemy rather than recognising the ideology and rejecting it. Neither were they statically placed in a position of oppositional or dominant reading because meaning is multi-layered, having contradictory spaces, and relates to a multiplicity of identifications and interests. However, what is evident is that these decodings are socially patterned, as these groups share the same frameworks of interpretation *on this issue,* based on identities mobilised in discourse. Whilst these socially shared meanings seem clear cut, it is recognised that they are never fixed and are always being refined through the interaction of textual understandings, socio-demographic factors and personal interaction.

These readings do constitute 'preferred readings' to the groups involved, as Wren-Lewis (1983) suggested, but using and identifying these decoding positions has allowed the scope for possible readings to be established, locating shared communities of meaning. Is it ultimately these 'preferred readings' which groups circulate in their own social circles which result in perpetually negotiated social meanings? It will continue to be a challenge to researchers to identify how these meanings are disseminated and the way participants act on them.

A case can be made for the interpretive production of meaning from this research, but what difference does it make for Muslims in terms of social practice? Their differential interpretations result in a cycle of empowerment and frustration which often has an alienating result. The effects have yet to be realised by future research.

Perhaps what I have (tentatively) provided here approximates the 'set of rules' (proposed by Morley, 1981) for decoding texts on Islam: cultural proximity, knowledge and media literacy. However, attempting to engage in a 'falsely universalising theory' obscures the diversity of social groups (Harding, 1986). Muslims are a heterogeneous group with different nationalities, sects, languages etc., as well as demographic differences. Given arguments regarding the increased religiosity of young Muslims, (verified here), would, for example, using different age groups produce different responses? These groups were constructed to be as homogeneous as possible in order to restrict the number of variables at play and offer 'a glimpse of culture' which could then be 'set in systematic relationship to other glimpses' (Fiske, 1994, p. 195). Part of the relevance of 'snapshots' of differently situated groups is that they contribute to understandings of them and subsequently contribute to meeting their needs (Wallston, 1981). It is hoped that this research can make an impact in this way.

Notes

1   Focusing specifically on English newspapers, but the use of 'British' refers to how these papers are commonly understood and reflects their national availability.

2   Some of the terms employed here are not done so unproblematically. What appears to be an essentialist construction of 'Britain', 'the British public' and 'the public sphere' in this article reflects the assumptions made and collectivities formulated by the press when constructing Muslim as 'other'.

3   The concept of cultural proximity is borrowed from Galtung and Ruge (1965). However, in relation to Muslims here, it represents religious proximity.

4   Although the consensus can sometimes be attributed to the homogeneity. The transcripts were problematised and discourse analysis implemented in order to examine the effects of the research context on the groups.

5   It is estimated that around 70 per cent of British Muslims are under the age of 25 (The Runnymede Trust, 1997).

6   Data from 'Leicester, Key facts: Ethnic Minorities, 1991 Census', Environment and Development Department, Leicester City Council, 1995.

7   Yet they also showed a degree of ignorance regarding other cultures, religions and appropriate terminology, one referring to 'Christianism' in society.

References

Ahmed, A. (1992), *Postmodernism and Islam: Predicament and Promise*, Routledge, London.

Ahmed, A. and Donnan, H. (1994), 'Islam in the Age of Postmodernity', in A. Ahmed and H. Donnan (eds), *Islam, Globalisation and Postmodernity*, Routledge, London, pp. 1-12.

Anderson, B. (1983), *Imagined Communities*, Verso, London.

Burgess, J., Harrison, C. and Maiteny, P. (1991), 'Contested Meanings: The Consumption of News about Nature Conservation', *Media, Culture and Society*, vol.13, pp. 499-519.

Cohen, R. (1997), *Global Diasporas: An Introduction*, UCL Press Ltd, London.

Corner, J. (1991), 'Meaning, Genre and Context: The Problematics of 'Public Knowledge' in the New Audience Studies', in J. Curran and M. Gurevitch (eds), *Mass Media and Society*, Edward Arnold, London, pp. 267-284.

Dahlgren, P. (1988), 'What's the Meaning of this? Viewers' Plural Sense-making of TV News', *Media, Culture and Society*, vol.10, no.3, pp. 285-301.

Duffy, K. B. and Lincoln, I. C. (1990), *Earnings and Ethnicity: Principal Report on Research*, Leicester City Council, Leicester.

Esposito, J. L. (1992), *The Islamic Threat: Myth or Reality?* Oxford University Press, Oxford.

Fiske, J. (1994), 'Audiencing: Cultural Practice and Cultural Studies', in N. K. Denzin and Y. S.Yvonna (eds), *A Handbook of Qualitative Research*, Sage, Thousand Oaks, California, pp. 189-198.

Galtung, J. and Ruge, B. (1965), 'The Structure of Foreign News', *Journal of Peace Research*, vol.2, pp. 64-91.

Gellner, E. (1983), *Nations and Nationalism*, Blackwell, Oxford.

Gilroy, P. (1997), 'Diaspora and the Detours of Identity', in K. Woodward (ed), *Identity and Difference*, Sage, London, pp. 301-346.

Hall, S. (1980), 'Encoding and Decoding', in S. Hall, D. Hobson, A. Lowe and P. Willis (eds), *Culture, Media and Language,* Unwin Hyman, London, pp. 128-138.

-- (1988), 'New Ethnicities', in J. Donald and A. Rattansi (eds), *'Race', Culture and Difference*, Sage, London, pp. 252-259.

-- (1992), 'The Question of Cultural Identity', in S. Hall, D. Held and A. McGrew (eds), *Modernity and its Futures,* Polity Press and Open University Press, United Kingdom, pp. 274-325.

Halliday, F. (1996), *Islam and the Myth of Confrontation: Religion and Politics in the Middle East,* Tauris, London.

Halloran, J., Bhatt, A. and Gray, P. (1995), *Ethnic Minorities and Television: A Study of Use, Reactions and Preferences*, University of Leicester, Centre for Mass Communication Research, Leicester.

Harding, S. (1986), *The Science Question in Feminism*, Cornell University Press, Ithaca.

Hippler, J. and Lueg, A. (eds) (1995), *The Next Threat. Western Perceptions of Islam*, Pluto Press, London.

Höijer, B. (1998), 'Social psychological perspectives in reception analysis', in R. Dickinson, R. Harindranath and O Linné (eds), *Approaches to Audience: A Reader*, Edward Arnold, London, pp. 166-183.

Jacobson, J. (1997), 'Religion and Ethnicity: Dual and Alternative Sources of Identity among Young British Pakistanis', *Ethnic and Racial Studies,* vol.20, no.2, pp. 238-256.

Knott, K and Khokher, S. (1993), 'Religious and Ethnic Identity among Young Muslim Women in Bradford', *New Community*, vol.19, no.4, pp. 593-610.

Mercer, K. and Julien, I. (1994) 'Black Masculinity and the Politics of Race', in K. Mercer, (ed.), *Welcome to the Jungle. New Positions in Black Cultural Studies*, Routledge, London, pp. 131-170.

Modood, T., Berthoud, R., Lakey, J., Nazroo, J., Smith, P., Virdee, S. and Beishon, S. (1997), *Ethnic Minorities in Britain: Diversity and Disadvantage*, Policy Studies Institute, London.

Morley, D. (1981), 'The Nationwide Audience: A Critical Postscript', *Screen Education,* no.39, pp. 3-14.

Paulis, P. B. (ed.), (1989), *Psychology of Group Influence*, Erlbaum, Hillsdale, New Jersey.

Poole, E. (1999), 'Framing Islam: An Analysis of Newspaper Coverage of Islam in the British Press', in K. Hafez (ed.), *Islam and the West in the Mass Media. Fragmented Images in a Globalised World,* Hampton Press, New Jersey, pp. 157-179.

Preston C., Keane, M. and Cheater, F. (1995), 'All You Ever Needed to Know About Running Focus Groups but were Afraid to Ask', *Audit Trends,* no.3, pp. 140-143.

Robins, K. (1991), 'Tradition and Translation: National Culture in its Global Context', in J. Corner and S. Harvey (eds), *Enterprise and Heritage: Crosscurrents of National Culture,* Granta Books, London, pp. 21-44.

The Runnymede Trust, Commission on British Muslims and Islamophobia (1997), *Islamophobia: A Challenge for Us All,* The Runnymede Trust, London.

Said, E. (1978), *Orientalism,* Vintage, New York.

Sreberny-Mohammadi, A. and Ross, K. (1995), *Black Minority Viewers and Television: Neglected Audiences Speak Up and Out,* University of Leicester, Centre for Mass Communication Research, Leicester.

Turner, J. C. (1985), 'Social Categorization and the Self-Concept: A Social-Cognitive Theory of Group Behaviour', in E. J. Lawler (ed.), *Advances in Group Processes,* JAI Press, Greenwich, CT, pp. 77-122.

van Dijk, T. (1988), *News as Discourse,* Lawrence Erlbaum Associates, New Jersey.

Wallston, B. S. (1981), 'What are the Questions in Psychology of Women? A Feminist Approach to Research, *Psychol.Women Q.,* vol.5(4), pp. 597-617.

Werbner, P. (1994), 'Diaspora and the Millennium: British Pakistani Global-Local Fabulations of the Gulf-War', in A. Ahmed and H. Donnan (eds), *Islam, Globalisation and Postmodernity,* Routledge, London, pp. 213-236.

Wimmer, R. D and Dominick, J. R. (1997), *Mass Media Research An Introduction,* Wadsworth Publishing Co, California.

Woodward, K. (1997), *Identity and Difference: Culture, Media and Identities,* Sage and Open University, London.

Wren-Lewis, J. (1983), 'The Encoding/Decoding Model: Criticisms and Redevelopments for Researching on Decoding', *Media, Culture & Society,* vol.5, pp. 179-197.

6 Deconstructing Identity: Multicultural Women and South African Situation Comedy

DOROTHY ROOME

Introduction

In reviewing the year 1996, a journalist for *The Independent,* Mapula Sibanda, suggests that:

> For South Africans, 1996 was a bold step towards reconciliation and transformation. All of us were by now familiar with the changes in our country - even some of those who were not willing to change - and most of us were ready to reconcile our differences to build a prosperous nation. (Sibanda, 1996, December 22)

Implicit in this comment is the concept of identity and a unified nation, a premise which has inspired some South Africans and dismayed others. To ascertain the extent to which this ideology was popular, I embarked on a reception studies project, interviewing four randomly constituted female focus groups who examined their culture and identity as they reacted to the popular situation comedy *Going Up III* (*GU III*). In the meeting between the focus groups and the text of *GU III*, another discourse emerged, created by the groups' cultural education and institutional practices.

In this paper the responses of the groups are referenced to illustrate how the micro-processes of viewing a television programme engage with the macro-structures of media and society. The research analysis maps the diversity of audiences in their reception of *GU III* but my purpose is also to evaluate whether a transformation and cultural reconciliation occurs in the cultural and ethnic processes which affect viewers' patterns of identification and differentiation. To assess possible disparity between the audience's response to the text and the intentionality of the local production team, the producer, writers and an actress/musician from Penguin Productions, were interviewed. Using comic realism, the production team depict a variety of South African identities through their portrayal of characters involved in addressing social and cultural issues in *Going Up III.*

The original concept behind the *Going Up* (*GU*) series was to reach a white viewership because whites could not understand Zulu. It was decided to use mostly English, as 60 per cent of viewers could understand English. Joe Mafela, co-writer and the male lead of the series, speaks fifteen languages. He says the concept for *GU* evolved from locating the production historically in the 1950s and introducing elements of the 1980s and 1990s by referencing contemporary situations. Richard Benyon, co-writer, maintains he never visualises a particular audience but he assumes he is a member of the audience and he has to surprise himself. While the cast and the writing workshop respond to the narrative as an audience would, he contends that he writes for himself, or rather, for the child in him, not consciously restricting his vocabulary but modelling it for that child.

Methodology

The use of focus groups in communication research in Africa has generally been successful because 'the group setting and relaxed atmosphere with which interviews are conducted encourage free flowing comments in a non-threatening environment' (McClean, 1992, p. 100). The objective for this ethnographic study was to search for similarities in viewers' decoding and responses as well as discrepant readings. The four randomly selected focus groups consisted of two Zulu groups, an English and an Afrikaans speaking group, five to eight women in a group with a minimum basic education - a total of 30 women. To establish the groups, I used the 'snowball' method where an informant acts as a source for locating other persons from whom data can be generated and then refers the researcher to additional persons with an accumulative result (Liebes & Katz, 1993, p. 25). Female associates provided access to various groups of women to establish the snowball sample. These women selected participants from their particular ethnic or cultural group and acted as facilitators for the group. Open-ended questions were designed to elicit responses to the text. I was present during the interviews but my presence did not inhibit the group as I participated in the discussions. At the end of the meeting with the group, participants filled in a questionnaire with details about education, age, salary, occupation and media preferences.

For a situation comedy to be 'successful', it should address changing cultural standards and operate as 'a site of negotiation of cultural change and difference' (Neale & Krutnik, 1990, pp. 237). *GU III* seems to successfully portray events occurring in a small well-established law firm, Cluver and Associates, located in the central business district of downtown Johannesburg. A *shebeen* or speak-easy is located on the top floor of the building, hence the 'Going Up' of the title. The main characters include Jabulani Cebekulu (played by Joe Mafela), a black helper, who wears a khaki dust coat, signifying his servile position; Mr. Reginald Cluver, the senior partner, an elderly colonial-style white lawyer, and Edward Tsaba, the black associate, representing the role of the new black elite in South Africa. Secondary characters include Mrs. Jakobs, the secretary; Squeeza, the black owner of the *shebeen*, and Klein Piet Gouws, a white Afrikaans-speaking security guard in the foyer of the building. Each episode is motivated by the introduction of new clients.

Two episodes were screened for the interviews. The first episode, 'The Case of the Historically Advantaged Pale Males', concerns changing identity in the new South Africa. Three white male Afrikaner construction partners arrive seeking advice from Cluver and Associates. They are puzzled about why they no longer receive government contracts. Jabu explains they need to become more representative of the new South Africa. They take this advice literally and change their names to African ones, and appoint gay men and lesbians, women and people with disabilities as board members. The second episode, 'Flexible Asian Models', concerns the use of pornographic video tapes. A female video maker has been asked by the Department of Public Works to make a corporate video on work-related tasks. The tapes are apparently very boring so a legal situation is pending in the office of Cluver and Associates. At the same time, a newly married young woman approaches Reginald Cluver about a divorce, because she has discovered pornographic tapes among her husband's possessions. In error, Jabu mixes up the public works tapes with the pornography tapes and certain problems ensue.

Cultural Capital

Pierre Bourdieu interprets 'cultural capital' as a circulation of meanings and pleasures which is difficult to control; it is different from a circulation of wealth, whose meanings and pleasures are harder to possess (Bourdieu, 1984, p. 99). 'Cultural capital' includes 'popular cultural capital', where meanings and pleasures that serve the interests of subordinate and powerless groups may be used as strategies to resist or oppose the value systems of the dominant ideology (Bourdieu, 1984, p. 120). Within the ostensible homogeneity of the groups, (Zulu, English and Afrikaans) a heterogeneity emerged among the individuals within the group when discussing the representations and relationship of characters or the politics of identity construction. The groups also articulated differences in their attitude to sexual and musical identity and certain moral lessons which were implicit in the text. In the groups' responses, conflicts sometimes occurred between modernity and traditionalism; in particular, a rift appeared in the perceptions of change between women of different socio-economic classes, where clear cut moral choices were portrayed as evidence of rapid social change. In some instances, the performance discourse was not comfortable or even familiar to the group and this fact affected the way the groups responded.

The English-speaking focus group was socially and economically advantaged and, because of their 'cultural capital', they could not visualise that Afrikaans speakers in the construction business might be so desperate for work they would cross the boundary of identity to become assimilated and change their names to African ones; they were amused by the absurdity of the logic intended by the writer, so theirs was a preferred reading. The Zulu groups' 'popular cultural capital' included their personal experience in fighting a system that had excluded them from any social or economic recognition; they understood the strategies employed by the Afrikaner men to take advantage of the situation so they failed to recognise humour in the situation thereby presenting a discrepant reading. The Afrikaans group resented the stereotype of Afrikaans men wearing short khaki trousers and being personified as so stupid that they were unaware of the economic changes of power in the society. Meanings the groups expressed validated their social experiences not their subordination. They conceived socially pertinent and pleasurable meanings from the semiotic resources of the text by asserting their social identity in negotiation with the structures of domination in South African society. During the interview sessions, discussion of values inherent in the professional and social problems of South African society occurred, especially the changing role of women in South African society.

In *GU III*, the Zulu focus groups enjoyed Jabu as the trickster/entertainer, giving a preferred reading. This indicates the successful adaptation of the African oral tradition, according well with Richard Benyon's comment that Mafela provides ideas - 'usually limp' - which are subsequently workshopped by the rest of the production team. Jabu's 'limp' contributions could indicate that, as an African from an oral culture, he is able to conceive situations directly relevant to the audience's daily life (Ong, 1982, p. 49). However, in the construction of Jabu's character, the racial stereotype of the 'slave figure, the native and the clown or entertainer' deliberately or unconsciously reproduces the ideologies of racism (Hall, 1990, p. 8). In adapting Mafela's ideas to create the 'entertainer' Jabu, 'a good man capable of putting out every gloss he likes on the world to achieve its approval', (Benyon interview, September 1996 [1]) the production team creates an ambivalence so that it is unclear whether the audience should be laughing at or with him.

The better educated Zulu focus group did not react to the humour and presented a negotiated reading. Although they admired Jabu's dexterity in contextualising how the Afrikaners could obtain contracts, at the same time they felt he was a crook who made sure things went well for himself. The less well educated Zulu group were impressed with the way Jabu took control of the clients from Cluver and provided answers 'partaking in every culture - he is too democratic'. The Afrikaans group offered a preferred reading as they had always previously associated Jabu with the greasy 'Chicken Licken'[2] advertisement and really disliked him, but in *GU III* he demonstrates how clever he is and gives an amusing performance. The most potent comment from this group characterised Jabu's flexibility in changing identity as 'incredible, as he remained at ease with himself so that he could always return to his inner core'. The English group's reading was also a preferred one, as they felt Jabu was a very likeable character, who 'knew what was going on'. They remembered him from his character in the 'Chicken Licken' advertisement and found him very amusing.

Comic Realism and the Allegoric Mode

According to a review in the *Mail & Guardian,* the series could be viewed as part of a Reconstruction and Development programme because the comedy 'lampoons present day South African society - warts and all' (Worsdale, 1996, p. 34). Another newspaper report suggests that comedy is on the increase because it is the flip side of paranoia, (*Sunday Times,* 8 September, 1996, p. 19) and in the context of the tragedies of the new South Africa, laughter is emerging as a positive response to fear, a gallows humour using personal experiences rather than faceless stereotypes. There is a general consensus that the crime rates are extraordinarily high in South Africa and that black, white, Coloured or Indian groups are highjacked, raped, robbed and killed without discrimination - hence laughter occurs as an attempt to oust fear. This type of humour is therefore attempting to deconstruct personal experiences into a 'logic of the absurd'.

The Afrikaans group were the least comfortable of all the groups regarding Mrs. Jakobs' viewing of pornography or the creation of sexual innuendo. Their reaction was manifested strongly during the discussion when most felt some form of censorship of printed pornography was essential. The Zulu groups laughed less frequently at certain jokes, indicating a possible lack of understanding of the words or lack of comprehension of verbal signifiers for concepts unfamiliar to them. They laughed when Klein Piet says 'boring' after he returns the corporate video tape, which he had thought was pornographic. However, in this example, the narrative had explained the concept and the literal meaning provided a set of derived meanings. The knowledge of the meaning evolves into an 'ideological', cultural or linguistic competence so that to understand a concept is to know those concrete events or objects to which it refers. At the end of 'The Historically Advantaged Pale Face Males', Jabu pronounces the common sense verdict that 'you can't change who you are, just by changing your name' so recuperating those who have tried to change their identity. Society is thereby returned to the status quo since the sitcom offers stability at the expense of change (Neale & Krutnik, 1990, p. 253).

Richard Benyon maintains that although comedy can provide a forum for confrontation of serious issues, it should not be pretentious (interview, September, 1996). He concedes that the *Going Up* series has elements of allegory: the building represents South Africa, the law office being the privileged white South Africa, with a modest non-white representation by a black lawyer and a coloured secretary, while Jabu floats between the black world of the *shebeen* and the white world of the law office. 'Allegory discloses the truth of the world...and represents a world where 'reality' and truth are found in the free play of signifiers' (Hendershot, citing Cowan, 1995, p. 5). The Zulu groups were particularly receptive to the allegorical mode, suggesting that Mr. Cluver symbolised the benevolent white priest in their church. They also maintained that the constant bickering and competitiveness between Mrs. Jakobs, the Coloured secretary, and Jabu was accurate as Coloureds[3] always try to denigrate blacks to improve their own situation. The better educated group saw Edward Tsaba, the educated black lawyer, as typical of many returning exiles, who could not even speak their mother tongue (in his case Sotho) and were complete misfits. This type of allegorical mode is polysemic, but as evidenced by the Zulu groups' response, it works through many layers of meaning, foregrounding signification rather than being.

The Creation of Characters as Stereotypes

In addition to the allegorical mode or 'vehicle for a melting pot' described by Durrant, *GU III* depicts stereotypical characters. But in comparing the interviews of the four members of the production team a subtle ideological split in their different perspectives about the series and the characters became apparent. In discussing the characters, Richard Benyon indicates that he liked the characters in *GU*, referring to them as 'all good guys', but *GU III* is really about criminals as in every episode criminals lie and attempt to squirm out of their misdeeds (interview, September 1996). This aspect was never mentioned in the interviews with Joe Mafela or Abigail Kubheka, the *shebeen* queen, Squeeza. Benyon argues that the translation convention used by Jabulani in *GU* becomes a mechanism whereby with both cunning and heart, he changes his boundaries. Jabu moves his identity from one side of the translation fence to the other, conversing in Zulu, Afrikaans and English, and this characterisation was recognised and endorsed by all the focus groups. Joe Mafela (interview April 1995) says he wanted to develop *GU* because, since the earlier Zulu production of *S'Gudi S'Naysi* had been so successful among Zulu speakers, he felt the audience would be widened by using English as well. Benyon, by contrast, never mentions language but says the character of Jabu is full of compassion for people who have problems. However, the Zulu focus groups saw him as self-serving. Contending that he hates comedy to moralise, Benyon says he prefers a politically incorrect sitcom in which people speak and respond to events the way they occur in South Africa, forgiving each other as they currently do. This perception of transformation and reconciliation is at odds with Benyon's comment that in real life there have to be consequences for things that people say to each other, although he admits he enjoys absurdist humour.

The 'Imagined Community' of Going Up

The South African Broadcasting Corporation (SABC) has been given the task of contributing to the development of a national identity and culture (Tomaselli & Teer-Tomaselli, 1994). Thus within the narrative of *GU* the 'imagined community', with its image of 'we' and 'us', is symbolised by the *shebeen* where people of different cultures mix (Van den Bulck & Van Poecke, 1996, p. 164). This 'imagined community' of the *shebeen,* which encourages patrons to consume excessive quantities of alcohol, is not seen by Mafela as a negative influence in society (interview, April 1995). Squeeza, the *shebeen* queen refuses service to a customer when she feels he has had too much to drink, and she might even request a fellow customer to escort an inebriated customer home. Mafela never mentions prostitution as a characteristic of the *shebeen,* but affirms that *shebeens* now have regular liquor licences and operate until 4 a.m. to accommodate men who work shifts. Kubeka admits prostitution might have been a problem in the past but says that recently the *shebeen* owners have been able to obtain a licence to sell alcohol and achieve respectability (interview, April 1995). She stresses this respectability, maintaining that the *shebeen* in the show is a business without prostitution. It is portrayed as a social club or community, where Jabu and his friends meet to discuss the day's events and have fun. Roberta Durrant's vision of the *shebeen* was to use it as a colourful space reminiscent of the old Sophiatown with its prohibition and the 'township jive' of the 1950s.

Traditional vs. Progressive Responses

The differing value systems for authoritarian control by the state were in evidence among the individuals of the Zulu focus groups. They argued vehemently about the validity of the 'traditional' concept of the *shebeen*. Some felt *shebeens* should be banned to prevent men wasting money that could be used for food and clothing for their children. However, some, who admired the *shebeen* queen for earning an honest living, argued that customers should exercise self-control, not disagreed with government intervention, as drinking was a personal matter. The concept of self-regulation as opposed to regulation by the community is perhaps more an emphasis on a political expression of individual liberty. This implies a transformation and cultural reconciliation since it confirms tolerance of, and respect for, other human beings with an emphasis on individual liberty and social justice.

Certain African cultures remain allied to the notion that deconstructing 'identity' is an attempt to erase old key concepts before the emergence of new concepts (Hall, 1991, p. 1). In a new South Africa, Africanisation falls into the category of being 'in the interval between reversal and emergence', (Williams, 1977, p. 123) - thus it cannot be thought about in the old way. But without a concept of Africanisation, important questions cannot be asked about transformation and cultural reconciliation. Kubheka agrees that the *shebeen* may be a negative representation for black society in South Africa, but many blacks regard visiting a *shebeen* as normal as going to church, even though attending church is less expensive (interview, April 1995). A person who visits a *shebeen* cannot be punished for doing so as it is a cultural tradition, signifying the community's interaction from previous times. Individuals drank genuine African brew from calabashes in the old days; today people drink African traditional brew and English beer or spirits from painted coloured tins, while listening to traditional music.

A positive response emerged from the less educated Zulu group who felt the atmosphere was so amiable and Squeeza's socialising with the customers was so friendly that it made them want to join the party. Both

English and Afrikaans groups spoke enthusiastically about the *shebeen* and compared it to the English pub scene, saying in the upscale northern suburbs in Gauteng, this was now the place to go, where one could have a drink, listen to music and meet all kinds of people. A preferred reading was presented, as a feeling of 'cultural tourism' emanated from both groups.

Sexual Identity and Pornography

The right to assume the sexual identity of one's choice has been addressed in the new Constitution for South Africa but the political implications of homosexuality are not universally accepted. In 'The Case of the Historically Advantaged Pale Males' episode, Richard Benyon creates a stereotype of a twittering pair of gay men whose presence on the board of the company makes the company politically correct. Consequently the Afrikaans construction company bids and wins contracts from the Government of National Unity. Jabu, the clown, lampoons the pair in his inimitable style, and the consequence is a double consciousness through the 'logic of the absurd' to promote heterosexuality and deny homosexuality as an abomination. These identity politics created by the production team emphasise how identities operate through exclusion with a construction of the marginalised subjects (in this example, the gay men) outside the field of the symbolic, where this identity excludes 'different' men.

Heterosexuality vs. Homosexuality

The response to the gay characters by the focus groups was a preferred reading and across three groups there was a reluctance to discuss in any detail how they felt about the representation. The English group side-stepped the issue easily by saying 'gays were not on' as far as the Afrikaans workers were concerned. Both Zulu groups also avoided the question, which had been a general one about the way construction men included women, people with disabilities and gay men and lesbians. Among the groups, there seemed to be a conspiracy of silence or 'absence' of discussion which confirmed that the production team's adherence to the ideology of heterosexuality was the preferred reading of the three groups. The Afrikaans group did not avoid the discussion of gays, some of whom admitted they disapproved of the life style, but three confessed they were more comfortable with gay men, finding gay women very aggressive. One woman divulged that her best friend's son of thirty had 'come out' but she had no reason to feel differently towards him.

In a 'classless' society technological revolutions can implement profound change, and here the issue of male and female sexuality arose in the discussion of the pornographic video tapes. In *GU II* and *III*, Mrs. Jakobs develops computer skills and uses equipment available to her at the law firm to teach herself African languages, trying to bridge the economic gap that can change her socio-economic status in the society. She uses a video cassette recorder for transcribing the contents of videos under legal examination, and she surreptitiously watches a pornographic video brought in as evidence. As Gray (1996, p. 118) suggests, the video tape recorder has been a 'major innovation in home entertainment' as the way women watch television and videos raises complex issues for them in their everyday lives. The hire or purchase of video tapes for viewing in the privacy of one's home means that women too can now watch pornography in the private space of their bedrooms with or without a partner.

Pornography and Sexuality

Traditionally there has been the assumption in South Africa that pornography is viewed only by men, but in the discussion with the focus groups it seems this perception is changing. This fact was evidenced by one group of Zulu women who stated that they watched pornographic videos with their partners. When discussing the lifting of censorship on pornography, certain of the thirty to forty year old women in both this Zulu group and one of the English groups stated that they watched pornography with their partners 'to help the relationship'. They felt that freedom of access to pornography meant they could explore their own sexuality and identity - a concept in complete contrast to the policies of the Director of Publications in South Africa (Duffy, 1996).

In the new South Africa, over a hundred films and publications are currently banned. This reneging on the promise of a transformation from the bad days of authoritarian apartheid rule suggests a 'reconciliation' towards the conservative element of the previous regime which had banned so many political writings, films and videos. This conservative response to new developments in mass culture echoes the British reaction to cinema in the 1920s and television in the 1950s, when 'moral reformers were...fearful for the effects of these new mass-produced cultural forms on those "weaker" members of society - women, children and the 'lower orders' in general - whom they sought to protect' (Gray, 1996, p. 119). This was reflected in the educated Zulu group, where one of the young women strongly recommended removing the tape after watching the video in bed with one's partner, to protect children from seeing pornography, as her children had a habit of entering early in the morning to play the video cassette recorder.

In the 'Flexible Asian Models' episode, the recently-wed Mrs. Kipling, after discovering the pornographic videos hidden in her husband's closet, consults Mr. Cluver about a divorce. Due to a mix up, when she decides to view them she discovers them to be boring educational tapes. At the end of the episode, still puzzled about why her spouse goes off at odd times to view these tapes, she plaintively questions Mr.Cluver who sloughs off her concern with 'It's a male thing'. The intention of the production team is to present the idea of watching pornography as 'a male thing' as well as a 'working man's activity' and they achieve the latter through the double entendre of the working class men being 'very stimulated' after watching the mixed up tapes.

But although this was a preferred reading by some of the older English-speaking group and one of the Zulu groups, there was also an attendant condemnation of pornography. Conversely, the younger women in all groups provided an aberrant reading of the text. They supported an unconditional lifting of the ban on pornography and, as women, indicated their interest in watching pornographic videos. As Gilroy (1996, p. 44) says, 'class relations are an integral part of capitalist societies but cannot explain politics', so within political movements frequently a divergence from the mainstream occurs among the women of the movement, the youth and those of different race.

Among these women of different political and socio-economic position, there were those who believed it was their right to view pornographic tapes as a free expression of their sexuality. The notion of self-regulation as opposed to regulation by the community emerges again, as it did with the control of *shebeens*, as the expression of individual liberty. This transformation from the apartheid years does not necessarily mesh with reconciliation since there are many individuals who would like to return to complete censorship of pornography. This 'porn free' view was expressed in strong terms by the Afrikaans group and the working class Zulu women, most of whom were Muslim. The reasons from both groups varied, depending on their subjectivity, but two women from the English group advocated censorship as a feminist discourse, since patriarchal power is regarded as the dominant power in society and as such, pornography exploits women's bodies. A woman from the English group and one from the Afrikaans proposed a liberal feminist position, placing the onus of censorship on the individual to view and respond to material as the woman sees fit. Definitions of pornography and erotica have been slippery at best so the mere fact that it is no longer illegal to watch pornographic videos indicates transformation in the country but not necessarily reconciliation.

Musical Identity

Abigail Kubheka explained how her musical talent has enabled her to sing all over the world, starting with the female group 'Skylarks' in the 1960s (interview, April 1995). At that time, blacks were not allowed to sing in the same cast with whites, but the owners of clubs kept a lookout for the police and when they arrived the black singers suddenly started washing dishes in the kitchen.

Frith contends that 'identity is mobile, a process not a thing and ...music making and music listening is best understood as an experience of this *self-in-process.'* (Frith, 1996, p. 109) The process of post-apartheid transformation is most evident in the *GU* series through the music, where blacks and whites participate together in dance and song; a relatively new experience for most people. Reconciliation is more subtle, as evidenced by the reaction of the focus groups. The introduction of popular music in *GU III* is part of the encoding by the production team to recreate the fun atmosphere of a *shebeen* from the 1950s and 1960s (Mafela interview, April 1995) with the dancing and singing creating a light hearted ambience. However Klein Pit's rap song in 'The Case of the Historically Advantaged Pale Males' episode conveys the production team's perception of a comedy of the absurd as Piet Gouws changes his name to 'Mr. Snowman' to promote his singing career. The text of Mr. Snowman's song plays with the meaning of 'toyi-toying',[4] moralising about changing identities and lampooning the political process while following the format and rhythm of a typical rap song.

Popular Music and Class

The 'self' manifested by the reaction of the various groups to the music in the episode was varied. The better educated, slightly younger middle class Zulu-speaking group disliked the music, as they felt it went on for too long and should be excluded completely. They contended that they never listened to any music, although as young girls they had sung in church choirs. However, among the other Zulu group were women actively involved in African National Congress (ANC) affairs, economically a mix of the very poor and not so poor; they really liked the music and said it reminded them of the music their mothers listened to as they enjoyed that 'township jive'. In addition, this group loved Mr. Snowman's rendition of the rap song. One of the woman said she enjoyed watching Piet Gouws as he was 'so *active*'. One of the English speakers explained how she 'really liked that sound'. These white women had previously indicated their reservations about black communities and the new government of national unity, yet questions about the music activated a positive response that indicated music provided a way of making sense of the new South Africa.

Music works materially, giving people different identities and placing them in different social groups so that it 'constructs our sense of identity through direct experience of the body, time and sociability by placing ourselves in imaginative cultural narratives.' (Frith, 1996, p. 115) However, taking an identity from rap music was rejected by the better-educated Zulu group, possibly because it represented a particular ethnic identity from which, as an emerging middle class, they wished to retreat. Since the abolition of apartheid, the class structure has begun to change and access to exclusive locations is not closed to people of colour if they can pay for entrance. The 1994 general elections in South Africa promised the democratic libertarian approach with reconstructive aspirations of race as the basis of change, and this is still integral and essential to the national consciousness - as evidenced by the television promotion jingle 'simunye' or 'we are one'.

Homogenisation and Multiculturalism

In the new era in South Africa, blacks have political power but the perception is that aside from the black elite, many black individuals and groups do not have economic or social power, and the negotiation to create a national and nationalising culture has been the task of the South African Broadcasting Corporation (SABC). Their task has been to construct a more homogeneous culture and the singing on television of 'simunye' or 'we are one' attempts to signify unity and homogeneity.

When Zulu women were asked what it meant to be South African, all articulated the SABC's 'simunye' indicating their positive reaction to the concept of a nation that has been homogenised; yet all were proudly Zulu in their cultural aspirations. Commenting on the process of reconciliation one woman who lives in the shacks and ekes out a living as an informal trader selling old clothes exclaimed 'Let them (the whites) accept us from their hearts and say they are sorry for what happened and then it's OK'. The English upper-class white group admitted South African society was changing and they were trying to relate to the changes.

National Identity

When the English group was asked to identify what it meant to be South African no one suggested an inclusive identity as the promotional piece 'simunye' advocates. Rather the answers were evasive and referenced only how fortunate they were to live in such a beautiful country; one woman in her early sixties said she was lucky to speak English, a language spoken world wide and a language of power. There was a lack of consensus about what it meant to be 'South African' but a construction of a cultural authority - 'English' – emerged, and a defiant use of 'Englishness' to signify an authoritarian inscription of the cultural sign. An anxious sense of identity seemed to be negotiating the image of 'English' so that in the process of accepting a social transformation these women were antagonistic and ambivalent. Any solidarity as a 'South African' in the oneness of 'simunye' was situational and strategic, to placate the reality of a black government. The generational gap expressed a sharp difference in the responses of those women in their forties who were more amenable about accepting a social transformation and confronting the black/white borderline. With the passing of time they indicated 'we'll get used to it, we'll have to - this is our country too'.

Kevin Robins (1996, p. 61) believes cultural change implies an ability to relinquish certain codes and symbols of living and values by giving up part of an inherited identity, observing that 'there is a basic fear about the mortality of the collective institution.' Similarly the focus group of white upper-class English-speaking women recognised the possible demise of their way of living as a privileged minority. The interaction with diverse cultural groups provides new experiences, modifying people's fears and prejudices by recognising the other as a culture apart, not an extension of the same culture, and thereby promotes a cultural dynamism.

Nation-building

Benyon had no intention of deliberately using a nation-building theme in the situation comedy series *GU*. However, he says, by resolving ridiculous conflicts, white and black characters probably achieved a type of nation-building. Benyon maintains that black audiences love the character of Cluver, the elderly white lawyer, but he is unaware whether or not white audiences also like this character. Jabu's character is sensitive to issues which are important to all South Africans. This nation-building ingredient in *GU III* is apparent through the positive reaction of black viewers to the white lawyer Mr. Cluver, but this phenomenon is a very different approach compared with the first of the series in 1990 when the situation was more politically sensitive in terms of a 'mixed [race] situation'. The Jabulani character broke the black stereotype; his major contribution has been to change the typical stereotype held by whites of a stupid, servile black into the smart hero of the series. It is his acumen, cunning and underhandedness that achieve results and motivate the story in ways Mr. Cluver, the white lawyer would never consider utilising.

The later series of *GU* deals with real issues relating to the fears of whites, as well as the hijacking fears of both whites and blacks. According to Benyon, although nation-building is not part of the production team's agenda and workshop sessions do not attempt to heal the country's wounds, the writing group for *GU* is sensitive to issues that are important to them.

In addition, the SABC, as a public broadcasting system, has extensive access to large audiences and a mandate to present a model of South Africa as a unified nation. Consequently promotional spots on SABC1 advocating 'simunye' or 'we are one' have been broadcast since the relaunch of the SABC in February 1996.

Transformation and Consumerism

Social class is not defined by a series of properties in terms of gender, age, social or ethnic origin but 'by the structure of relations between all the pertinent properties which give [a] specific value to each of them and to the effects they exert on practices' (Bourdieu, 1984, p. 106). With the demise of apartheid in South Africa the notion of 'a unified nation' has been complicated with the sudden enfranchisement of more than 35 million people and the introduction of a totally new system of democracy. Today the media provide 'advice' for black viewers' conduct in the new business-oriented environment. Appropriate western dress codes, personal hygiene, (use of deodorants, soaps) 'correct' care of children, education and the admonishment to people 'don't do crime' are constantly broadcast.

In striving to attain a certain social position, the new South African citizen has to acquire skills to access a position in the middle class or bourgeoisie. Instead of community-based ethics, the focus now is on the development and encouragement of personal goals, with 'self' being valorised. Explicit codes about monitoring bodily functions, manners and etiquette are recommended to viewers. Thus the language of autonomy, identity and self-realisation provides a stable grid of regulations so that the newcomers to democracy may obtain instruction about 'self'. This process has also meant changes in the laws regarding pornography and a more open approach to sexuality is emerging through television programmes which discuss many previously taboo subjects.

Conclusion

'Humour is ambivalent, it involves no commitment and its meanings change according to the circumstances of its utterance' (Palmer, 1987, p. 224). In social realist comedy such as *GU*, the audience witnesses the breaking of established social codes. Ideology becomes the site of struggle, and the meaning is determined by reference to the role it plays in the class struggle at any given point in time and place. The assigning of meaning can change at any time according to the place and time created, the purpose for which it was used or the identity of the participants.

In the ethnographic research the four focus groups responded according to their cultural background but all identified with the narrative and characters. As an audience they constantly reiterated their heterogeneity, disagreeing with each other as ethnic groups and yet within those groups, unbeknown to them, there were links with groups from the other ethnicities. The educated Afrikaans group rejected the presence of pornography in the society as did part of the Zulu group and the English group. However, there was consensus among a few of the younger members of the Zulu and English group about viewing pornographic videos and agreement that it is incumbent on men to make a practical contribution to household chores and provide openness in sexual communication. The sharing of these values implies a crossing of boundaries which indicates transformation from those rigid pockets of separateness reminiscent of apartheid. Again the most significant transformation occurred in the *production* of the series where a mixed black and white production team created a sitcom for heterogeneous South African audiences, providing their individual unique Eurocentric or Afrocentric perspective.

Notes

1   I would like to thank Dr. Ruth Teer-Tomaselli for kindly undertaking to interview Richard Benyon for me based on questions I prepared.
2   Joe Mafela was universally known as S'Dumo from the character he played in the TV series *Sgudi's Snaysi* for which he won 'Most Popular Personality Television Award'. He was also the actor in the fried chicken commercials on television.. Names like 'S'Dumo Special Burger' and 'Joe's Full House Chicken' are part of the take-away chicken chain's permanent menu.
3   'Coloured' has become a designation still worn with pride by this community as during apartheid in the hierarchical structure of the society members were elevated above blacks (Adam, 1971).
4   'Toyi-toying' was a political protest dance used in protest marches during apartheid.

References

Adam, H. (1971), *Modernizing Racial Domination: The Dynamics of South African Politics*, University of California Press, Berkeley.

Bourdieu, P. (1984), *Distinction: A Social Critique of the Judgement of Taste*, Cambridge, MA, Harvard University Press.

Duffy, J.G. (1996), 'Bottom falls out of sex industry', *Mail & Guardian*, 24-31 December.

Durrant, R. (Producer), (1996), Episodes 4 and 24. *Going Up III*, Penguin Films, Johannesburg.

Frith, S. (1996), 'Music and Identity', in S. Hall and P. du Gay, (eds), *Questions of Cultural Identity*, Sage, London, Thousand Oaks, pp. 108-127.

Gilroy, P. (1996), 'British Cultural Studies and the Pitfalls of Identity', in J. Curran, D. Morley and V. Walkerdine (eds), *Cultural Studies and Communications*, Arnold, London, pp. 35-49.

Gray, A. (1996),'Behind Closed Doors: Video Recorders in the Home', in H. Baehr and A. Gray (eds), *Turning It On: A Reader in Women and Media*, Arnold, London, New York, Sydney, Auckland, pp. 118-129.

Hall, S. (1980), 'Encoding/Decoding' in S. Hall, D. Hobson, A. Lowe and P. Willis (eds), *Culture, Media, Language*, Hutchinson and Centre for Contemporary Cultural Studies, Birmingham, pp.128-138.

-- (1990), 'The Whites of Their Eyes: Racist Ideologies and the Media', in M. Alvarado and J. O. Thompson (eds), *The Media Reader*, Trinity Press, Worcester, pp. 7-23.

-- (1996), 'Introduction: Who Needs Identity?' in S. Hall and P. Du Gay (eds), *Questions of Cultural Identity*, Sage, London, Thousand Oaks, pp. 1-17.

Hendershot, C. (1995), 'Postmodern Allegory and David Lynch's *Wild at Heart*',*Critical Arts*, vol. 9, no. 1, pp. 5-19.

Liebes, T. and Katz, E. (1993), *The Export of Meaning: Cross Cultural Readings of Dallas*, Polity, Oxford.

McLean, P.E. (1992), 'Methodological Shortcomings of Communication Research in Southern Africa: A Critique Based on the Swaziland Experience', in S. T. Kwame Boafo and N. A. George (eds), *Communication Research in Africa: Issues and Perspectives*, African Council for Communication Education, Kenya, pp. 89-108.

Neale, S. and Krutnik, F. (1990), *Popular Film and Television Comedy*, Routledge, London.

Ong, W. J. (1982), *Orality and Literacy*, Methuen, London.

Palmer, J. (1987), *The Logic of the Absurd*. British Film Institute, London.

-- (1994), *Taking Humour Seriously*, Routledge, London, New York.

Robins, K. (1996), 'Interrupting Identities: Turkey/Europe', in S. Hall and P. Du Gay (eds), *Questions of Cultural Identity*, Sage, London, Thousand Oaks, pp. 61-86.

Sibanda, M. (1996), 'Looking Back', *Independent*, Johannesburg, 22 December.

Tomaselli, K. and Teer-Tomaselli, R. (1994),'Reconstituting Public Broadcasting: Media and Democracy During Transition in South Africa', *Communicare*, vol. 13, no. 2, pp. 44-65.

Van Den Bulck, H. and Van Poecke, L. (1996), 'National Language, Identity Formation and Broadcasting', in S. Brahan and A. Sreberny-Mohammadi (eds), *Globalization, Communication and Transnational Civil Society*, Hampton, Cresskill, N. J, pp. 157-177.

Williams, R. (1977), *Marxism and Literature*, Oxford University Press, Oxford.

Worsdale, A. (1996), 'The Restoration of Comedy', *Mail & Guardian*, 24-31 October.

7 'Indians are Like That': Negotiating Identity in a Media World

S. ELIZABETH BIRD

The American Indian as Cultural Icon

It's one of the most celebrated images of the American Indian[1] - a tight close-up of a middle-aged man, his stoic face speaking for the suffering of generations, watching the despoilment of his ancestral lands by the pollution of the white man. His agony is revealed by the single tear forming in the corner of his eye. This 1972 public service advertisement, targeting environmental pollution, became an American popular icon, solidifying the environmentally-conscious, spiritual 'noble savage' as the prevailing archetype of the Indian. The actor who posed for the shot, 'Iron Eyes' Cody, seemed to personify that archetype in his professional and personal life.

More than 20 years later, when Cody died, his personal identity began to unravel, as it emerged that his real name was Espera (or Oscar) DeCorti, an Italian-American with no Indian ancestry. He had lived out his life as a kind of 'going native' fantasy, marrying an Indian woman, adopting Indian children, and acting as an Indian spokesman. He was only the latest in a line of famous Indian 'wannabes' that included Englishman Archie Belaney, known as 'Grey Owl' (Francis, 1992).

The celebrity of Cody illustrates many elements that make the role of the American Indian in popular culture so distinctive, not only in the United States, but also elsewhere. The original inhabitants of the Americas, decimated in what amounted to genocide, are still one of the most disadvantaged groups in the country, suffering from high levels of poverty, unemployment, and sickness.[2] At various times they have been stereotyped as savages, cannibals, sexual predators, and shiftless, drunken losers (Berkhofer, 1979). Yet simultaneously, they have been exalted as noble, spiritual - the true symbol of America. White people have also been 'playing Indian' for a century or more, and they still do, meeting at weekends all over the United States and Europe, to dress in Indian regalia and act out Indian rituals (DeLoria, 1999). Indian shamans, real and spurious, have become rich from teaching white people supposed Indian lore (Whitt, 1995). According to mainstream culture, 'real' Indians are wise, calm, spiritual and live in a kind of mythical netherworld.

So images of Indians in contemporary popular culture are one-dimensional, with a heavy overlay of romanticism. A now substantial body of literature documents the representation of Indians in popular literature, television, and film, (e.g. Berkhofer, 1979; Francis 1992; Churchill, 1994; Bird, 1999), while contemporary Indian life is rarely represented. Occasional films such as the Indian-directed *Smoke Signals*, a funny and honest portrayal of modern reservation life, cannot compete with the narrative resonance of such blockbusters of noble savagery as *Dances with Wolves*.

This intertextual melange of imagery suggests that American Indians as symbols are a potent presence in North American and European cultural narratives, but one wonders whether these narratives speak in any way to Indians themselves. As cultural studies scholars have long argued, we cannot presume to read off the cultural meaning of anything through textual analysis alone. Yet few scholars have studied audience response to American Indian representation from the standpoint of either Indian or non-Indian audiences. Hanson and Rouse (1987, p. 57), having acknowledged the consistency of the noble savage imagery in contemporary culture, write, 'far less certain is the precise connection between the familiar caricature of the generic Indian and the more complex set of beliefs and attitudes that individuals actually had concerning Native Americans.' My purpose in this study was to explore this connection, extending the discussion not only to how white audiences respond to representations of Indians, but also to how Indians respond to and imagine representations of themselves.

Hanson and Rouse (1987), using a social scientific survey of students' attitudes to Indians, conclude that their (mostly white) respondents' perceptions tend to be positive, rejecting the older stereotypes of war-like, primitive people, and claiming to value the contributions of diverse Indian cultures. They paint a picture of a rather open-minded population, who value diversity (a message they were probably used to receiving in the sociology and anthropology classes from which they were recruited). Their respondents rated television and movies as their most important source of information about Indians.

Yet Hanson and Rouse's data also point to the acceptance of stereotypes. For instance, the students associated Indians with rural and traditional life-styles, and tended to think of them as living in the past. Respondents agreed that Indians tend to be 'submissive' and 'withdrawn,' even as they disagreed that Indians were 'lazy,' 'weak,' 'undependable,' or 'unpatriotic,' all of which might have described popular perceptions in the 19th century.

I believe this study shows that by the late 20th century, college students knew how to give an appropriate response to a survey on racial attitudes, and few are likely to offer strongly pejorative comments. Although these students rejected the old Western stereotypes, they appear to have internalised the more contemporary stereotype, without seeing it in any way as derogatory. Prevailing American attitudes would not favor 'submissive' and 'withdrawn' as positive descriptions of most Americans, yet it seems unlikely that these students meant these terms as negative. Rather, they accepted the stoicism and laconicism of Indians as part of the 'noble savage' paradigm. While Hanson and Rouse read their results as indicating a breakdown of stereotypes, I believe they merely suggest a shifting to a 'positive' stereotype that reflects a self-conscious 'political correctness.'

Support for this comes from my own research that compares Indian and white responses to *Dr. Quinn, Medicine Woman*, an Old West television series that featured Cheyenne characters. This research, documented more fully elsewhere (Bird, 1996), concluded that the largely stereotypical presentation of Indians was accepted as authentic and unremarkable by white audiences, while Indian viewers found it inauthentic, irritating, and one-dimensional. A typical contrast was in response to an episode in which the main Cheyenne character is unjustly imprisoned by the Army, yet refuses to protest. A white woman remarked approvingly: 'Indians are like that. You know, they can be very intense emotionally but able to suppress it and not show it' (Bird, 1996, p. 253). Indian viewers were angered, arguing that 'his manhood was suppressed,' and the character was not allowed to show normal emotions. 'He just ... put his head down, made him look pitiful. That kind of pissed me off' (ibid., p. 256).

Thus, I suggest that while contemporary perceptions of American Indians are not generally 'negative,' they are still narrow, and ultimately objectifying. Hanson and Rouse's students may have known the right things to say, but their perceptions of Indians are still framed in a particular way, with the media as central agents. As Thompson (1990, p. 219) puts it, a central role of the media is the 'public circulation of symbolic forms', and the Indian is undoubtedly a symbolic construction in America and elsewhere. Indians themselves simply do not find symbolic representations that resonate in any way with their own experiences and identity.

Media and Identity

My earlier study was based on analysis of qualitative focus groups with Indians and non-Indian people, and points to the importance of open-ended methodologies in drawing a more subtle picture of audience response, one that begins to get at the way media representations connect with people's sense of identity. As defined by Woodward (1997, pp. 1-2), 'Identity gives us an idea of who we are and of how we relate to others and to the world ...Identity marks the ways in which we are the same as others who share that position, and the ways in which we are different from those who do not.' For instance, a central character in *Dr. Quinn* was Sully, a glamorous, long-haired loner who 'knows the ways' of the Cheyenne. White viewers, especially women, saw in him an ideal hero: 'He stands up for women and...blacks...and American Indians...he's always doing the right stuff,' commented one (Bird, 1996, p. 255). Sully unproblematically fits with a white sense of identity related to the Old West, in which the role of the good white man is to speak for the oppressed, but ultimately to guide them toward the inevitable progress of civilization. He comes from a long line of border-crossing mountain men, which can be traced back to early pioneer narratives and the novels of James Fenimore Cooper, and he became a staple in the Western narratives of Europe, such as the German novels of Karl May. He is the personification of the 'going native' fantasy (Baird, 1996). For all its mainstream resonance, this narrative violates Indians' own sense of identity. They recognized the theme: 'I can't think of one movie that there hasn't been this white guy that has somehow been part of their culture' (Bird, 1996, p. 255). But they resented it strongly: 'Here's another white person fixing the Indians' (ibid.); 'I know a lot of old stories...I can't ever recall one where anyone talked about a long-haired, light-skinned, hairy guy that helped my tribe' (ibid., p. 256).

Discussing the relationship between identity and media representations, Woodward writes, 'Representation as a cultural process establishes individual and collective identities, and symbolic systems provide possible answers to the questions: who am I? what could I be? who do I want to be?' (1997, p. 14). For whites and Indians, the experience of watching the *Dr. Quinn* Indians and wannabes is diametrically opposed – whites' identity is validated and authenticated, while Indian identity is denied and erased.

Indian participants in my study spoke about how media representation is so entrenched that it may be impossible for conventional media to provide the kind of narratives that speak to Indian identity. An Ojibwa participant spoke of the need to transcend conventional media and reinvent identity: 'I think what's coming up now is virtual reality experience...We're going to have something more than T.V., where our people will win the game' (Bird, 1996, p. 259).

The Media-Creation Exercise

My first study indicated that Indian people do believe media representations are important, both for their sense of personal identity and literally as mediators, filtering relationships between themselves and others. The daily experience of American Indians is that white people constantly see them through the lens provided by the media. The 1998 film *Smoke Signals*, written by Sherman Alexei, a Coeur D'Alene Indian, includes a sequence in which the two young central characters take a long bus trip from Washington State to the South West. The more confident Victor instructs his nerdy, bespectacled friend Thomas how to look like a 'real Indian,' exhorting him to let his long hair flow free, 'look stoic,' and 'look like you've just come back from hunting a buffalo.' Thomas protests that their tribe were fishermen, but Victor knows that the generic image of Indians is a buffalo hunter: 'This isn't 'Dances with Salmon', you know!'

With this in mind, I devised a study aimed to offer a more subtle and nuanced understanding both of white perceptions of Indians, and of how Indians might re-imagine the role of media in representing themselves. Working in Duluth, Minnesota, I recruited 10 groups, each with four participants (although two groups ended up with three, due to last-minute drop-outs). Two consisted of white women, two of white men, two of Indian men, two of Indian women, and two were mixed Indian/white. Since the task involved a group planning exercise with minimal direction and supervision, I decided it would be most effective if the members already knew each other; usually one individual was contacted, and he or she was then asked to recruit three friends/acquaintances. The result was a pool of 38 participants, ranging in age from 17 to 58, with an average age of 30. Each participant was compensated with a check for $50.

The groups were told that their mission was to design a fictional television series they would want to watch regularly.[3] It could be any genre (sitcom, drama and so on), and could be set anywhere, at any time period. The programme should include a cast of characters, both major and minor, and the group had to decide who they were and how they related to each other. Their goal was to design the programme in as much detail as possible, providing a character history, developing a detailed story for the first episode, and outlining some of the storylines that would happen over the next six weeks. At the end of the estimated two hours, they summarized their decisions on forms provided. The sessions were also audio-taped, and the transcripts analysed. The only restriction was that at least one character should be white, one American Indian, and one a woman, although none of these had to be a leading character. I hoped to avoid focusing the groups' attention too heavily on the issue of Indian characterisation; they were simply told that the project was a creative experiment. After full instructions, coffee, and soft drinks were provided and the researcher withdrew while the groups talked.

Clearly, this is not an 'audience response study' in the familiar sense; there is no media text to view, and no viewers watching and decoding. This choice emerges out of a growing dissatisfaction among audience researchers about the limitations of response studies. In a media-saturated culture, it is no longer possible to separate out the 'effects' of particular media (if it ever was), and the goal must be to reach a more holistic, anthropological understanding of how people's world views are patterned by the media, and how the media are inserted into their daily lives. As Drotner (1994, p. 345) argues, for media ethnographers this implies a move away from specific reception studies: 'in empirical terms the context of investigation is widened to include areas beyond the immediate situation of reception...media ethnographers apply a variety of methods in order to better grasp the dynamics of mediated meaning-making... as part of everyday life.'

Most of the groups began in varying degrees of despair, discussing how impossible the task was, and wondering about the point of the exercise. However, all eventually got down to the task, and produced a variety of creative ideas (the $50 payment proved crucial, turning the exercise into a 'job' to be done properly, rather than a frivolous activity). Several groups began with drama, but almost all ended up creating comedies or 'comedy-dramas,' often discussing how humour can deal with serious issues in a non-threatening way, a point echoing Drotner's (1994, p. 353) observation that when she asked young people to create their own videos, 'humour...was the genre everybody could agree upon.'

In the end, each group transcript averaged over 40 pages, providing a wealth of ethnographic detail about how people actually integrate generic conventions, stereotypes, and everyday experience in a mediated world. All groups talked at length about their need to have programming to which they related, and all drew to varying degrees on their own experiences. While there was much to be gleaned from the exercise, I will focus here on the implications of the American Indian characterisation, and in the interests of brevity, I will omit discussion of the mixed white/Indian groups at this point.

Whites Represent Indians

In analysing the white groups, I was interested in the extent to which their own creations would connect to the *Dr. Quinn* study, in which white audiences appeared to have naturalized familiar stereotypes, and did not

110

appear very interested in the development of Indian characters. To a great extent, that turned out to be true.

The first white group comprised four women: a 58-year-old office worker, a 35-year-old administrator; a 32-year-old university admissions worker, and a 42-year-old secretary. Their favorite shows were all sitcoms: *Frasier, The Nanny, Friends,* and *Wings,* respectively. Significantly, they began by talking about their favorites, and formulating how 'their' show would fit in this genre. Soon, they created a sitcom, *Dents and Tangles,* in which a young husband-and-wife team (Scott and Jennifer) run a connected hairdressing salon and body shop [car repair garage]. Tired of big city life, they have moved home to Duluth to start their business. The action will focus around their struggles to make it, amid an array of supporting characters. They develop detailed character sketches of the characters. For instance, Jennifer is described in writing: '27 years old, BBA degree, cosmetology background. Excited to start her own business and establish herself as a manager. Her relationship with Glenn (Scott's dad) will be complicated, as she and Scott see themselves as equals professionally. She's very stylish.' Seven characters are given this kind of detailed description.

At various moments, someone remembers that an Indian character is needed. One suggests, 'maybe an Indian girl could be one of the best stylists and have her be really flashy and beautiful,' citing the Disney cartoon *Pocahontas.* Later, the same woman mentions Marilyn, a character in the series *Northern Exposure,* set in Alaska and featuring several Native characters: 'she was good, her heritage came through and she was really very quietly intelligent.' Others agree, and it is quickly decided that Marilyn could be exported from that series intact: 'We could have her make some one-line saying at the end of the show... And in some episodes you could have her say something and leave the shop in the middle of the show, something rather, um ... prophetic, as though she knew the outcome of the situation.'

All in all, this group's result was revealing. The discussion of Marilyn was cursory compared to the detailed development of other characters, and the group relied entirely on an already-existing media character, while all other characters emerged through dialogue about personal experience and knowledge. *Northern Exposure's* Marilyn was unusually well-developed (although still sketchy compared to the white characters; see Taylor, 1996), yet the version imported to *Dents and Tangles* was one-dimensionally stereotypical - wise, spiritual, silent. In discussing the events that would ensue in the first few episodes, the group detailed the escapades of even the minor characters, except for Marilyn, as someone occasionally remembers and says something like, 'Oh yes, then Marilyn comes in, says something wise, and all that.' It's hardly a stretch to imagine professional TV programmers developing their characters in much the same way.

The second white female group consisted of a 30-year-old community organiser, a 36-year-old secretary, a 37-year-old community organiser, and a 38-year-old 'home-maker/mom.' All were regular television watchers, whose favourite programmes were *Northern Exposure*, *ER*, and the female-oriented sitcoms *Grace under Fire* and *Roseanne*. Perhaps reflecting their combined preferences, they developed a contemporary 'comedy/drama' called *Mesabi North*, featuring the everyday lives of a mixed group of people in a Duluth apartment building. This group set out to make the situation 'funky,' featuring an eclectic mix of types. With much laughter, they seem be gently satirising the tendency in American shows to showcase a 'diverse' cast. They begin by casting the Indian character, who will be the apartment owner/manager:

> M: She's Native American, she's trans-gender ... She's our main character right now.
>
> S: She's a vegetarian. She's into Earth stuff, you know keeping the environment clean.
>
> M: That's where that funky smell comes from.
>
> S: She's got some funky smells coming from her apartment, incense you know,
>
> G: Hippie stuff.
>
> S: Crystals, all the crystals and all the rocks around her.

Soon they decide that this central character will be white, but 'How about ...there was an American Indian elder living in the building?' This is met with approval: 'sort of like a mother, spiritual advisor?' The group goes on to describe a range of deliberately stereotyped characters - a single, Latina mother, a gay couple, a lesbian couple, a Hmong immigrant family, and so on. They assert that the humour will emerge from the interaction among them: 'and then also a better understanding of different lifestyles...maybe,' commented one. Even though all the characters are stereotypical, the group provides much more detail for some; the gay male couple is quite fully realised, with details of occupations, hobbies, and personal appearance, as the group refer often to their own gay friends. They have more trouble with the Indian woman, as they grope for appropriate descriptions:

S: Selma's our Native American Elder Women.

M: Yup, elder lady ...

S: What's Selma's last name? She don't need a last name, we just go by Selma.

M: It could be like Selma Morning Star.

L: I like Selma Morning Star.

M: Make her last name sound more Native American ... Blackfeather...or...

S: Sunbear

M: Blackhawk...or

S: Brownbear, Selma Brownbear.

M: Or Redbird ... She has beadwork classes and she sells her beadwork at the pow-wows in the summer.

G: Not just beadwork. She does it all.

S: Weaving and basket making and makes rugs ...

In the plot outlines for the first few weeks, Selma gets little mention, after one episode in which other tenants think she is smoking pot (she is actually burning sage in a ritual). Once again, the group has drawn heavily on existing symbolic forms to create their character, and then cannot think what to do with her.

Both white male groups were slightly younger than the women. The first comprised a 25-year-old jeweller, who favoured the sitcom *In Living Color*, a 25-year-old graphic artist, and a 23-year-old student, both of whose favourite programme was *Friends*. They name their program *Crazy Horse*, setting it in a conservative Southern community, where a couple is trying to open a casino. At one point, the group gets into a long digression about the enormous (and presumably shady) profits made by Indian casinos. This group was probably the least engaged of any, constantly having to return to task, while drinking whisky and becoming progressively inebriated. Their characterisation is weak, and they are immediately flummoxed by the need to include an Indian character. Their first attempt is strikingly stereotypical:

K: OK, how 'bout the setting is a jewelry store in like, downtown Duluth, and they have to deal with all the drunk Indians that come in.

J: Hey ... one could be a recurring character

K: There you go.

However, they move on, and eventually decide on a male Indian, married to a white woman, who opens a casino in the South. Again drawing on stereotypes that Indian casino profits probably derive from white expertise or Mafia connections, one suggests: 'How 'bout, the thing that's really pissing him off is the wife runs it and he's the Indian guy. So he's gotta stay home and take care of this little kid. Or he's like a janitor or something.' They go on to discuss the humour involved in having the Indian try to hide his ancestry while running an Indian casino, settling on his name as Todd Crazy Horse. They continue to explore various characteristics for Todd, having him sexually involved with casino employees, while his wife fumes, and taking direction from the Mafia. They talk often about 'dialogue between Todd and Mary Beth which would outline humorous conflict resulting from his heritage,' but cannot come up with specifics. In the end, it is clear they have no idea how to develop the character, although they do a more coherent job with his wife and other supporting characters.

The second white male group included a 25-year-old cook, a 24-year-old student, and a 27-year-old 'unemployed graduate student,' whose favourite programmes are *Seinfeld*, the fantasy drama *Hercules*, and *Friends*. Between them they developed a rather rich scenario for their sitcom, *The Other Lebanon*, centered around a bar in a Colorado town, originally settled by 19th century Lebanese immigrants. Conflicts emerge between the locals and 'rich, yuppie ski resort people,' who are becoming increasingly numerous. This group was explicitly interested in not being stereotypical, and introduced some interesting characters, such as a highly-educated bartender and a female garage owner, both very detailed. They tried hard with the Indian character, beginning with a false start in which they visualise a group of students as central characters: 'But um, there'd be a chaperone, and build off the image of the wise American Indian, somebody that's kind of calm.' This was rejected as clichéd, and the group settled on their character: 'There's an Indian women, she's a good musician. She plays rock music, to traditional Irish, to Patsy Cline...She owns a profitable, kind of alternative movie theater...She's not a shaman or anything.' However, once established, the group found it difficult to know what to do with her, only mentioning her once again, to reiterate that she would defy expectations in terms of her musical repertoire. Meanwhile, their other characters and scenarios were described carefully and thoroughly.

Indians Represent Themselves

The white groups were clearly most comfortable with stories and characters that fit both their own lives and the mainstream media genres they experience every day, genres that take the white experience for granted. Minority viewers often have to read against the grain, and view representations through a lens that places ethnic identity in the forefront. Lind (1996), following Cohen (1991) and others, stresses the importance of 'relevance' in audience interpretations of media - the fact that cultural identity is a crucial framing device through which people view media imagery. American Indians, like other minorities, spend their lives acutely aware of their ethnicity, and of media representations of it. In my *Dr. Quinn* study, for example, white focus groups rarely initiated discussion of Indian representation, taking it for granted. I usually had to raise it as a topic, something that never happened with the Indian groups, who raised it almost immediately.

So it was not surprising that the groups in this study all took the opportunity to create programmes that explicitly explored issues of Indian identity and life. The first male Indian group included four pre-medical students, aged 33, 20, 27, and 32. They listed their favourite shows as *ER*, the mostly Black sitcom *Fresh Prince of Bel Air*, *Seinfeld*, and *Star Trek: Next Generation*. Their comedy, *Red Earth*, evolved through a series of ideas that all involved people as outsiders, beginning with one participant describing his own life: 'Coming from a reservation, becoming urbanized...and going back to the reservation...Being accepted in your traditional beliefs verses the societal beliefs ...I actually wrote a story on my own a long time ago...I called it "The Glass Culture."' Others then discussed having a white female doctor trying to be accepted on a reservation, an Indian doctor trying to fit into suburban America, or an Indian student's struggle to become a doctor.

This prompted reflection from other group members as they talked about the differences among minority experiences: 'Even if you are a minority, the Black struggle is hard to relate to the Native American struggle...You got a Black ...brought over here from another country. What is their stake in this?...But what can you tell a Native American? I have to be here, that's all.   Struggle's totally different.' Initially, the group is concerned that they keep the programme accessible, not alienating the mainstream by focusing only on Indians, but gradually the ideas become more and more 'theirs.' The next scenario is a rewrite of history, in which the Indians fight back, forming a majority, with 'casinos all over America.' Indians buy back all the land, and kick the intruders out. This iteration was called *Return of the Buffalo* – 'one of the Indian prophecies, when the Buffalo get replenished the wars will start and then the Indians will take the land back.' In another development, 'It'd be real funny if some aliens came to the planet and said 'all Native Americans stay here, and all non-Native Americans get out.''

C: And then you'd have everybody in the world trying to find out who they married back in there. Yes, I'm 1/2,000ths. I need to be over here, and then you have a little line [queue] that says, 'tribal papers'....'

S: ... and you ask them what kind of Native American and they'll say Cherokee. Cause every white person I talk to says, 'yeah, I got some Indian in me.' What kind? "Oh, Cherokee."

C: I mean you gotta have a show that Native Americans take over something ... even the apes took over...God, *Planet of the Apes*. We can have *Planet of the Indians*...We could have *Rain Man* ... Anytime he sees a white person he just pees on them.

M: It's called *Red Earth*.

The idea of an Indian/alien takeover takes hold, with 'buffalo being teleported down here...Just like *Independence Day*...all you see is a dark cloud.' The mother ship, in the form of a giant teepee, invades Washington, D.C., using buffalo dung as bombs, and forces a meeting with the white, female President ('so we take care of the woman and the Anglo in one'). Later they adapt the idea, positing an Indian planet which is exploring distant lands, the first being Earth. They send a scout (George, who takes his name off the Washington Monument) to Earth, and he has to make contact. No-one believes his story, and he ends up in the jail, the 'nuthouse,' or the 'drunk tank.' Ideas flow as his survival skills are tested:

C: He spends his night on the town. He's running round these white people with hatchets...You can see George Scout stripping the bones...

S: George goes driving.

R. George searches for a mate.

S: See George in Central Park roasting...

S: His ass...

C: A human being on a stick…

M: Want some white meat?

R: Man, white people be complaining about this show. Scare the shit out of that grad student too.

C: He'll say, "Is this what they really think about me? They look at me like I'm food!"

R: George starts selling drugs for extra money.

S: Starts selling drugs out of the Washington monument.

Eventually George meets, but eats the President, then goes home to Red Earth, and 'everybody's pissed at him because he's changed.' Although they now know 'the Earth is an evil place,' the invasion proceeds. Observes one participant, 'suddenly it's become a dark satire.'

The second Indian male group included a 41-year-old video producer and social worker, a 39-year-old unemployed man, a 46-year-old counselor, and a 36-year-old cook. Their favourite TV choices were sports, *Northern Exposure*, news, and the classic sitcom *M*A*S*H*. They created a drama 'with comedy' called *School Days*, set in the 1960s in an Oklahoma Indian boarding school.[4] Like the first group, their discussion gained an increasingly strong Indian identity as the time progressed. They began with a stereotyped scenario of a white couple who consult an Indian elder for enlightenment, but gradually the seeker of truth evolves into Joe, an Indian man who has lost his identity in a white world, and the elder is his grandfather. As this happens we learn, through flashbacks, about his life growing up in the oppressive boarding school (something two of the participants had experienced). As one participant says, 'this Indian…is being tormented by the matrons of the boarding school for trying to hold on to his ways…But he goes on to become well-educated and graduates, maintaining his identity all the way through. No matter what they put him through. A lot of it's never told…That our people have success stories.'

They envisage the young man visiting home, having been taught not to speak Ojibwa at the school: 'he knows the language but he doesn't dare speak it …and then maybe he kinda hides it from his grandpa that he's being locked into a room or that he's being punished for singing or for praying or using the medicines.' The series would humorously explore relationships among students as they defy the authorities, while also featuring compassionate teachers and friendships among students and staff. Remembering that a white character is required, the group creates Miss

December, the school principal. 'Everything she talks, everything she says is demeaning...she's a cold-hearted bitch.' The group saw humour as crucial, and media as a key to reducing prejudice:

> Prejudice is based on ...you don't have the knowledge...The thing we battle the most is stereotypes...No matter how successful we are, we're just an Indian or we're just a Black, or we're just a Mexican. So you turn that into humor...You turn that whole thing around and what you're doing while you're laughin', while you're learnin', is you're correcting stereotypes, and learnin' how to laugh at them, together.

The Indian female groups also tackled the issue of identity directly. The first group were students, aged 17,18, 19, and 21. Their favourite shows were *Fresh Prince*, news, and *Seinfeld*. Opting immediately for a comedy, they began by laughing about a reservation setting 'with everyone going around saying 'How!'' Tossing ideas around, they mention the white 'wannabe' – 'you know there's always one non-Native always just hangs around the Indians.' They move on to visualise an Indian school, not unlike the previous group's, with a cast of Indian students and a mean, sadistic white teacher. Then one member suggests they 'make it about something that you would never even think of an Indian being - how 'bout a car salesman?' The group runs with this, playing with stereotypes of Indian reservation life all the way. They name the series *Rez Rider*, a common term for the kind of beaten-up car found on reservations, deliberately contrasting that with the super-car that was the star of the old series *Knight Rider*. Their star is Melvin Two Hairs, an Indian car dealer in the exclusive Los Angeles suburb of Brentwood. He sells expensive foreign cars, and the humour revolves around the reservation lifestyle he maintains in the ritzy neighbourhood. His 'company car' is 'Rusty,' the Rez Rider, which is described as a character itself: 'the typical rusted, taped-up, reservation ride.' They create the car in rapid dialogue:

> D: You know, you have maybe a flash light for a head light...

> M: ...and you can only get out one side. And you have to open it from the outside.

> L: You have a plastic window in the back...

> T: ...Duct taped seats, powder compact for rear view mirror...

> D: You know, you have all your bumper stickers from the pow-wow just holding your fender up...

L: 'Red power.'

D: And you know, like his muffler is being held up by an old belt. Then the antenna is the clothes hanger. You ever seen that?

L: And you don't even have reverse. You gotta get out and push it.

D: A truck, one of those little bitty ones, that can only fit one person... somebody heavy, like totally hogs the seat. And everybody has to ride in the back, and it only gets to go up to 45 miles an hour...and oh ...he's gotta have that one-eyed, three-legged dog sitting right there in the passenger seat.

Melvin is married to Ruthie, and they have 'hellion' five-year-old twins, 'like little rez kids who, when they see people they're sneaking up on them...and they're all dirty. All crusty.' The requisite white character is a rich, sophisticated widow who keeps buying cars from Melvin, and being shocked by his reservation ways. One day Ruthie serves dinner:

D: And instead of having a whole, expensive dinner, it's fry bread, mutton and beans.

L: And some commod. orange juice [government commodities given to reservations].

T: Oh, and then they have that big block of butter. And the wrapper's still on it: 'For Reservation.'

Nevertheless, Mrs. Dubois is a classic 'wannabe,' constantly hoping Melvin will teach her about Indian lore and tradition. The message coming from the group is that whites need a dose of reality when it comes to Indians - and the squalor of reservation life, even as comedy, is that reality, not the spiritual savage.

The second Indian female group included a 27-year-old social services secretary, a student who did not give her age, a 34-year-old human services case manager, and a 29-year-old educator. Their favourite programs were *ER*, *Star Trek Deep Space Nine*, and *Star Trek Voyager*, and they created a comedy-drama called *Migizi Way*. Like the other Indian groups, they quickly decide to explore stereotypes, suggesting, 'we would like to see a show that did what *Cosby* did for Blacks...Have some role models...' They choose a present-day setting: 'We don't need any more historical, romantic Indian pictures. We want reality here.' They go on to debate whether 'reality' is what they really want: 'get the rez humor out there ...that's funny. But just how much of the real life rez do you want to expose?' Eventually, like the other groups' stories, their scenario grapples with Indian people's movement between two worlds. In their tale, Mary, a 35-year-old Indian woman, returns to a reservation in Minnesota, about to give birth to her fourth child. Her husband has just been killed in a drunk driving accident, and she had been making a living as a writer/illustrator in the white world. Now she returns to her live with her husband's family, and over the next few episodes, experiences a rebirth herself, as she rediscovers her cultural identity. Episodes would feature Mary's struggles with bureaucracy; for instance, her husband was an enrolled tribal member, while she has to fight to prove to authorities that she is a 'real' Indian. The token white character is Steve, a good-looking publisher who is excruciatingly 'politically correct;' he is 'always asking if saying this would be offensive.'

Negotiating Identity in a Media World

We know that television does not mirror reality (nor do people want it to), but that it refracts back a sense of reality to which people may or may not relate. The mainstream American majority are offered countless opportunities to recognise themselves in the genres that tell the familiar tales. As Livingstone (1999, p. 100) writes, 'media cultures provide not only interpretive frameworks, but also sources of pleasure and resources for identity-formation which ensure that individuals…have a complex identity of which part includes their participatory relations with particular media forms.'

The program scenarios created by the white participants in this study told tales that felt quite familiar, reflecting their own taste for mainstream sitcoms. The main players were people like them, and they pulled from a wide cultural repertoire in which people like them might interact. They had difficulty placing the required Indian characters in their scenarios, and they were largely unable to develop their personalities. They drew heavily on media-generated stereotypes of nobility and stoicism; even when they consciously attempted to subvert those stereotypes, they did not know how to 'write' the characters. This is particularly striking when one remembers that northern Minnesota, where the study was done, has a fairly significant Indian population, unlike many regions in the United States.

For the Indian participants, the media world is clearly one they must negotiate. Although some did like popular sitcoms, the range of their favourite TV programmes was quite different, with news and sport getting mentions, and appreciation for fish-out-of-water sitcoms like *Fresh Prince*. Several appreciated the *Star Trek* series, in which cultures often collide. Their scenarios spoke vividly about how it feels to be an outsider, and they revel in the chance for Indians to be stars and winners. Their white characters, although often unsympathetic, are drawn from the personal experience of living as an Indian in a white world, and not so much from media images. The same can be said for their Indian main players – they are acutely aware of the prevailing Indian media stereotypes, and reject them angrily, in a way that speaks volumes about being marginalised in a world of alien media imagery.

I conceived this exercise as an attempt to extend the study of media reception in creative directions, as advocated by recent theorists such as Seiter (1999) or Abercrombie and Longhurst, (1998). As Ang (1996, p. 72) puts it, we are moving toward 'an ethnographic *mode of understanding*, in the sense of striving toward clarifying what it means, or *what it is like*, to live in a media-saturated world' (italics in original). For most white Americans, to live in a media world is to live with a smorgasbord of images that reflect back themselves, and offer pleasurable tools for identity formation. American Indians are permitted only an identity they do not recognise, and which they reject with both humour and anger, making us wonder if their own tales of alternative identity will ever be told.

Notes

This study was funded with a Grant in Aid from the University of Minnesota Graduate School. Thanks go to my graduate assistant David Woodward, who helped set up and transcribe the interviews in 1996.

1   While 'Native American' is also used, I use 'American Indian,' which is preferred in Minnesota.

2   Latest data show that in spite of revenue derived from gambling operations in some states, the overall living conditions for American Indians have declined, with unemployment over 50% in many reservations (Associated Press, 2000).

3   I am indebted to Renee Botta and Carolyn Bronstein for sharing an unpublished paper using a similar methodology. In quoting transcripts, I do not attribute statements, except when quoting group exchanges, when initials are used to distinguish contributors.

4   Thousands of Indian children were forcibly removed from their families and educated in Government funded boarding schools, from the 19th century into the second half of the 20th, with the goal of 'cultural assimilation.'

References

Abercrombie, N. and Longhurst, B. (1998), *Audiences*, Sage, London and Thousand Oaks.

Ang, I. (1996), *Living Room Wars: Rethinking Media Audiences for a Postmodern World*, Routledge, London and New York.

Associated Press (2000), 'Casino Revenues Haven't Helped most Indians,' *St. Petersburg Times*, 3 September.

Baird, R. (1996), 'Going Indian: Discovery, Adoption, and Renaming Toward a 'True American,' from Deerslayer to Dances with Wolves,' in S.E. Bird (ed.), *Dressing in Feathers. The Construction of the Indian in American Popular Culture*, Westview Press, Boulder, pp. 195-210.

Berkhofer, R.F. (1979), *The White Man's Indian*, Vintage Books, New York.

Bird. S.E. (1999), 'Gendered Representation of American Indians in Popular Media,' *Journal of Communication*, vol. 49, no.3, pp. 61-83.

Bird, S.E. (1996), 'Not My Fantasy: The Persistence of Indian Imagery in *Dr. Quinn, Medicine Woman*' in S.E. Bird. (ed.), *Dressing in Feathers*, Westview Press, Boulder, pp. 245-262.

Churchill, W. (1994), *Indians are Us: Culture and Genocide in Native North America*, Common Courage Press, Monroe, Maine.

Cohen, J. (1991), 'The 'Relevance' of Cultural Identity in Audiences' Interpretations of Mass Media,' *Critical Studies in Mass Communication*, vol. 5, pp. 442-454.

Deloria, P.J. (1999), *Playing Indian*, Yale University Press, New Haven.

Drotner, K. (1994), 'Ethnographic Enigmas: The 'Everyday' in Recent Media Studies,' *Cultural Studies*, vol. 8, no.2, pp. 341-57.

Francis, D. (1992), *The Imaginary Indian. The Image of the Indian in Canadian Culture*, Arsenal Pulp Press, Vancouver.

Hanson, J. R. and Rouse, L. P. (1987), 'Dimensions of Native American Stereotyping,' *American Indian Culture and Research Journal*, vol. 11, no. 4, pp. 33-58.

Lind, R.A. (1996), 'Diverse Interpretations: The 'Relevance' of Race in the Construction of Meaning in, and the Evaluation of, a Television News Story,' *Howard Journal of Communications*, vol.7, pp. 53-74.

Livingstone, S. (1999), 'Mediated Knowledge: Recognition of the Familiar, Discovery of the New,' in J. Gripsrud. (ed.), *Television and Common Knowledge*, Routledge, London and New York, pp. 91-107.

Russell, R. (1999), 'Make Believe Indian' *New Times Los Angeles Online*, 8-14 April.

Seiter, E. (1998), *Television and New Media Audiences*, Oxford University Press, Oxford.

Taylor, A.M. (1996), 'Cultural Heritage in Northern Exposure,' in S.E. Bird (ed.), *Dressing in Feathers*, Westview Press, Boulder, pp. 229-244.

Thompson, J.B. (1990), *Ideology and Modern Culture: Critical Social Theory in the Era of Mass Communication*, Polity Press, Cambridge.

Whitt, L.A. (1995), 'Cultural Imperialism and the Marketing of Native America,' *American Indian Culture and Research Journal*, vol.19, pp. 1-32.

Woodward, K. (ed.) (1997), *Identity and Difference*, Sage, London.

PART II
NEGOTIATING IDENTITY
THROUGH ALTERNATIVE
MEDIA USE

8 Learning about Turkishness by Satellite: Private Satisfactions and Public Benefits

MARISCA MILIKOWSKI

Introduction

When I started my research into the influence of Turkish satellite television on Turkish viewers in the Netherlands, I already knew that by 1995 almost 50 per cent of Turkish families in the Netherlands had equipped themselves with a satellite dish, in order to be able to watch Turkish channels. I also knew that 50 per cent was a lot, comparatively, and that the mass adoption of the new technology had happened with record breaking speed.[1] I soon learned that the most popular channels on satellite were heavily commercial. What people primarily enjoyed, it seemed, was the sheer abundance of entertainment, information and infotainment on offer. The public Turkish channel, TRT-International, which is offered on Dutch cable, was often described in uncomplimentary terms. It was called dull, dry, official and officious.

The most difficult problem I faced was a conceptual one. It had seemed reasonable, when proposing the research, to assume some kind of relationship between Turkish television viewing and integration. But now I felt trapped. By linking the interest in Turkish television to integration, I had set up myself for a journey into that badly charted field of social and political influence. I did not know where to start. What kind of influence could I have been thinking of?

Some conceptual narrowing-down had to be done, but how to narrow down the influence of such a continuous firework of entertainment and information as offered by the popular channels in question? Even a very modestly priced dish, I now knew, offered a choice of at least three different commercially-financed channels, whose only common denominator in this case is that they are Turkish channels. Many people don't stop at that, and buy a dish that gives them a much wider choice. All of the ten or so Turkish satellite channels offer their own variety of information and entertainment, whose only commonality is that they are in Turkish.

By stating the problem in these terms, its solution became more obvious. The central concept could only be Turkishness. And the central question must therefore concern the influence of Turkish satellite television on the 'Turkishness' of Turkish people in the Netherlands. This, of course, led to a series of new questions. For what *is* Turkishness, other than an administrative category? Any specific answer to that question consists of a more or less subjective and context-dependent choice of attributes. In the anthropological literature, such features go by the name of 'boundary markers' (Barth, 1969, 1996; Baumann and Sunier, 1996; Vermeulen and Govers, 1996). So in a conceptual sense the question would become if and how Turkish transnational television affects prevalent markers of Turkishness in the context of Dutch society.

Between the summer of 1997 and December 1998, a total of 50 Turkish-Dutch people were interviewed about their experiences with, and their ideas about, Turkish satellite television. In the first phase of the data collection, 30 people were interviewed individually. The questionnaire contained some closed and many open questions. Its aim was to make people talk about their TV-experiences, habits and preferences, as well as about their political and cultural views. The large majority of these respondents were young adults, aged between 20 and 30, but some older and some younger people were also interviewed. The second part of the data collection consisted of focus group discussions, in which another 20 informants participated (see also Ogan and Milikowski, 1998; Milikowski, 1999, in press). In this chapter, I will use the material to take a closer look at the influence of Turkish television on two groups of boundary markers: political-cultural and social-cultural ones.

Dutchness and Turkishness

A boundary, such as the one between 'Dutchness' and 'Turkishness', consists of contrasts. Such contrasts always have an objective and a subjective part. An objective contrast is the difference in religious affiliation and tradition. The dominant tradition in the Netherlands is Christian, and so are most 'native' affiliations. The dominant tradition in Turkey is Islamic, and so are most 'Turkish' affiliations. Muslims want mosques as Christians want churches. Such differences are fairly straightforward, and easy to determine. The subjective interpretation of such a difference is largely up to the parties concerned. It is possible to enlarge religious difference into a 'clash of civilisations' and throw up bulwarks against one another. It is also possible to treat religious difference as a fact of social life, and make provisions accordingly (Rath, Penninx, Groenendijk and Meijer, 1996;

Buijs, 1998; Lindo, 2000). The first approach builds a boundary like the Berlin Wall, while the second one builds something like a garden gate.

The boundary I am interested in is far from symmetrical (Penninx, 1988). 'Dutchness', in general, is represented by a well-organised, affluent and liberal society with a population of 16 million people who communicate in Dutch – if not in English. 'Turkishness', on the other hand, is represented by no more than 300,000 (which is less than two per cent) of these inhabitants, whose march through the institutions of Dutch society has only just begun. It is necessary to mention this, because it puts the boundary we are dealing with into perspective. It is Dutch society that lays down most of the rules and conditions by which the game is played, and any society has ways and means to invite or discourage participation. However, an immigrant group itself also has a considerable influence on its social and civic success in the new society. For instance, it can also choose between the 'barbed wire' or 'garden gate' definitions of the various differences it encounters, and either encourage or discourage participation in the various institutions of the new country (Vermeulen, 1992; Vermeulen and Penninx, 1996).

When immigrants from Turkey started on their course of settlement in the Netherlands, Dutch society was congratulating itself for having taken the worst stings out of the boundaries of class and religion with which most citizens had grown up. Working class kids had begun to flock into the universities; Catholics and Protestants had shed many of the bonds and automatic affiliations formerly prescribed by their religion; and women of all backgrounds and denominations had successfully fought against the rules, customs and beliefs that hindered their personal and collective emancipation. It had become a widely shared conviction that inherited identities – notably those of class, gender, religion, ethnicity and political affiliation – should not constrain individual lives. This conviction is written in the first article of the Dutch constitution, which states that 'all who are in the Netherlands are treated equally in equal cases. Discrimination on grounds of religion, philosophy of life, political persuasion, race, gender, or on any ground whatever, is not allowed.' Of course, the constitution also makes provisions to guarantee the classical civic rights and freedoms of organisation and expression. But in the dominant contemporary consciousness, the concepts of progress and fairness were very strongly associated with individualisation.

This made for a considerable difference with the new immigrants. Many Turkish families found the egalitarian free-and-easy behaviour of the Dutch offensive, and desired to protect 'Turkish culture' against the alien intrusions of the new environment. So how would Turkish television affect this state of things? Its popularity raised several anxieties in the

Netherlands. One fear was that Turkish television would lead to an even stronger preoccupation with Turkish affairs, at the cost of participation in Dutch social and civic life. Another fear, sustained by a controversial study from Germany (Heitmeyer, Müller and Schröder, 1997) suggested that Turkish television would brainwash people into anti-liberal and anti-integrationist attitudes. The assumption behind this latter fear was that that even if Turkish audiences in the Netherlands did not intentionally embrace such 'non-western' values, they could not help being infected with them just by watching Turkish programmes. It is easier now than it was then to see that this assumption was not only outdated in its conception of media influence, but also ideological in its conception of Islam and Turkishness. At the time Turkish satellite television came in, the 'Rushdie Affair' was still fresh, and fears of a new wave of political totalitarianism in the form of Islamic fundamentalism had been stirred up during the Gulf War.

Now that eight years have past since the first Turkish dishes were installed, it is evident that these fears have been unfounded. Turkish immigrants, though indeed watching a lot more television from their country of origin than immigrants from Morocco and Surinam, and identifying strongly with other Turks (Cadat and Fennema, 1996), *also* take a closer interest in Dutch civic life and participate more actively in Dutch institutions (Fennema and Tillie, 1999). It is not a matter of either/or, it seems. The explanation given by Fennema and Tillie is that civic interest and behaviour is a cultural resource in itself. By this reasoning, the political content of people's convictions is less important than their inclination to organise and participate as a way of getting things done (see also Putnam, 1993).

Ideological Turkishness

In the course of my research I was often struck by the partisan nature of people's reflections on Turkishness. This is perhaps less surprising when one takes Turkey's problems into consideration. An important element of nationality is the location of a country's borders, and those of Turkey are contested, politically as well as militarily. A second point of serious national disagreement concerns the secularist foundation of the Turkish State. In the Atatürkish order of things, the organisation of the Islamic religion belongs to the domain of the state, with the army watching against transgressions. From this particular perspective, alternative forms of religious organisation can be easily conceived as threats to the integrity of the state. This is also a divisive issue among Turkish people in the Netherlands (Lindo, 2000). Against the background of these and other conflicts, it is easier to

128

understand why definitions of Turkishness raise some anxieties. I will illustrate this nervousness with two examples.

The first example comes from my interview with Mr. Ali Yalman, whom I visited in his home in Amsterdam. He is in his forties, married to a Turkish woman, and father of three children. Mr. Yalman is an electrician by training, but spends much of his time in a neighbourhood centre, helping Turkish children with their school work. He also volunteers as a coach for the football team of his 8-year-old son. Mr.Yalman is an enthusiast of Turkish television and of much else. He proudly shows me his state-of-the-art electronic equipment, which includes a new sophisticated satellite dish. When you press the number of any of a hundred and twenty channels on the remote the dish starts searching the sky for you, and picks up the desired signal within seconds. It costs a packet, he says, but what do you expect, it is the best on the market! After this demonstration, my host starts on a lecture about Turkey and its glories. It is all there in the book he shows me. See? These are the dates, and these are the proper maps. It is important that I get this stuff right, he says, because he has noticed that the average Dutch person is completely ignorant about the subject. Also, talking to other Turks could easily set me wrong, since many Turkish people talk political and/or religious nonsense. Hence the lecture, which will hopefully inject some sense in me.

The fear that I would get the wrong ideas about Turkishness by talking to certain people, or by visiting certain meetings, is what many of my Turkish informants had in common. In the summer of 1998, I visited a rally organised by the Dutch and German branches of Milli Görüs (National Vision), a Turkish Islamic organisation. I was interested in going there because Milli Görüs, a group that does not agree with the Atatürkish conception of state secularism, had recently attracted a lot of political attention as a 'fundamentalist threat'. I wanted to see what would happen at that all-day meeting in the Amsterdam Arena, the football stadium of Ajax, holding 50,000 people and rented out during the off-season for cultural activities. The stewards and box office staff were at first somewhat suspicious of our motives. But after having explained that our interest in the affair was purely academic we were let in and allowed to enter one of the entrances marked 'women', leading to a women-only section on the second rung. The stadium was rapidly filling up with families, many of whom had come from Germany. In several respects the spectacle was new and extraordinary to me. I had never seen so many women with headscarves in one place. When the times for prayer were announced, the people put their food boxes away, climbed a flight of stairs, rolled out their prayer mats and knelt down side by side in the corridors of the stadium. All of this was unfamiliar to me. Yet the atmosphere of the rally was also, in a sense, familiar. What was going on in the stadium reminded me somewhat of the communist Summer Festivals that I had visited with my family when I was a child. People picnicked, met friends, listened to singers, and waited for the high moment of the political speech, which would be celebrated with rounds of applause. What also contributed to the feeling of familiarity was the working class atmosphere of the present rally and the feeling of 'united we stand' that it generated.

But the response of my companions, a Turkish graduate from the University of Istanbul, and an American professor with strong ties to Turkey was very different. They were shocked and offended by the events. According to them, this rally was a disgrace to Turkey and its people and my response only went to show how naive I was about things Turkish. They did not trust me to make any further judgements for myself and gave up translating. There was no need for me to understand the speeches, I was told, because these were all nonsense. Instead, my companions offered me their own judgements and interpretations. The Welfare Party had just been banished, and rightly so. In Turkey such a meeting could never be held. All these headscarves, and all this praying in the corridors – this was not normal Turkish behaviour. What business did the Dutch Government have to allow such a meeting to take place? And so on and so forth. Just entering a Turkish scene, it seemed, was enough for my academic companions to be stung into a highly ideological, political partisan mode of information processing. So how would Turkish satellite programmes affect such a politicised scene?

Television Talk

'It is just television, you know', an informant said when I asked her to show me a programme she liked. She could not understand the academic fuss. When she switched on the TV, I saw what she meant. What came on was a well-known game show that looked at if it had been copied from Dutch television – or the other way around. Being bilingual and liking that kind of programme, my informant used to watch both until the Dutch *Wheel of Fortune* was cancelled. Another women told me that she preferred to watch *As The World Turns* on satellite, because on Dutch television it lagged two years behind. Popular films are also shown much earlier on Turkish than on Dutch channels. That Turkish television dubs where Dutch television subtitles is seen as a drawback by some people, who prefer a native speaking Robert de Niro to a Turkish speaking one. But to those who are less literate in Dutch, or less literate in any form, the dubbing is most welcome. To one young girl watching a movie on satellite, this was a compromise that relieved her of the burden of translation. 'Now I can watch a film with my parents without my father asking every minute what is going on.'

All the same, most of the people I have talked with are, for one reason or another, critical of the television culture on satellite. An often-heard complaint is that these channels are too glaringly commercial. Advertisements pop up everywhere, preferably at what are, from a viewer's perspective, the worst moment. No programme is safe from commercial intrusions, which are timed to grab people's attention at all costs. It is not funny any more, a respondent complains. 'You are watching a football match, and when the ball goes out a second window immediately opens to show a commercial. It is impossible to concentrate that way. Where is the ball? Where is the car? It drives you crazy.'

According to a number of respondents, Turkish satellite television is also 'too commercial' in the sense of cheap and silly. There is too much violent infotainment, too much gossip posturing as news, too much attention for popular stars at the cost of serious information, they say. But others like the satellite for that very reason. 'When I was a kid we used to watch TRT with my grandparents', a girl says. 'It was all serious dull stuff, about the state and the government.' She has had her fill of it, she says, and welcomes the light touch of the commercial channels.

The commercialisation of Turkish television culture has affected the public face of social life in yet another way (Oncü, 1995; Staring and Zorlu, 1996; Tekinalp, 1996; Tokgöz, 1996). Under its influence, the political and religious identities of channels have become less and less visible. 'For example, Kanal 7 is supposed to be an Islamic fundamentalist channel, but I don't see much difference', an informant says. Young people don't mind even when they notice: they take television politics less seriously anyway. Older people are often more critical of this particular change. One informant told me that her aunt, who is in her seventies, refuses to watch 'the satellite', because the lack of political seriousness and predictability offends her. In her view, a channel should distinguish itself from the competition by its selection and coverage of news. Commercialisation, however, works in the opposite direction. Just as happens elsewhere, Turkish commercial television channels are driven to compete for audiences, advertising and sponsorship. As a result, political and religious distinctions disappear into the background. The implicit message is that such difference is all very well, but should not interfere with general audience appeal. And just as elsewhere Turkish audiences have responded in kind and now zap between channels more freely (Ang, 1996).

Cultural minorities are understandably more anxious about loss of identity than are cultural majorities, and the Turkish immigrants were no exception. Like others before them, Turkish immigrant families have done their best to re-establish the mainstays of life as they knew it (Böcker, 1994), and to protect themselves against the onslaught of 'Dutch culture' which was associated in particular with its post-sixties features. In doing so, they became in some respects more Turkish than they had been at home. The boundaries were defensively drawn, and they were heavily patrolled. The focus of the defence was on issues relating to the organisation of sexuality, gender and family which is where traditional and post-traditional values often clash (Gillespie, 1995; Barth, 1996; Baumann, 1996). Growing up as a Turkish person in Dutch society was not easy. Girls in particular used to be closely watched, and punished for transgressions (de Vries, 1987). Many considered this unpleasant, or even unfair, but they often lacked the knowledge and authority to question the rules, or the assumptions behind them. As a result, 'being Turkish' could become a prison with no acceptable exit. Turkish girls certainly did not want to become 'Dutch' if that would imply losing their Turkishness. They wanted it both ways: to be more free and equal and to be Turkish too. In the past, their parents could maintain that such a combination was impossible, but now Turkish television tells different.

Various stories told by young women attest to the helpful role of Turkish television in getting their points across. One girl gleefully recounts how she has got her mother to acknowledge the possibility that she might have a boyfriend. My informant had carefully prepared the scene. That evening, the rights and wrongs of sexual relationships before marriage would be the subject of a talk show on satellite, so she had said: '...Mum, let us watch this programme together.' A women-only audience would be best, she had judged, because the presence of her father might just tip the scales to her disadvantage. The viewing occurred in silence. 'My mother did not open her mouth once. But she took it all in. And the next day, when we were in the kitchen together, she asked: do you have a boyfriend?' Though such a strategic use of the medium is rather special, many stories do contain an element of 'enlightenment' brought about by satellite television. That Dutch television features similar viewpoints and behaviours in abundance is well known, but in the eyes of many Turkish parents this only affirmed the essential difference between these cultures. Within such a 'two cultures' framework, seeing a Turkish actor acknowledge his homosexuality on television has the opposite effect of seeing a Dutch actor doing so. The same goes for other customs and viewpoints which had acquired the status of boundary markers. Turkish commercial satellite television has made several informants more aware that the Turkishness they grew up with was in fact a very defensive definition of Turkishness. 'My parents have stood still while most people in Turkey moved on', a respondent said. 'The reason is that they were afraid of the Dutch. They were afraid that they would lose their children.'

The Good, the Bad and the Indifferent

So what is the bottom line? Am I proposing that, in contradiction to common sense beliefs, Turkish satellite television exerts a *positive* influence on social-cultural integration in the Netherlands? A colleague asked me this question recently, and after some hesitation I answered 'yes'. Because that *is* in fact the headline version of what I have been arguing above. Yet I am not satisfied to leave it there, and will use the present opportunity to discuss some of the problems raised by this particular headline. The first problem concerns the definitions of integration and culture, and I will briefly explain how I understand them. The second problem concerns the notion of television effect. In an earlier version of this chapter, I have taken others to task about their dated and ideological assumptions regarding the influence of television. Am I now saying that television *does* have a big influence, but that fortunately in this case it is a good one? These questions are the subject of this final section.

What do people understand by cultural integration? Most often, they understand that sharp distinctions fade away, either because a minority gives up some of their distinct customs and beliefs, or as the result of a more mutually conceived transaction, whereby the culture of the dominant majority also changes somewhat. What these perspectives have in common is that they both depart from what some authors have called a romantic conception of a national culture. In this conception, sharing a national culture means sharing a particular set of traditions and ideas. The alternative conception of sharing a national culture focuses on institutional participation. What is shared here is the institutional framework, not the beliefs and interests such institutions serve to bring together. Though these conceptions are associated with different viewpoints on integration policy,[2] they are not mutually exclusive and both have something to contribute to the issue of Turkish satellite television.

If we look at the issue from the institutional perspective, the first observation to be made is that freedom of information and communication is an important national institution, though by no means an exclusively Dutch one. That this freedom has ultimately been respected, regardless of the fears of bad alien influence, means that Turkish and Moroccan cultural tastes have been *de facto* accepted as part of the contemporary Dutch cultural scene. Many Turkish people have been fearful that their dishes would be banned, which would have confirmed their sense of being second class citizens (Gomes, 1998). From the institutional perspective, the acquisition of acceptance is a form of integration in itself. This may sound like a rather abstract point, but it must be made to put my cultural argument in its proper perspective.

This cultural argument is not that Turkishness and Dutchness will cease to exist as categories denoting certain different customs, beliefs, or skills. A good example is language. When people watch a lot of Turkish television their Turkish will remain fluent, or even become more fluent, as has happened to members of the second generation. A command of the Turkish language does not of course mean that people are not also fluent in Dutch. But it does signify a difference between Dutchness and Turkishness, since hardly any other inhabitant of the Netherlands speaks Turkish. Islamic holidays are another example. It would be no surprise to find that these holidays will get a boost from seeing them celebrated on TV, as is also happening to Turkish popular music. Indeed, many informants have told me that the special affinity they feel to Turkish people, Turkish landscapes and/or Turkish cultural sights and sounds is affirmed by what they see on Turkish television. My argument, in sum, is not that distinct cultural features will fade away or vanish under the influence of commercial television. In some respects, they may even become more prominent.

What I do think is that Turkish commercial satellite television helps to reduce cultural difference to more manageable proportions. During the last decades, several factors have conspired to lend a Berlin Wall-like aspect to the Dutch-Turkish cultural boundary. On the international scene we have seen efforts to replace the ideological frontiers of the Cold War with an equally encompassing 'clash of civilisations' between the West and the Islamic parts of world. This view of things has a high scare potential, not least in Turkey itself, whose very future is predicated on the proposed frontline. In such an ideologically charged context, the contribution of commercial television could be to take some sting out the fight. On the Dutch national scene, the choice of boundary markers distinguishing Turkish from Dutch culture was partly affected by circumstances that no longer prevail. While many of the older generation of Turkish immigrants had no formal education to speak of, the large majority of their children graduate within the Dutch educational system, some of them at the highest levels (Crul, 2000). An additional difference is that, other than their parents, most members of the second generation have grown up in a city. These are cultural changes in their own right (Bruner, 1972; Luria, 1974). Similar developments, with similar cultural effects, can now be witnessed going on in Turkey itself.

This leaves me with the question of how much power we may grant television to influence people's outlook and behaviour? In such general terms, this question may well be unanswerable. So it is fortunate that the influence of Turkish television can be explained in a rather down to earth fashion. Of course it is true that most people do not change their lives and outlooks just because people on television tell them to. But it is also true that certain forms of edification are actively sought and appreciated. In her study of Italian families in Belgium, Michielsen (1991) found that many women loved RAI Uno because it allowed them to explain Italy to their children. Gillespie (1995) bears witness to the gratifications obtained from watching Indian films and soaps by Asian families in the UK. Turkish satellite television in the Netherlands is, I think, welcomed for comparable reasons. The opportunities it offers for closeness and communication is evidently appreciated. At the same time, these popular channels address certain subjects and legitimate certain changes that are probably not so unwelcome anyway. Few parents are so rigid in their beliefs that they wouldn't rather give in on some issues than risk a break with their children. And few children have such a bad relationship with their parents that they would prefer an angry conflict to a peaceful solution.

Notes

1   Turkish immigrants established several records in one stroke, according to the Veldkamp Survey held in 1995 (see Veldkamp 1996a, 1996b). They were the most eager adopters of the satellite dish (leaving the Moroccans far behind), champion TV-watchers (34 hours per week on average) and champion watchers of television from their country of origin (80 percent of the viewing time). But note that these figures were based on self-reports. Also, they may refer to the number of hours the television set is on rather than to the number of hours it is really attended to.

2   This was well demonstrated during a recent debate about integration in Dutch parliament. The debate had become necessary in view of the public excitement following the proclamation of a multicultural drama by politically influential liberal publicist. The author contended that integration had failed and that Dutch liberal culture would not survive unless citizens woke up to defend it. Interestingly, the majority of the Dutch parliament countered this move from the romantic side by placing itself in an institutional position.

References

Ang, I. (1996), *Living room wars: Rethinking Media Audiences for a postmodern world*, Routledge, London.

Barth, F. (1969), *Ethnic groups and boundaries: The social organisation of cultural difference*, Little and Brown, Boston.

-- (1996), 'Enduring and emerging issues in the analysis of ethnicity', in H. Vermeulen and C. Covers (eds), *The anthropology of ethnicity: Beyond ethnic groups and boundaries*, Spinhuis, Amsterdam, pp. 11-32.

Bauman, G. (1996), *Contesting Culture: Discourses of identity in multi-ethnic London*, Cambridge University Press, New York.

Bauman, G. and Sunier, T. (1996), *Postmigration ethnicity*, Spinhuis, Amsterdam.

Böcker, A. (1994), *Turkse migranten en sociale zekerheid: Van onderlinge zorg naar overheidszorg?* [Turkish migrants and social security: From mutual to public care?], Amsterdam University Press, Amsterdam.

Bruner, J. S. (1972), *The relevance of education*, Norton. New York.

Buijs, F. J. (1998), *Een moskee in de wijk* [A mosque in the neighbourhood], Spinhuis, Amsterdam.

Cadat, B.Y. and Fennema, M. (1996), 'Het zelfbeeld van Amsterdamse migrantenpolitici in de jaren negentig' ['The self image of Amsterdam migrant politicians in the nineties'], *Amsterdams Sociologisch Tijdschrift*, vol.22, no. 4, pp. 655-681.

Crul, M. (2000), *De sleutel tot succes* [The key to success], Spinhuis, Amsterdam.

de Vries, M. (1987). *Ogen in je rug. Turkse meisjes en jonge vrouwen in Nederland* [Eyes in your back: Turkish girls and young women in the Netherlands], Samsom, Alphen aan den Rijn.

Fennema, M. and Tillie, J. (1999), 'Political participation and political trust in Amsterdam: civic communities and ethnic networks', *Journal of Ethnic and Migration Studies*, vol. 25, no.4, pp. 703-726.

Gillespie, M. (1995), *Television, Ethnicity, and Cultural Change*, Routledge, London.

Gomes, F. J. (1998), 'Satelliettelevisie: Verleden, heden en toekomst' [Satellite television: Past, present and future], MA thesis, University Amsterdam.

Heitmeyer, W., Müller, J. and Schröder, H. (1997), *Verlockender Fundamentalismus: Türkische Jugendliche in Deutschland*, Suhrkampf, Frankfurt am Main.

Lindo, F. (2000), *Heilige wijsheid in Amsterdam* [Holy wisdom in Amsterdam]. Spinhuis, Amsterdam.

Luria, A.R. (1976), *Cognitive Development: Its cultural and social foundations*, Harvard University Press, Cambridge Mass.

Michielsen, M. (1991), *Italia Mia*, Acco, Amersfoort.

Milikowski, M. (1999), 'Stoorzender of katalysator? Turkse satelliet televisie in Nederland' [Turkish satellite television in the Netherlands], *Migrantenstudies*, vol.15, no. 3, pp. 170-191.

-- (in press), 'Exploring a Model of De-ethnicization: The case of Turkish television in the Netherlands', *European Journal of Communication* and 'Zapping between Dutch and Turkish: Satellite television and Amsterdam Turkish Migrants', in F. Pierre Gingras (ed.), *Migration and Identity*. Routledge, London and Toronto.

Ogan, C. and Milikowski, M. (1998), 'Television helps to define 'home' for the Turkish women of Amsterdam', *Journal of the World Association for Christian Communication*, vol. 43, no.3, pp. 13-22.

Oncü, A. (1995), 'Packaging Islam: Cultural Politics on the Landscape of Turkish Commercial Television', *Public Culture*, vol. 8, no 1, pp. 51-73.

Putnam, R. D. (1993), *Making Democracy Work: Civic Traditions in Modern Italy*, Princeton University Press, Princeton N.J.

Penninx, R. (1988), *Minderheidsvorming en emancipatie: Balans van kennisverwerving t.a.v. immigranten en woonwagenbewoners 1967-1987* [Minority formation and emancipation], Samsom, Alphen aan den Rijn.

Rath, J., Penninx, R., Groenendijk, K., and Meijer, M. (1996), *Nederland en zijn Islam* [The Netherlands and its' Islam], Spinhuis, Amsterdam.

Slijper, B. (1999), 'Twee concepties van liberale tolerantie in een multiculturele samenleving'. [Two concepts of liberal tolerance in a multicultural society], *Migrantenstudies*, vol. 15, no 2, pp. 83-96.

Staring, R. and Zorlu, S. (1996), 'Turkse migranten en satelliet-teevee' [Turkish migrants and satellite TV], *Migrantenstudies*, vol.12, no.4, pp. 211-221.

Tekinalp, S. (1996), 'Mainstream-Centering Political Views in Turkish Elections', in D. L. Paletz (ed.), *Political communication Research, Approaches, Studies and Assessments*, vol. 2, pp. 145-163, Ablex, Norwood N.J.

Tokgöz, O. (1996), 'Women's Images and Issues in Turkish Election Advertisements', in D. L. Paletz (ed.), *Political communication Research, Approaches, Studies and Assessments*, vol. 2, pp. 163-171, Ablex, Norwood N.J.

Veldkamp (1996a), *Media-onderzoek Etnische Groepen 1995* [Media Use by Ethnic Groups 1995], NOS, KLO, Hilversum.

Veldkamp (1996b), *Invloed Schotelantennes op kijkgedrag Turken en Marokkanen* [The influence of Satellite Dishes on the Viewing Behaviors of Turks and Moroccans], Veldkamp, Amsterdam.

Vermeulen, H. (1992), 'De cultura. Een verhandeling over het cultuurbegrip in de studie van allochtone etnische groepen' [De cultura. A discussion of the concept of culture in studies of allochtonous ethnic groups], *Migrantenstudies* vol. 8, no 2, pp. 14-30.

Vermeulen, H. and Covers, C. (1996), *The anthropology of ethnicity: Beyond ethnic groups and boundaries*. Spinhuis, Amsterdam.

Vermeulen, H. and Penninx, R. (1996), *Het democratisch ongeduld: De emancipatie en integratie van zes doelgroepen van het minderhedenbeleid* [The democratic impatience: The integration and emancipation of six target groups of Dutch minority policy], Spinhuis, Amsterdam.

9 Diasporic Audiences and Satellite Television: Case Studies in France and Germany

ALEC G. HARGREAVES

Introduction

The advent of cable, satellite and digital technology is revolutionising the supply of television programmes to domestic consumers, offering major new opportunities to minority ethnic groups and other previously marginalised audiences. Little more than a decade ago, Europe's immigrant minorities enjoyed virtually no access to television broadcasting from their countries of origin. In most of the countries where they had settled, technological constraints combined with tight regulatory controls meant that television broadcasting was limited to a handful of channels, few of which made any significant efforts to address minority audiences. Today, throughout western Europe scores or even hundreds of channels – including stations based in the countries where immigrant minorities have their origins – can be accessed at the touch of a switch by cable or satellite.

Writing at what in retrospect now seems quite an early stage in these developments, Appadurai highlighted their actual or potential impact in the formation of ethnoscapes, i.e. diasporic identities 'spread over vast and irregular spaces, as groups move, yet stay linked to one another through sophisticated media capabilities.' (Appadurai, 1990, p. 306) Cable and satellite television, together with other forms of electronic communication such as the telephone and the Internet, are undoubtedly helping to overcome the physical and technological barriers which until recently seemed to condemn many migratory groups to gradual detachment from their countries of origin. Some have seen in these developments a welcome opportunity to strengthen links between diasporic populations and their 'home' countries[1] (Kettane, 1999). Others have warned of the dangers of 'ethnic segmentation', with differential patterns of media consumption leading to new or reinvigorated barriers of ignorance and incomprehension between minority and majority ethnic groups in countries of immigrant settlement (Husband, 1998).

139

Drawing on fieldwork conducted among Maghrebis in France and Turks in Germany, this chapter argues that the impact of cable and satellite TV among minority ethnic audiences is more complex than is often thought. Cultural flows among diasporic groups cannot be adequately understood within a simple, bi-polar model constructed around the 'home' countries of migrants on the one hand and the societies in which they have settled on the other. Viewing patterns among minority ethnic audiences need to be seen within a more complex multi-polar framework in which ethnicity, while certainly a factor, is not always the dominant force. Viewing choices are partly determined by other forms of difference traversing ethnic groups, such as age and gender, as well as by the growing diversity of programme sources, which is steadily widening the options open to domestic consumers. At the same time, inequalities in the ownership and control of broadcasting systems continue to impact differentially on the capacity of ethnic groups to shape the programme outputs available to them.

This chapter is divided into two main parts. The first of these considers the new and rapidly evolving context in which the viewing patterns of diasporic groups are shaped. The second examines in greater detail the viewing choices of the Maghrebi and Turkish minorities in France and Germany respectively.

New Viewing Horizons

While the long-term implications of greater programme choice have yet to fully unfold, one important consequence is already clear. The old idea of television as a central force in the construction or consolidation of national consciousness as the prime locus of collective identities is being steadily eroded (Robins et. al., 1997). Until recently, television undoubtedly tended to strengthen national identities. Technological constraints limited television broadcasting to a relatively small number of channels, regulated and in many cases owned by the states in which they were located, and their broadcasting range seldom extended far beyond national boundaries. These channels focused primarily on the national societies to which they broadcast. Except for the United States, which supplied a significant proportion of programmes broadcast by many European channels, most foreign countries were either seen through the filter of domestic programme-makers or largely ignored. Although some states made fairly generous provision for sub-national regional variations, few made more than minimal efforts at addressing immigrant minorities (Frachon and Vargaftig, 1995).

Cable, satellite and digital technologies have now greatly expanded both the number of channels available for programme delivery and the distances across which they can be broadcast. Since the early 1990s, continental Europe's two largest groups of recent immigrant origin – Turks, who have settled principally in Germany, and Maghrebis, concentrated mainly in France – have been served by a growing range of television stations based in their countries of origin. At first sight, it may be tempting to conclude that one set of national broadcasters is simply being joined and/or displaced among minority ethnic audiences by others operating within what is still a basically national optic. Turkish stations cater essentially for Turks, whether at home or abroad, Algerians in France can now watch Algerian TV, while Moroccans and Tunisians also have their national channels.

But patterns of programme supply and demand are more complicated than this. Two of the first Arabic-language satellite channels to become available in Europe were the Egpytian-based ESC and the Saudi-financed MBC, broadcasting from London. Neither Egypt nor Saudi Arabia has a significant expatriate population in western Europe. These channels have, however, picked up sizeable audiences among Maghrebi and other Arab minorities in Europe, as well as in North African and Middle Eastern states (Mostefaoui, 1997). If anything, these stations are liable to strengthen pan-Arab, rather than national identities. More recently, a number of stations serving diasporic groups without a 'home' state of their own have also taken to the air. Kurds, for example, are targeted by MedTV (Transnational Communities, 1999), while BRTV serves Berber-speaking viewers (Amalou, 2000). Both stations are filling gaps left by national broadcasters in Turkey and the Maghreb, where the Kurdish and Berber minorities – who also make up a sizeable component of the expatriate populations of these countries – have been ignored, repressed or marginalised by mainstream media institutions. In this way, satellite broadcasting is eroding the grip of national broadcasters not only in countries of immigrant settlement but also in the 'home' states of diasporic groups. For while ESC, MBC and other pan-Arab channels such as Al Jazeera (El-Sherif, 1999) are building audiences that stretch across national affiliations, stations such as MedTV and BRTV are chipping away at a sub-national level.

Yet this too is only part of the picture. Numerous American stations are now widely available by cable and satellite throughout Europe and the Mediterranean basin, where they are further eroding nationally-defined audience boundaries. And lest it be imagined that hitherto untainted national cultures are suddenly being subjected to unprecedented centrifugal forces, it should not be forgotten that the programme schedules of 'national' broadcasters in Europe, as indeed in Turkey and the Arab world, have seldom been purely national. In varying degrees, American imports or derivatives have long been a staple ingredient of prime time schedules on French, German, Turkish and Maghrebi channels. The popularity of American-made soaps, movies and sitcoms bears witness to the fact that national broadcasting boundaries have never been wholly synonymous with the diffusion of purely national cultures and identities. A significant element of hybridity was already present in most 'national' broadcasting systems even before the advent of cable and satellite, and this shows no sign of abating. For this and other reasons, it is impossible to read off the cultural composition of their programme outputs or the collective affiliations of their audiences from the national location of broadcasting organisations.

When the number of channels available for programme delivery was small, the construction of audiences as national communities was favoured not only by the technological constraints limiting broadcasting range more or less within national boundaries, but also by regulatory and ownership patterns dominated to a large extent by nation-states. In France, for example, until as recently as fifteen years ago all television channels were state-owned, and in most western European countries publicly owned stations remain a significant part of the media landscape. Xavier Gouyou Beauchamps, Chairman of France Télévision, which runs France's main publicly owned stations, speaks of 'their function in constructing social cohesion, which stands out as their *raison d'être* today.' (Beauchamps, 1997) According to Beauchamps, 'in a fragmented democratic society, general interest television channels are spaces that are able to bring people together and forge common identities. [These channels] help to shape the collective imagination, that invisible substratum of our national identity.' (Beauchamps, 1997) But publicly owned channels openly committed to this vision of the nation-state now command only a minority of the national audience in France. They are being elbowed aside by private operators for whom the maximisation of profit is more important than the defense of the nation-state.

It is true that when privatisation was first introduced into French TV, in the mid-1980s, continued scarcity of channels and reliance on terrestrial technology encouraged commercial stations to maximise their audience share by offering 'general interest' programming constructed around a highest common factor that was national in scale. But this was a pragmatic, rather than a principled policy. Private ownership has grown in tandem with new broadcasting technologies that have greatly expanded the number and range of TV channels, so there has been a rapid growth in the number of specialist stations aiming to make profits by serving segmented markets within as well as across national boundaries. In this way, changes in

142

patterns of ownership and control are reinforcing the tendency of technological developments to erode the significance of national boundaries in the construction of television audiences (Robins et. al., 1997, pp. 29-31; Becker, 1997, p. 111).

In the new league of media ownership which is now emerging, most of western Europe's immigrant minorities have yet to establish themselves as significant players. Stations such as MedTV and BRTV, led respectively by Kurdish and Berber activists based outside their 'home' countries, are the exception, rather than the rule. Influential Arabic-language stations broadcasting from within Europe are mainly owned and run by Middle Eastern states or proxies. The London-based MBC, for example, is financed by Saudi capital. Similarly, stations such as TD1, broadcasting by cable from within Germany to the Turkish minority, depend largely on imports of 'home' country programmes; little of their output is produced locally by programme-makers rooted in the minority audiences at which they are aimed. Satellite broadcasting is therefore tending to replicate the long-standing marginalisation of minority ethnic groups as suppliers of programmes on terrestrial TV. Although broadcasting organisations based in countries of immigrant settlement are often significant forces in the media landscapes of the countries in which expatriate minorities have their origins, minority ethnic programme-makers seldom have the opportunity to address 'home' country audiences. It would therefore be wrong to see the new patterns of programme production, distribution and consumption which are now emerging as a mutually reinforcing loop within which diasporic and 'home' country populations are being drawn steadily closer together.

Some of the paradoxes involved in these new programme flows may be illustrated with reference to the case of France and Algeria. Until the end of the 1980s, most Algerians could receive only a single television station, run by the state-owned ENTV, over which the ruling FLN party exercised tight control. The FLN's grip on power began to weaken in 1988, when young Algerians frustrated by poor economic opportunities and political corruption took to the streets. The bloody repression of their demonstrations went virtually unreported by ENTV. The only television pictures to reach Algeria were seen on a handful of domestic satellite receivers, which were just beginning to bring access to French stations, on which there was high profile coverage of these events (Hakem, 1995, p. 72). Over the next few years, as the political situation in Algeria moved through a brief period of liberalisation into one of quasi-civil war, ownership of satellite receivers grew rapidly. With ENTV still presenting heavily selective coverage skewed in favour of the authorities, satellite relays of French TV became the main platform on which Algerians watched opposition – and sometimes government – politicians debating the issues confronting their country. By the mid-1990s, most Algerians were thought to have access to satellite stations. Although it is impossible to quantify with precision the impact of these channels, it is not difficult to find examples of French stations affecting people in Algeria. For instance, a woman in Algeria interviewed on French TV in 1993 was forced to flee the country when her comments, relayed back into Algeria by satellite, made her a target for death threats from Islamist 'guerrillas' (Bernard, 1995). Later it was suggested that French TV pictures of expatriates voting in France during Algeria's 1995 presidential elections helped to increase the turnout within Algeria itself in the face of Islamist intimidation, though there is no way of confirming this (*Le Monde*, 1995).

Interestingly, French press reports suggested that the parallel acquisition of satellite TV by Algerian families in France was one of the factors in the relatively high turnout rate noted among the expatriate population during the same elections (Bernard and Herzberg, 1995). Again, there is no way of verifying this more widely, but several respondents of Algerian origin interviewed during the fieldwork described later in this chapter did say that they had been inspired to vote by watching Algerian satellite TV coverage of these elections.

Although it is likely that satellite television is in some ways helping to strengthen a sense of collective identity among Algerians on both sides of the Mediterranean, it would be a mistake to conclude that this is the sole or even dominant effect of satellite TV among dispersed populations of this kind. Pictures of Algerian expatriates engaged as actors in the democratic process are extremely rare on French television. Viewers watching by satellite in Algeria, like those in France, find that French TV more usually ignores the Algerian immigrant minority or circulates negative stereotypes of it (Hargreaves and Perotti, 1993). In its own way, Algerian satellite TV presents an equally selective and misleading picture of the 'home' country, glossing over internal problems and divisions in favour of more bland images (Amari, 1995). While first-generation members of the Algerian diaspora, nostalgic for the land of their birth, may be relatively happy to acquiesce in this rose-tinted vision, their children and grandchildren have other viewing priorities (discussed below). And when viewers in Algeria tune in to French channels, few if any of them do so in the hope of seeing pictures of expatriates in France. Much more commonly, they seek a mixture of news and entertainment unobtainable on domestic stations.

Far from converging with the aid of satellite TV, Algerians at home and abroad seem in many ways to be looking past each other: migrants in France are wallowing nostalgically in images of the 'home' country that are increasingly at odds with the experiences of those who live there, while viewers in Algeria are mesmerised by images of First World opulence beyond the reach of their Third World purses. These paradoxes are neatly encapsulated in a scene in Merzak Alloauche's film *Salut Cousin!* (1996), where the young protagonist, freshly arrived from Algiers, is astonished to find his expatriate relatives in France glued to Algerian satellite TV while he and his peers back home think the only channels worth watching are French.

Thus while satellite television is undoubtedly transforming flows of information and entertainment between the 'sending' and 'receiving' countries of international migrants, its impact on diasporic audiences and those in their country of origin is by no means uniform. The limited access of minority ethnic programme-makers to satellite stations means that 'home' country viewers see little of the diaspora. And while immigrant minorities can now access a rapidly expanding supply of stations from their countries of origin, they are more selective than is often thought in their choice of programmes, as we shall see in the remainder of this chapter.

Minority Ethnic Viewing Choices

Relatively little empirical research has so far been conducted on the consumption of cable and satellite TV among immigrant minorities in Europe. The findings to date are limited almost entirely to single-country studies.[2] To help fill this gap, I have been conducting research among minority ethnic groups in France, Germany and Britain, using a standardised methodology. As the fieldwork among South Asians in Britain is not yet complete, the findings are not yet available, but the research carried out among Maghrebis in France and Turks in Germany is now complete and the results show striking similarities.

It is clear from both samples that minority ethnic groups do not function as monolithic blocks. They are traversed by many forms of variegation, with generational and gendered differences particularly significant in shaping patterns of media consumption. The viewing preferences of second- and third-generation Turks and Maghrebis have much in common with those of majority ethnic German and French youths. Ethnic differences are more pronounced among first-generation Turks and Maghrebis, compared with the general population in the countries where they have settled. But although Turkish and Maghrebi migrants equipped with satellite or cable are strongly inclined to watch stations broadcasting from their countries of origin, few of them are entirely monocultural in their viewing choices. Most watch at least some programmes on German or French channels, and sometimes other stations too. Different forms of 'pick and mix' are further complicated by gendered differences as well as by variations in the types of channels available in different households.

The following analysis is divided into four sections. The first of these describes the methodology used in the research. The second examines the range of viewing options open to different households together with the role of living room politics and other factors in the process of channel selection. The main channel choices of individual respondents are analysed in the third section, while the fourth considers a number of explanatory factors.

Methodology

Maghrebis and Turks are, of course, broad ethnic categories within which many sub-groups may be distinguished by linguistic, religious or other criteria. There are significant differences, for example, between the Kurdish minority and majority ethnic Turks. Maghrebis are divided not only by the national boundaries separating Algeria from Tunisia and Morocco but also linguistic differences between Arabic- and Berber-speakers. With Kurdish and Berber satellite stations now available alongside those broadcasting in Turkish and Arabic, these are likely to be reflected in different viewing habits among the various sub-groups within the Turkish and Maghrebi minorities. As the samples in the present survey were quite small – about a hundred interviewees in each country – it was not possible to adequately reflect within them each of these sub-groups. Instead, it was decided to concentrate mainly on families where Arabic and Turkish were the mother tongues. Had greater resources been available, it would also have been valuable to include samples of Berbers and Kurds.

The research was designed to elucidate not only the role of variables such as gender and generation in shaping personal viewing patterns but also the ways in which individuals are affected by inter-personal dynamics within the home. To this end, the interview schedule included a number of questions about viewing patterns in the household as a whole, as well as a series of questions focusing on individual respondents. As far as possible, interviews were conducted on a one-to-one basis, so that participants were not inhibited or otherwise influenced by the presence of other family members. By putting the same questions to all interviewees, it was possible to cross-check some of the answers, especially those relating to the behaviour of the household as a whole. The interviews, structured mainly around closed questions with a smaller number of more open questions, were conducted by female interviewers of Maghrebi and Turkish origin. This meant that the interviews could be conducted where necessary in Arabic or Turkish and also facilitated interviews with female respondents without the presence of male relatives, which might otherwise have been more difficult to arrange.

In Germany, interviews were conducted in 30 households with a total of 93 Turks plus one majority ethnic female respondent married to a Turk, while in France 104 Maghrebis and one Belgian woman married to a Moroccan migrant were interviewed in a total of 27 households.[3] Participants were located in urban areas typical of those in which immigrant minorities are concentrated: in industrial towns such as Montbéliard and Lyon in France and in German cities such as Berlin, Munich and Darmstadt. The socio-economic profiles of respondents were weighted towards the lower end of the income scale, broadly in line with the status of the Maghrebi and Turkish minorities as a whole. In Germany, the sample was divided equally between male and female respondents. In France, 43 male and 61 female Maghrebis were interviewed. The samples were designed to be sensitive not only to gender but also to generational differences. They included 41 first-generation and 63 second-generation Maghrebis, together with 37 first-generation, 46 second-generation and 10 third-generation Turks.

Where first-generation Turks and Maghrebis migrated to Germany or France as adults, the second generation was either born in the country of settlement or brought there at a young age by adult migrants, while the third generation was born of second-generation parents. These generational distinctions are closely related to differential processes of acculturation. As members of the first generation spent all their early years in Turkey or the Maghreb, they have been less formatively influenced by German or French culture than have the second and third generations, raised mainly or exclusively in Europe. Second- and third-generation Turks and Maghrebis are of course also exposed within the family home to the cultural heritage of their migrant parents or grandparents, but they are generally less immersed in this than the older generations. As will be seen below, generational differences in the prior acculturation of viewers play a key role in their consumption of satellite and cable channels.

Differences of age, generation and gender are also at work in hierarchically-structured family relationships. With only three exceptions, all the second-generation Maghrebi participants were living in their parents' homes. While most of the Turkish households in our sample were headed by first-generation respondents, five were headed by second-generation couples and seven were headed by a first-generation Turk married to a second-generation spouse. As a general rule, parents enjoy greater authority than their children in spaces such as the living room, where the main television set is usually located, and this gives them greater control over the process of channel selection. Although almost half the homes in our Turkish sample had at least one extra set in a room belonging to one or more younger members of the family, female respondents watched these less frequently than their male counterparts. Second-generation female Turks living in parental homes equipped with more than one set were in fact twice as likely to watch in the living room as on a bedroom set. These ratios were reversed among second-generation Turkish males, two-thirds of whom watched mainly on bedroom sets. Bearing in mind the greater authority generally enjoyed by parents in channel selection on the living room set, young female Turks appear to have less independence than their male counterparts in the channel selection process. It is possible that this helps to account for the generally higher proportion of Turkish programmes viewed by second-generation females when compared with the proportion among second-generation males. Gendered differences of this kind were less in evidence in the viewing patterns of young Maghrebis. In multi-set Maghrebi households, girls were evenly divided between those watching mainly in the living room and those watching mainly in the children's room(s), while boys were only slightly more inclined to watch mainly in their own room(s).

Viewing Equipment and Channel Selection

Differences in the range of programmes available to respondents were another significant element in shaping viewing choices. Two sets of factors were of major importance here: the range of satellite and/or cable channels available to different households and the number and location of television sets within each home. There was a TV set with satellite and/or cable access in the living room of each of the sample homes. In most Maghrebi households and almost half of the Turkish households, there was a second set in another room. Some homes also had a third set. Most of the second and third sets were located in the bedrooms of younger members of the household. While most of the bedroom sets in Turkish homes had access to cable and/or satellite, almost all those in Maghrebi homes were restricted to terrestrial channels.

As no Arabic-language channels were licensed for transmission on cable networks when the fieldwork in France was carried out, in 1996, interviews were conducted solely in homes able to access Arabic-language stations by satellite. In Germany, where the fieldwork was conducted in 1998, the situation is more complex (Becker, 1997). TRT-International, a Turkish state-owned station, has been available via cable in many parts of Germany since the early 1990s. Cable subscribers in Berlin can access not only TRT-International, but also TD1, a German-based station serving the Turkish minority with a mixture of imported and locally made programmes, as well as daily or occasional Turkish-made programmes on stations such as the Open Channel. In addition, a wide selection of Turkish channels – commercial, state-owned and religious – can be accessed by satellite across the whole of Germany. There are thus considerable differences in the range of Turkish channels available in different households, with cabled homes outside Berlin able to receive only TRT-International, while those with satellite can access far more 'home' country stations. Significant variations in viewing patterns were found to be associated with the particular range of stations available in different households.

The interview schedule included a series of questions about the channels to which each set was most frequently tuned (irrespective of who was watching), the decision-making processes involved in channel selection and the stations most frequently watched by each individual respondent. In some households, there were inconsistencies in the responses of different interviewees concerning the channels most frequently selected (irrespective of personal preferences), but in most homes a clear picture emerged. In Germany, Turkish stations predominated on the living room set in the great majority of homes. The dominance of Arabic-language stations on the living room sets of Maghrebi households was somewhat less pronounced. There was agreement in just over half of the Maghrebi households (14 out of 27) that the living room set was tuned mainly to 'home' country channels and in some cases a number of other Arabic-language stations, such as the Egyptian-based ESC, a popular source of movies and soaps. Respondents in another quarter of the homes reported that French channels predominated. In two of the Maghrebi households participants said French and Arabic channels enjoyed roughly equal screen time on the living room set. Responses in three other homes were inconsistent or contradictory, with parents reporting that French channels predominated while their children said Arabic stations were to the fore. In Turkish households, bedroom sets were tuned primarily to German and a few other non-Turkish channels such as Eurosport and MTV. Bedroom sets in Maghrebi households were able to receive only terrestrial channels, so French stations enjoyed a monopoly on them.

It is likely that the conflicting answers given in response to some of these questions reflected differences in personal tastes. Younger viewers who thought Arabic stations were given too much screen time may have confused their personal feelings with the actual time given over to different channels, while parents with contrasting tastes may have fallen prey to a similar confusion in reverse. Tensions of this kind became very evident when interviewees were asked to identify the person(s) by whom programme choices were normally made. All agreed that outside the living room area, programme selection was controlled by the occupants of the room in which the set was located. Almost all these sets were in the bedrooms of younger viewers, who used them to watch a diet of mainly or exclusively French, German or American stations. Channel selection in the living room was subject to more complex family dynamics. Here respondents in the same household often gave different and sometimes contradictory accounts of the process by which channels were chosen. In several cases, for example, parents said their children made the selection while the children themselves said their parents were in control. In households where participants agreed that power was unevenly distributed, parents, especially fathers, were usually seen to be dominant. In other homes, although the father was often perceived by other family members as having a dominant role, this perception was not always shared by the father himself. Participants in many households spoke of quarrels erupting over channel selection. In some homes there was agreement that channels were chosen by the family as whole or by different members of the family at different times. In several single-set homes, for instance, children were allowed their choice of channel in the afternoons, while the parents took control in the evening. Overall, however, there can be little doubt that parental authority, embedded in the wider fabric of family relations, tended to give parents greater control than their children over channel selection on the living room set.

Personal Viewing Choices

Respondents were asked to name the channels which they personally watched most frequently for each of a range of TV genres stretching from films and soaps to news and current affairs. As the question concerned only the main personal choice of channel for each genre, the responses do not provide an exhaustive picture of all the stations which may have been watched, even if only briefly, by each participant. But the combined responses for all genres given by each respondent provide a revealing indication of the main preferences of different viewers.

Several trends emerge clearly. 'Home' country channels are far more popular among first- than among second-generation respondents, but this tendency is less pronounced among Maghrebis than among Turks. Among our sample, almost a quarter of Maghrebi migrants reported watching French stations more commonly than Arab channels, compared with only two Turkish migrants (both female) who cited solely or mainly German channels. In general, the audiences gained by French channels among female Maghrebis seem to be greater than those enjoyed by German stations among female Turks. Second-generation males are less likely than their female peers to watch 'home' country stations, and this tendency is particularly pronounced among young Maghrebis, whose preference for French channels is very marked indeed when compared with the levels of interest shown by second-generation Turks for German stations.

The relative – though not complete – domination of 'home' country channels on living room sets reflected the attractiveness of these stations in the eyes of migrant viewers. In multi-set homes, almost all first-generation Maghrebis said they normally watched the living room set, but second-generation respondents were more likely to watch in their bedrooms, where only French channels were available. In Turkish homes, too, there was a broad, but less pronounced, tendency for the attraction of 'home' country stations to weaken across succeeding generations. On living room sets where first-generation Turks dominated the channel selection process, Turkish stations were preeminent, except in cabled homes outside Berlin, where the only Turkish station available was TRT-International. In most homes headed by a first-generation respondent and a second-generation spouse, Turkish channels predominated on the living room set. The homes of second-generation couples were more evenly divided between those where Turkish channels predominated and those giving priority to German stations. Where second- and third-generation viewers living in the parental home were able to control channel selection, most obviously in their own bedrooms, German stations dominated, together with a sprinkling of other non-Turkish channels such as MTV and Eurosport.

Beyond these generational, gendered and inter-ethnic variations, one other general feature was very apparent: a significant element of hybridity in the channels named by most respondents, except for second-generation Maghrebis. Only a handful of Maghrebi migrants cited solely 'home' country stations. Alongside 'home' country stations, many also watched other Arabic-language channels ranging from the entertainment-oriented ESC and the news-led MBC to various Middle Eastern stations specialising in religious programmes. Yet even when other Arabic-language stations are included alongside 'home' country channels, these held a monopoly among only about a quarter of first-generation Maghrebis. Almost three-quarters reported watching at least some French stations. While the stations named by almost half the Turkish migrants were exclusively Turkish, the remainder watched at least some German channels. Three fifths of second- and third-generation Turks cited a mixture of German, Turkish, and in some cases other (often American) channels.

Explanatory Factors

At least three sets of factors appear to be at work in the diverse viewing patterns found among minority ethnic audiences: differential processes of acculturation, variations in the perceived quality of programme options, and hierarchically structured relationships within the family home. While acquiring functional competence in the linguistic and other codes of the countries in which they settle, migrants generally remain more attached to the cultural heritage of their country of origin. By contrast, children and grandchildren born and educated in the country of settlement are more deeply immersed in its cultural codes, which they often master more effectively than those of their migrant forbears. Where first-generation Turks and Maghrebis turn enthusiastically to 'home' country stations out of nostalgia for the land of their birth, second- and third-generation members of minority ethnic households are more inclined to watch German, French or American channels of the kind favoured by their majority ethnic peers.

This trend appears to be more pronounced among second- and third-generation Maghrebis than among their Turkish counterparts. Although no directly comparable data exist on linguistic, religious and other cultural practices among Turks in Germany compared with Maghrebis in France, surveys covering both minorities within France indicate that the erosion of pre-migratory cultures is more rapid among Maghrebis than among Turks (Lapeyronnie, 1993; Tribalat, 1996). This may be partly due to the higher rates of illiteracy among Maghrebi migrants, making it more difficult for them to transmit written cultural forms to their children and grandchildren. In addition, Turks in France have greater rates of endogamy than Maghrebis, and second-generation Turks are also more prone than second-generation Maghrebis to marry first-generation spouses, whose fuller immersion in the cultural codes of the 'home' country helps to further reduce cultural erosion among the diaspora. As similar tendencies appear to be at work among Turks in Germany, it is probable that their attachment to pre-migratory cultures is eroded less rapidly than is the case among Maghrebis in France. One of the practical consequences of this is that second-generation Maghrebis generally face greater linguistic obstacles than their Turkish peers in the comprehension of 'home' country stations.

Viewing choices are shaped not only by patterns of prior acculturation but also by perceived differences in the range and quality of channels. In Algeria, where the largest national group among the Maghrebi population in France has its origins, satellite television, like terrestrial broadcasting, is heavily state-controlled. With a narrow range of satellite channels, Algerian television appears less attractive to the diaspora in France than the wider range of Turkish channels, many of them commercially owned, available to expatriates in Germany (Kettane, 1999). Where Algeria, Morocco and Tunisia each offers only a handful of domestically-based channels, a much greater diversity of Turkish channels is available, with marked differences between state-controlled, profit-oriented and religiously-based stations (Aksoy, 1997). To enjoy a comparable range of stations in Arabic, Maghrebi viewers have to look beyond the narrow confines of their 'home' state.

In Turkish households with satellite receivers, commercial stations such as Show, ATV and Kanal D are by far the most popular Turkish channels. While broadcasting in the Turkish language, these channels draw on popular forms of American-style programming to a far greater extent than state-controlled stations based in the Maghreb. Significantly, Turkish TV was found to have its weakest following in cabled homes outside Berlin, where the state-owned TRT-International was the only Turkish channel available. In the six sample households of this kind, Turkish programmes clearly predominated on only one set. In two other cabled homes, German stations predominated on the living room set, while there was no clear pattern in the remaining cabled homes. It is evident that ethnic affiliations are not on their own sufficient to determine viewer choices. Where 'home' country viewing options are restricted to a state-owned monopoly, these may prove insufficiently attractive compared with commercial stations based in the country of settlement, which enjoy strong audiences in many of the Turkish cabled homes.

The number and location of TV sets within the home, together with hierarchical relationships among family members, also play a significant role in personal viewing patterns. These help to explain the overwhelming predominance of French channels among second-generation Maghrebi participants. While most of the bedroom sets in Turkish homes had access to cable and/or satellite stations, all the bedroom sets in Maghrebi households were able to receive only terrestrial (i.e. French) channels. Consequently, second- and third-generation Turks watching in their own rooms could dip into Turkish as well as German and other channels, whereas second-generation Maghrebis were unable to flip to Arabic-language or other non-French stations if they wished to.

This does not mean that second-generation Maghrebis are becoming narrowly Gallicised in their cultural orientations. Many of the programmes they watch on French TV are American imports or significantly influenced by American models, and they have a strong appetite for more of this. When asked if they wanted extra channels, most Maghrebi migrants pronounced themselves satisfied with the 'home' country and other Arabic-language stations to which their satellite dishes had now given them access. By contrast, most of their children said they wanted access to extra stations, foremost among which were American-style channels such as MTV, TNT and CNN.

Conclusion

Few, if any, participants were completely monocultural in their programme choices. Among Turks, as among Maghrebis, it was clear that most respondents were exposed for at least part of the time to a mixture of programme sources. Even among second-generation Maghrebis, whose viewing patterns were heavily weighted towards French channels, responses to other questions nevertheless indicated a perceptible impact upon them arising from exposure to Arabic-language stations, which they evidently saw from time to time on living room sets. Asked whether they felt more or less interested in what was happening in their parents' country of origin since the installation of the satellite receiver, heightened interest was evinced by almost two-thirds of second-generation Maghrebis. Nearly one in two also said they felt closer to their parents' 'home' country. Concerning events in France, about a third of respondents (both first- and second-generation) reported a reduced level of interest since the installation of the satellite dish; except for a handful of second-generation viewers whose interest in French affairs had increased, the remainder of the sample reported no change. Yet only two interviewees (one first-generation male and one second-generation male) said they felt less at ease in France since they had access to satellite TV; most reported no change in this respect, while one in seven among both generations said they felt more at ease. Thus while satellite channels may be helping to strengthen affective links between respondents and their 'home' country, this does not seem to have provoked any significant increase in dissatisfaction with France as a place in which to live.

The findings among Turkish respondents were very similar. They show clearly that, in their sense of social involvement, migrants and their descendants are not engaged in a zero sum game. It is quite possible to feel a heightened sense of interest in one society without this necessarily implying loss of involvement in another. While the vast majority of first-generation respondents, both male and female, reported feeling closer to Turkey, very few said they felt less at ease in Germany. Most female immigrants and two fifths of their male counterparts said they felt more at ease there. While a clear majority of both sexes reported increased interest in what was happening in Turkey, only a handful said they were less interested by events in Germany and a third said their interest in these had grown. Somewhat paradoxically, perhaps, it would appear that the presence of a 'virtual' Turkey on TV screens in Germany may be helping the Turkish diaspora to feel more settled there.

As noted earlier, it would be far too simple to equate the watching of Turkish channels with a wholly conservative attachment to pre-migratory cultures. The programming on many of these stations is itself hybrid, often drawing on American entertainment models while broadcasting in the Turkish language. To a lesser extent, this is also true of many Arabic-language stations. While Turkish and Arabic-language channels may respond to nostalgic impulses among older expatriates, for younger viewers they may be part of a more complex process of cross-cultural mixing in which the lines of demarcation between 'home' and 'receiving' countries as well as other, particularly American, cultural models are increasingly blurred. In many ways, therefore, satellite television is helping to strengthen among diasporic groups feelings of attachment to multiple cultural spaces, rather than a monolinear reversion to ancestral roots.

Notes

1   While this expression is commonly used to denote the land in which minority ethnic groups have their origins, it should not be forgotten that in a very substantive sense, their home is now in the country where they have settled. This is especially true of second- and third-generation members of minority ethnic groups. In different ways and in varying degrees, diasporic populations often regard more than one place as home. To avoid giving the misleading impression that their 'true' home is the 'home country' from which their parents or grand-parents migrated, the expression is placed here in quotation marks.

2   Media consumption among Turks has been examined in France by Gokalp et. al., (1997) and in Germany by Sen (1995), while Schothorst and Verzijden (1996) have conducted similar investigations among a range of minorities in the Netherlands.

3   Where relevant to the dynamics of channel selection and related matters in the behaviour of the household as a whole, the answers of the two female respondents of European origin are drawn on in our analysis of the interview data, but they are not included elsewhere.

References

Aksoy, A. (1997), 'Reaching the Parts State Television Does Not Reach: Multiculturalism in Turkish Television', in K. Robins (ed.), *United Nations World Television Forum. Programming for People: From Cultural Rights to Cultural Responsibilities*, RAI/EBU, Rome, pp. 54-63.

Amalou, F. (2000), 'Les Berbères ont désormais leur propre télévision', *Le Monde*, 21 April.

Amari (1995), 'Zapping fou à Alger', *Télérama*, hors série, Algérie: la culture face à la terreur, pp. 70-71.

Appadurai, A. (1990), 'Disjuncture and Difference in the Global Cultural Economy', in M. Featherstone (ed.), *Global Culture: Nationalism, Globalisation and Modernity*, Sage, London, pp. 295-311.

Becker, J. (1997), 'Taking Turkishness Seriously: The Rise of Turkish Media Culture in Germany', in K. Robins (ed.), *United Nations World Television Forum. Programming for People: From cultural Rights to Cultural Responsibilities*, RAI/EBU, Rome, pp. 104-117.

Bernard, P. (1995), 'Fazia Meziane, une femme algérienne libre', *Le Monde*, 5-6 May.

Bernard, P., and Herzberg, N. (1995), 'Plus de 600 000 immigrés algériens en France ont commencé à voter pour l'élection présidentielle', *Le Monde*, 12-13 November.

Beauchamps, X. G. (1997), 'Télévision publique et cohésion sociale', *Le Monde*, 24 April.

El-Sherif, O. (1999), 'Letter from The Levant. Al Jazeera: Mirroring Change in Qatar', http://www.star.arabia.com/990624/OP1.html.

Frachon, C., and Vargaftig, M., (eds) (1995), *European Television: Immigrants and Ethnic Minorities*, John Libbey: London.

Gokalp, A, et al. (1997), *L'immigration turque et kurde: la dynamique segmentaire,a la nouvelle donne générationnelle et le nouvel ordre communicationnel*, Fonds d'Action Sociale, Paris.

Hakem, T. (1995), 'Tombées du ciel', *Télérama*, hors série, Algérie: la culture face à la terreur, pp. 72-73.

Hargreaves, A.G. and Perotti, A. (1993), 'The Representation on French Television of Immigrants and Ethnic Minorities of Third World Origin', *New Community*, vol. 19, no. 2, pp. 251-261.

Heytmeier, W., Müller, J. and Schröder, H. (1997), *Verlockender Fundamentalismus: Türkische Jugendliche in Deutschland*, Suhrkampf, Franfurt am Main.

Husband, C. (1998), 'Differentiated Citizenship and the Multi-Ethnic Public Sphere', *Journal of International Communication*, vol. 5, nos 1-2, pp. 134-148.

Kettane, N. (1999), 'Media and Immigration in Europe', in *Cultural Diversity – Against Racism. European Media Conference 20-21 May 1999*, Westdeutscher Rundfunk, Cologne/European Monitoring Centre on Racism and Xenophobia, Vienna, pp. 145-147.

Lapeyronnie, D. (1993), *L'Individu et les minorités: La France et la Grande-Bretagne face à leurs minorités*, Presses Universitaires de France, Paris.

Le Monde (1995), 'Les expatrés algériens ont commencé à voter pour le référendum constitutionnel', 26 November.

Mostefaoui, B. (1997), 'The Penetration of European Communication Groups in the Maghreb', *Bulletin of the European Institute for the Media*, vol. 14, no. 1, pp. 6-7.

Robins, K., Cornford, J. and Aksoy, A. (1997), 'Overview: From Cultural Rights to Cultural Responsibilities', in K. Robins (ed.), *United Nations World Television Forum. Programming for People: From Cultural Rights to Cultural Responsibilities*. RAI/EBU, Rome, pp. 11-45.

Sen, F. (1995), *Die Mediengewohnheiten der türkischen Bevölkerung in Deutschland*, Zentrum für Türkeistudien, Essen.

Schothorst, Y., and Verzijden, D. (1996), *Media-onderzoek Etnische Groepen – 1995*, KLO, Amsterdam.

Transnational Communities (1999), 'Capture of PKK Leader Causes Worldwide Kurdish Protest' http://www.transcomm.ox.ac.uk/wwwroot/traces.iss5pg1.htm.

Tribalat, M. (1996), *De l'immigration à l'assimilation: enquête sur les populations d'origine étrangère en France*, La Découverte/INED, Paris.

10 Sami Media – Identity Projects in a Changing Society

ELI SKOGERBØ

Introduction

The Sami are the indigenous people of the Nordic countries, scattered over the northern parts of Russia and Finland and the northern and central parts of the Scandinavian Peninsula. This area makes up Sápmi, the traditional Sami territories. The population is small, probably not more than 80,000 altogether, with the largest group of between 30,000 and 50,000 living in Norway. Sweden has a Sami population of around 10,000 to 20,000, Finland's population is between 2,000 and 4,000 and Russia's population is about 2,000. This situation, of one people divided into four different states, creates problems for identity-formation and cooperation as well as institution- building among Sami peoples.

This is also the case with Sami media, as they are confronted not only with four different states which have different policies towards indigenous people, but also with different systems of media regulation. In addition, Sami audiences speak a number of different languages, of which only some are mutually understandable. This article reports the results from a project on content, usage and conditions of Sami media that was carried out on behalf of the Sami Parliament in Norway in 1999-2000 (Skogerbø, 2000). The project was designed to map how Sami audiences and media workers experienced their own media situation.[1] This chapter is focused on one of the most controversial issues in modern Sami political discourse, that of identity construction, and the roles that Sami and Norwegian media take in these processes.

In Norway, the northernmost province of Finnmark[2] houses the largest number of Sami, which is reflected in the fact that several municipalities in the province are bi- or multilingual. The kingdom of Denmark-Norway from the 16th century onwards colonised Finnmark and gradually the balance of the population shifted from a majority of Sami to a majority of Norwegians. There was, at the same time, immigration from Finland and Russia which turned Finnmark into a multiethnic society several hundred years ago. In Sweden and Finland, the provinces of Norrland and Lapland, respectively, have the largest number of Sami. In this chapter, I will concentrate on the situation for the Sami in Norway, as most of my data is from this country. However, there are many parallels between the situation in Norway and the situation in Sweden and Finland.

From the beginning of the 19th until the late-20th century the Sami were subjected to harsh assimilation policies. Assimilation of Samis and other minorities can be viewed as the opposite side of the coin from the identity-formation and nation-building processes that took place in the emerging Norwegian state in this period. The results were the prohibition of Sami languages in schools and education, the oppression of Sami cultural expression and the implementation of laws and regulations that forced people to deny their identities. Among these was the Norwegian Act on Acquisition of Land in Finnmark of 1902 that required that landowners must speak Norwegian at home and have Norwegian names.

The result of these assimilation policies was the loss of language, culture and identity among large groups of Sami. In large areas of Sápmi, Sami languages are no longer spoken. In Norway, Sami is rarely heard outside the central Sami areas in Finnmark. Even when people speak one of the Sami languages, they may not be able to read and write it, as their entire education has been in Norwegian. Large groups of people living in areas where Sami is spoken have until quite recently experienced becoming illiterate in their mother tongue. This situation also creates specific conditions for the media.

After World War II, legislation and regulation which discriminated against the Sami and other minorities was gradually abolished. Nevertheless, it was in this same period that the Sami language(s) ceased to be the mother tongue for large groups of Sami. People stopped using the language in everyday life, and most importantly, parents stopped speaking Sami to their children. There are probably several reasons for this, but one explanation can probably be found in the extensive modernisation and reconstruction programmes initiated in Norway after World War II.

Finnmark was almost completely destroyed when the Red Army drove German forces out of the province in 1944, as the Nazi forces burnt and ruined everything that could be used by the enemy. Several other places and towns in northern Norway were also bombed during the war, partly by Allied forces, partly by German forces. Although these events must have had an enormous impact on the Sami population, as a large number of Sami communities were destroyed, in official Norwegian war history they are rarely described in other than Norwegian terms. That is, there are hardly any indications in Norwegian history books that a large number of the people who had their homes burnt and were evacuated to other parts of the country were Sami, many of whom did not speak Norwegian and therefore had a particularly difficult time in southern Norway.

These tragedies allowed for the launching of a major reconstruction programme immediately after the war, designed and led by successive Social Democratic governments. The ideas inherent in these programmes aimed at creating a modern Norwegian society, leaving little room for small and different cultures. One aspect of these programmes was a massive centralisation of primary and secondary schools, forcing children to leave home at the age of seven to live in boarding schools where only Norwegian was allowed. Also in areas where children could still stay at home, they had to attend a large central school instead of smaller village schools, where Sami had been spoken if not taught. In order to save their children from racism and discrimination, many parents in this period decided that the children should learn Norwegian instead of Sami. Sometimes but not always, people also denied their Sami origins and identity altogether. All over Northern Norway, Sami communities 'disappeared', sometimes to be 'rediscovered' or redefined in more recent times.

The modernisation programmes probably had the indirect effect of legitimising both public and private racism and discrimination. Traditional Sami ways of living were regarded as backwards and pre-modern, and the language continued to be prohibited in schools and was not used in public administration. Even today, Sami history and politics to a large extent still remain outside the curricula in Norwegian schools, colleges and universities. As a consequence, knowledge about Sami language, culture and society among Norwegians is severely limited, in spite of the fact that the Sami minority has now been politically recognised as an indigenous population.

Sami is a Fenno-Ugric language related to Finnish and Estonian that should be described as a language group rather than one language, as most different variants are not mutually understandable. In Norway, at least three Sami languages are in written and spoken usage, and UNESCO lists all of them as threatened languages (Davvi Sami, Julev Sami and Máttá Sami). If we add the Sami languages spoken in Finland, Russia and Sweden, the list become even longer. Thus, in itself, the Sami language situation causes problems because the languages are not mutually understandable. None of the Sami languages are related to the Scandinavian languages, and Norwegian-language speakers generally do not understand them. In addition, one of the effects of the assimilation processes described above, is that the majority of Sami people are most likely to speak Norwegian, Swedish or Finnish, that is, the majority languages in the states in which they are citizens. Norwegian and Swedish are mutually understandable but Finnish is not, a fact that also has implications for media usage, reporting and institutionalisation.

In the past 30 years, the rights of indigenous peoples have increasingly been put on the agenda. Within multinational states, indigenous peoples have mobilised, demanding political rights and compensation for loss of territories and other forms of injustice committed by the majorities in the past. In political thinking, such demands have been discussed and justified with reference to theorists like John Rawls (1973) and Will Kymlicka (1995). Kymlicka in particular has drawn attention to the importance of culture in determining the value of citizenship. In Norway, Nils Oskal (1999), following Kymlicka, has argued that citizens who, for ethnic or linguistic reasons, are excluded from the majority culture of a state, do not share the benefits and goods that the majority enjoy. Specific rights for indigenous peoples should be looked upon as a compensation for non-selected difference in life chances and life conditions that minorities experience because they are not members of the majority culture.

As a result of increasing demands from the Sami people, combined with increasing recognition of such demands, the political and cultural situation for the Sami minority has improved over the past 25 - 30 years. In the late 1960s, the prohibition of the use and teaching of Sami in schools was abolished. A major conflict over the damming of a river in Finnmark in 1979-80 put the focus on the violation of Sami cultural rights, and caused substantial revisions in Norwegian policy making. As a direct outcome of the conflict, the Commission on Sami Rights started its work in 1981. The Commission submitted its first report in 1984, recommending a revision of the Constitution and the setting-up of a Sami Parliament. The amendments to the Constitution were made and the Sami have been recognised, politically, as an indigenous population with certain territorial and cultural rights. The first Sami Parliament was opened in 1989, and consists of 39 representatives, elected in 13 constituencies spanning all of Norway. In Sweden, a Sami Parliament was opened in 1993, whereas the Finnish Sami Parliament, which had existed in another form since 1973, has been restructured to follow the same form as its neighbours. The Sami Parliaments have consultative powers in relation to the national parliaments.

In order to have the right to vote, Sami citizens have to register in a separate Sami register, thereby obtaining an ethnically defined citizenship in addition to the national citizenship. The criteria for registering are partly objective, as a person is eligible for the Sami register if her parents, grandparents or great-grandparents speak or spoke Sami, and partly subjective, as she also must identify herself as Sami. In 1997, the Commission on Rights submitted its final report to the Norwegian government, in which rights to land in Finnmark were discussed.[3] The

Report recommended that the Sami Parliament and the provincial authorities in Finnmark jointly took over the administration and management of what is currently state-owned land in the province. The recommendations have given rise to a heated political debate, in which old tensions between ethnic groups have (re)surfaced. In our content analysis of the coverage of issues related to Sami culture and society in Norwegian newspapers, news about the debate on territorial rights made up about 35 per cent of the total number of articles in our sample collected in 1999. This gives an idea of how controversial the issue is in the non-Sami population. In the media produced for and by Sami, the issue was less dominant, as these media present a more diverse picture of Sami society.

Concerning the media, certain regulations are implemented that cater specifically for Sami media while some instruments are designed for ethnic and cultural minorities altogether. Among the first, the public service obligations to have programmes directed at the Sami minority that are imposed on broadcasting institutions with a nation-wide coverage are most important. As discussed below, the Norwegian Broadcasting Corporation (NRK) has set up a separate Department for Sami programming. The Norwegian press subsidy system has a specific fund for Sami newspapers and allocations from the fund is the reason why three Sami newspapers are published regularly. In addition, there are public resources available for local radio and television producers serving ethnic and cultural minorities, but these are of less importance in the total media structure.

Sami Media – in the Midst of Identity Conflicts

In 2000, not only the political but also the cultural situation for the Sami minority is improving. The Sami languages are regaining some of their position, both formally and informally. Sami is being taught as both a first and a secondary language in primary and secondary schools in a number of municipalities. In the central Sami areas, Sami is used as an official language in addition to Norwegian, and it is less usual for Sami-speakers to teach their children Norwegian only. However, in Norway perhaps as many as half the Sami population do not speak any Sami languages. In our survey, no more than 43 per cent reported speaking Sami at home and not more than approximately 20 per cent knew how to read and write it.[4]

Consequently, language provides the origins of community and consensus, as well as cultural cleavages and conflicts in Sami society. Sami media are in the midst of these cleavages, and have always been so. During the past hundred years, several attempts have been made at starting and maintaining Sami newspapers, and the main problems have always been tied to the question of which language a newspaper should be published in, and what area it should cover. These issues are still at the front of the Sami media debate as Sami media face challenges related to the fact that their audiences cannot be defined by linguistic criteria. At the same time, language is one of the strongest markers for Sami identity and culture. Many of the political instruments that are used to ameliorate the effects of assimilation policies are directed towards reinforcing and strengthening the Sami languages, and for several media institutions, producing news in Sami languages is regarded as their raison d'être. These conflicts are also evident in the way audiences use and think of Sami media, as the following paragraphs will show.

NRK Sámi Radio – Public Broadcasting in Sami

In 2000, there are a number of different media that are produced by and for the Sami minority both in Norway and in the other Nordic countries. Among these, the daily broadcasting services in Sami of the Norwegian Broadcasting Corporation (NRK) are the most central ones. *NRK Sámi Radio* broadcasts six hours on weekdays and a couple of hours at weekends, most of the time only in northern Norway and in the capital, as the station shares a frequency with another NRK radio channel.[5]

Radio broadcasts in Sami were initiated on NRK long before the Sami were recognised as an indigenous population with specific rights. The first weekly 10-minute programmes were started in 1946. NRK, which is still the dominant public service broadcaster in Norway, was then the only radio station in the country, broadcasting on one channel only. It is still unclear *why* the institution began broadcasting Sami-language programmes, as NRK in this period favoured one national programme. Neither regional programmes, use of dialects nor other breaks with the focus on national unity and standardisation of language were tolerated or encouraged by the head of NRK. Historians point to several explanations, ranging from the zealousness of individuals within NRK who simply wanted to broadcast in Sami languages, to arguments that by broadcasting in Sami, listening to foreign, that is Finnish, and potentially 'dangerous' broadcasts would be prevented. In Norway, as elsewhere in the late 1940s, anti-Communist sentiments were rising. As Finland, at that point in time, was under a strong influence from the Soviet Union, contacts with the country were to some extent considered a security risk by Norwegian authorities (Hætta, 1984; Dahl & Bastiansen, 1999).

The amount of programmes in Sami slowly but gradually grew until the mid-1970s when the radio station physically moved to the centre of the core Sami areas, and was established as a separate entity within the NRK. The staff grew from about six in 1976 to about 60 in 1999 and the number of broadcast hours have risen from 407 in 1992 to 1637 in 1999. In order to solve the problem of distribution, *NRK Sámi Radio* for the past few years has been planning a common Nordic digital radio channel in cooperation with its sister stations in Sweden and Finland. By mid-2000, these plans were more or less abandoned as the Digital Audio Broadcasting (DAB) technology seems to have failed.

NRK Sámi Radio has a unique position both as a Department within the Norwegian Broadcasting Corporation and within the Sami community. The director of *Sámi Radio* is part of the top executive administration in the NRK and the resources allocated to the Department have been generous in the past ten to fifteen years, both in terms of economy, staff and technical equipment. Neither the Swedish nor the Finnish sister stations enjoy similar privileges within their mother companies.

Sámi Radio has a profile corresponding to that of a department within a public service broadcasting institution. It aims to attract a broad audience, but carries a number of programmes for specific audience segments too, such as youth, religious groups, and linguistic minority groups within the Sami community. The programme slate consists of about seven daily newscasts and a number of magazine programmes with a broad popular profile, many of them concentrating on culture, current events and music. During weekends, the programmes are restricted to about one hour of news and sports.

In addition to the daily radio broadcasts, *Sámi Radio* produces TV programmes and news and current affairs slots for the national and regional newscasts on NRK's nationwide TV channels. There was a weekly children's programme and one satirical talk show series in 2000 and other programmes which were broadcast sporadically and at non-prime time hours. Among these is a monthly magazine programme that features current issues and documentaries on Sami culture and society. TV news slots produced by *Sámi Radio* and broadcast on NRK's national news were also scarce and amounted to only 20 slots in 1999. From 2001, *Sámi Radio* will be producing a daily television news service for NRK's leading TV channel, NRK1.

Not only in terms of programme profile but also in terms of the objectives, *Sámi Radio* shares some characteristics with the traditional European public broadcasters. In the same way that its mother institution NRK forged a national identity and a national standard language, at the turn of the millennium *NRK Sámi Radio* has taken on the project of identity construction.

We are going through a phase in which the Sami society is being transformed from a traditional to a modern society. Sámi Radio will contribute to the construction of the modern Sami society. Through our activities as a programme producer we will contribute to making it possible for Sami people to identify themselves as Sami. This is an ideological objective and one of the main arguments why Sami broadcasts should exist. (author interview with Nils Johan Heatta, Head of NRK Sámi Radio, 29 September 1999)

The idea that public broadcasters were and should be instruments directed at modernisation and identity-formation was widespread in many European countries until the 1970s. Since then, these objectives have been toned down or removed from the agenda of these institutions. Increased competition and loss of monopoly positions for the public broadcasters, combined with increased recognition by political authorities that most nation-states are multicultural and consist of a number of different ethnic, cultural and religious groups, have made it difficult if not impossible for these institutions to focus only on *one* national identity at the expense of others.

In a number of different ways, these insights have benefited *NRK Sámi Radio*. Its position has been strengthened as a consequence of the struggle to obtain territorial and political rights and by the recognition of the Sami as an indigenous people. In the first place it has become legitimate to use the radio station as an instrument in the construction of a modern Sami society, as the Head of *Sámi Radio* points out:

NRK Sámi Radio defends the right of the Sami people to set up a society of our own. This is neither controversial nor problematic within the NRK. There is more political acceptance for these views today than there were ten – fifteen years ago. (author interview with Nils Johan Heatta, Director of NRK Sámi Radio, interview 29 September 1999)

In the second place, *NRK Sámi Radio* has been upgraded both in institutional terms, i.e. to a separate unit within NRK, and in terms of resource allocation. The position in the internal hierarchy is also witness to the changes that have taken place regarding the position of the Sami as a cultural minority, at least as conceptualised by the management of the public broadcaster. In 1999, the Head of *NRK Sámi Radio* described the resources of radio as very satisfying. Whether this situation will last, remains to be seen.

Sami Newspapers – Balancing Market Demands and Cultural Objectives

In 2000, three Sami newspapers are published, all of them in Norway and issued in three neighbouring municipalities in Finnmark. Two of them are published bi-weekly in Davvi Sami (*Áššu*[6] and *Min Áigi*[7]); the third (*Ságat*[8]) is mainly a Norwegian-language newspaper, which is published three times a week. The three newspapers have, to a certain extent, different profiles and content, but they also compete in the same local and regional markets, a factor that continues to make survival problematic. *Ságat* is the oldest of the three, as it was started in 1956 as a Sami language newspaper. All of them are owned and edited by Sami and produced and directed at a Sami audience, but they have different political and ideological affiliations. *Áššu* and *Min Áigi* are partly owned by political organisations such as the National Association of Norwegian Sami and Norwegian Sami Reindeer Herders' Association, in addition to having Norwegian newspapers among their major owners. Both newspapers belong to the radical faction in the Sami political community, and the editors-in-chief emphasise that the newspapers are instruments of identity-formation and cultural mobilisation as well as being news media:

> The paper is a news channel and source of information for the Sami people and it is also an instrument in the ongoing process of re-establishing and developing the Sami language in the sense that it makes people used to reading news in Sami. In practice these two objectives are equal: we work actively with the language and, at the same time, we contribute to the formation of the Sami society. The mediation of news theoretically has first priority but in practice this is not always the case. (author's interview with Håkon Isak Vars, editor of *Áššu*, 13 October 1999)

Min Áigi's editor-in-chief points out that the newspapers have several missions, as they perform the roles of news media by providing information and seeking to live up to standards of critical journalism and, at the same time, take on specific cultural obligations:

> Our objective is to be a critical Sami newspaper that should cover the entire Sami area. At the same time, we are a source of knowledge concerning language, we maintain it and develop it from an oral to a written language. We have a double mission, meaning that Sami journalists take on more cultural responsibility than most Norwegian journalists. (author's interview with Ann-Irene Buljo, editor of *Min Áigi*, 29 September 1999)

Ságat has a longer history than the other two, as it was started in 1956. For the first few years it was published in Davvi Sami but since the beginning of the 1960s the dominant language has been Norwegian. During the political mobilisation of the Sami people in the 1970s, *Ságat* held a moderate and conservative position in the debate on Sami minority rights within Norwegian society. In 1979, a Sami-language newspaper, *Sami Áigi,*[9] was started as a competitor and politically radical alternative to *Ságat*. Since then, *Ságat* has profiled itself more clearly as a Sami newspaper writing in Norwegian:

> Our objective is to serve the many Samis who do not read or write a Sami language as well as non-Samis interested in Sami politics. Our job is to write about issues that concern Samis; that is why we are here, and we are also receive press subsidies for doing just that. However, Sami issues may be several things: what happens in the Sami Parliament always concern Samis, but a decision-making process by local authorities in a municipality like Nesseby (i.e. one of the bilingual municipalities in Finnmark) can also be classified as such. (author's interview with Oddgeir Johansen, editorial staff member of *Ságat*, 26 September 1999)

Sámi Áigi went bankrupt in 1993, after a turbulent period in terms of both politics and economics. The controversy that surrounded *Sámi Áigi* explains why there were two Sami-language newspapers in the same geographical area in 2000. In spite of the common interests in maintaining and developing the Sami language, *Áššu* and *Min Áigi* have somewhat different profiles. Both were founded in 1993, *Min Áigi* as a direct successor of *Sami Áigi*, *Áššu* as an editorial and political alternative to *Min Áigi*. Accordingly, there are linguistic and political differences between the three newspapers that not only create a differentiated newspaper market for potential readers and subscribers but also cause conflicts and controversies between the media actors in the debate on Sami media policy and politics.

Áššu is the most clear-cut local newspaper of the three. Most of the articles and issues in the newspaper originate in the local community where it is published, Kautokeino, or in the neighbouring areas. The paper draws heavily on local history and culture both by printing historical and traditional material, such as Sami fairy- and folktales, and by concentrating on local news.

> We want to take care of Sami traditions, particularly through the emphasis we place on culture. We print, for instance, folktales as part of the effort we make to maintain traditions of storytelling and histories that the old people know. Culture is high on our priority list. *Áššu* started as a 'cultural' newspaper but since there was a demand for more news, we are more of an

166

ordinary newspaper today. (author's interview with Håkon Isak Vars, editor-in-chief, *Áššu*, 13 October 1999)

The dilemma described by *Áššu*'s editor-in-chief, that of being a newspaper for a local audience and at the same time being an instrument for preserving and maintaining culture and language, is common to all Sami media. They are caught between two objectives, that of being cultural agents, in which developing and maintaining the language is central, and that of being sources of information and identification for the entire Sami population. *Áššu* has chosen a line closer to the first than the second objective, but the choice is controversial. Articles about reindeer herding, which today is being modernised and included in the corporate negotiation structures in the same manner as agriculture and fishing, is embedded in long traditions in the community, but is, at the same time, a central issue in the relationship between Sami society and the state. Conflicts concerning profits, environmental issues, and inherited rights are as central in newspapers as they are in Sami politics. *Áššu* also has a profile dominated by individuals, not by activists representing organised or political interest organisations.

Min Áigi also has the characteristics of a local newspaper, but its profile is dominated more by politics than culture. It can be described as an arena for activists involved in Sami politics, the Sami Parliament, political organisations and other organised interests. The newspaper covers a wider range of issues than *Áššu*, and is the only one of the three newspapers which publishes international news, particularly news about indigenous peoples elsewhere in the world. *Min Áigi* can also be described as more 'modern' than *Áššu*, in the sense that the newspaper focuses on organised interests and spends fewer resources on transferring culture and history from one generation to another, and it does not cover religious issues in spite of the fact that religion is an important factor in the Sami society and culture.

The third newspaper, *Ságat*, can be characterised by the attention it gives to local politics and, in particular, local authorities, and local democracy. Local politics and issues related to local communities dominate its news stories. Nevertheless, the newspaper covers a much larger geographical area than *Áššu* and *Min Áigi* as it has access to the non-Sami-speaking audience who live outside the central Sami areas. However, the editorial staff in *Ságat* have a conception of Sami identity that differs somewhat from the expressions used by representatives of the Sami-language media:

Ideally, the newspaper should cover all Sami communities around the country, but it is not possible. People living in local communities widely apart from each other are not interested in reading about the same issues. To be Sami is not a conspiracy - Samis are surprisingly ordinary people and interested in the same things as other people. We have to make such considerations. At the same time, the newspaper is Sami because being Sami is something special. (author's interview with Oddgeir Johansen, editorial staff in *Ságat*, 26 September 1999)

The different conceptions of what comprises identity and what it is to be Sami are expressed in the priorities and profiles of *Sámi Radio* and the three newspapers. Language is the dominant marker of a Sami identity in *Áššu, Min Áigi* and *Sámi Radio*, a criterion not accepted by *Ságat*'s editors. *Ságat*'s audience are Sami whether they speak the language or not, and they are more or less integrated in Norwegian society. Yet there are several interesting similarities between *Áššu* and *Ságat*, too. *Áššu* serves a community where the dominant language is Sami, and draws heavily on local ways of living. As such, the language and its reporting on reindeer herding, which is an important source of income in its local area, corresponds with cultural and economic characteristics in Kautokeino. The same characteristics apply to *Ságat*, which is dedicated to reporting issues relevant to Samis in many different local communities where Norwegian is the dominant language.

Min Áigi and *Sámi Radio* cannot justify their choice of language with reference to their local audiences. Both are geographically located in Karasjok, where Sami is less used than Norwegian and, in addition, representatives for both institutions emphasise that they should not only report local news but should cover the entire Sami area. Reporting in Sami is, for these media, important for upgrading, modernising and legitimising the use of the language on a daily basis, and can be interpreted as a strategic choice in order to reconstruct Sami culture and identity. The risk run by choosing this strategy is, of course, that the media reach only a part of the Sami audience.

The fact that the three newspapers are published in three neighbouring constituencies means that, to some extent, they are competitors for the same markets, both needing to attract advertisers, readers and subscribers. None of the newspapers have resources that allow them to have an extensive coverage of the entire Sami area and this is part of the explanation of why they are more similar to the local Norwegian press than to regional or national newspapers.

The Views and Preferences of the Sami Audience

The audience of *NRK Sámi Radio* is, ideally, the entire Sami population in Norway. The co-operation with *Sámi Radio* stations in Sweden and Finland makes many of the programmes available to the Sami population across the national borders in Sápmi, too. The newspapers have a similar objective concerning their audiences, but since their geographical coverage does not extend far outside their local communities, the potential readership is constrained.

In the autumn of 1999, a survey of media usage was carried out, in which 930 individuals, of whom more than 80 per cent were registered as Sami voters, responded to a questionnaire concerning media usage and opinions about media use and media performance. Respondents were asked a number of questions relating to media usage in general, about which media they identified as their own, i.e. which ones they themselves defined as Sami, and where they collected information about issues related to Sami society, culture, economy and politics. The questions did not focus on preferences for specific programmes and types of programmes. Instead, the survey was directed at answering questions about the quantity and quality, in terms of covering issues and themes of specific interests for a Sami audience, of the media that were accessible for them. Forty-three per cent of the respondents spoke a variant of Sami at home, mainly Davvi Sami (39 per cent), but also Julev Sami (2 per cent) and Máttá Sami (2 per cent). The remaining respondents were Norwegian-speakers or used other languages. Only half of the Sami-speakers could read and write Sami, which means that whereas listening to the radio is possible, reading newspapers or magazines published only in Sami is not. The linguistic cleavages in our sample may or may not match the actual situation in the audience, as there exist no statistics about how many people speak the languages, let alone how many who know how to read and write in them.

The results of the survey revealed a number of tendencies. First, it showed that Norwegian local newspapers, one of the Norwegian national radio channels (NRK P1) and NRK's regional radio and television news are the most widely and frequently used media among Sami, just as they are among Norwegians. The two Norwegian television channels with a nation-wide coverage - NRK1 and TV - are, not unexpectedly, used daily by a large majority of Sami viewers. Further, Norwegian local newspapers and Norwegian regional radio and television news were the most important sources of information about Sami politics, culture and economy, followed closely by *NRK Sámi Radio*. *Ságat* was also a relatively important source of information amongst Sami audiences, as was, to some extent, *Min Áigi*, in particular concerning Sami politics. *Áššu* was less important as a source of information than *Ságat* and *Min Áigi* concerning all issues.

There are several explanations why so many Samis prefer Norwegian media to Sami ones, in particular, newspapers. The most obvious reason is *language*: people have little or no interest in media that are published in a language they do not understand. Since over 50 per cent of our sample does not speak Sami, the Sami-language media were bound to be less used and be less important than the Norwegian-language ones. Among the Sami-language media, *Sámi Radio* is most important, undoubtedly because it is less demanding to listen to a radio broadcast than to read a newspaper.

Yet the differences in usage and importance of the media produced by and for Sami on the one hand, and Norwegian media on the other, cannot only be explained by reference to language. The fact that *Ságat*, which is published mainly in Norwegian, is less important as a source of information than *Sámi Radio*, Norwegian local newspapers and Norwegian regional radio and TV news, illustrates this point. This can probably be explained by the fact that *Ságat* is published three times a week whereas radio news are broadcast several times each weekday, and most local newspapers are published five or six times a week. What is interesting and, to some extent, disturbing about these figures is the finding that Norwegian media are used more frequently and are more important than the media that are produced by Sami journalists and editors and directed at Sami audiences. The explanations for these findings are related to the linguistic and geographical cleavages that run through Sápmi.

These cleavages are confirmed by some of the results from the survey analysis. The respondents were asked the extent to which they agreed or disagreed that Sami media should be published in Sami mainly. The question split the audience in two almost equally large parts: one part disagreed, fully (23 per cent) or partly (13 per cent), that Sami should be the main language, the other part agreed fully (23 per cent) or partly (23 per cent) with the proposition. A similar pattern emerged when people were asked to agree or disagree with a view that placed *Sámi Radio* as the most important Sami medium according to their personal opinion. These results show deep and lasting structural conflicts and the linguistic cleavages are reinforced by geographical differences.

Geographically, the survey showed that *Sámi Radio*, *Áššu* and *Min Áigi* had most of their audience in the central Sami areas[10] that also are the strongholds of the Sami language. In these constituencies, more than 60 per cent of the audience listened to *Sámi Radio* at least twice a week, and the two newspapers each reached a large majority of the audience in these two constituencies. Outside this area, usage of these media dropped dramatically. The main explanation is again language, but the differences are larger than expected. As the project did not analyse the contents of radio news or radio magazines we know little about the alternative explanations for large variations among audiences, but the variations cannot altogether be related to language, as radio consumption is also very low in constituencies where a substantial part of the population are Sami-speakers. An alternative explanation may be that *Sámi Radio* did not manage to attract an audience outside the central Sami areas simply because the programmes were too focused on issues that are relevant for this audience segment only.

These findings would be of little importance if there were other media that catered for the audience segments that *Sámi Radio, Áššu* and *Min Áigi* seem to leave out: *Ságat* reached some of these. Its circulation is twice the size of that of *Áššu* and *Min Áigi* and it covers larger geographical areas. Yet the survey showed that some groups and geographical areas fell outside the interest fields of all Sami media, nor were these groups catered for by Norwegian local newspapers or by any other news media, as the following paragraphs will show.

Representation of Sami Culture and Society in Norwegian Media

As part of the project mapping the Sami media situation, a content analysis of 19 Norwegian newspapers and four news programmes was undertaken for a period of two weeks in the winter of 1999. Most of the 19 newspapers were local, covering one or only a few municipalities and they were, with one exception, selected from traditional Sami areas in northern and mid-Norway. The exception was *Aftenposten*, Norway's largest quality newspaper, which is published in the capital, Oslo. Oslo, which is a city with 500,000 inhabitants, probably has quite a large Sami population, although no more than 250 people registered to vote in the 1997 election to the Sami Parliament. The content analysis was intended to provide answers to questions concerning how the majority media in Norway represent and cover Sami culture, politics and other issues. After having defined the criteria, which should classify articles and news slots as dealing with Sami matters, articles were coded according to form and main theme. The coding was intentionally made simple and directed at getting as precise results as possible.

Previous studies have shown that ethnic and cultural minorities have problems getting access to majority media in the first place and if they do get access, they are often treated as exotic, different and belonging to the 'other' (Husband, 1994; Lindstad and Fjellstad, 1999). In spite of these studies, however, we expected to find a somewhat different pattern

171

concerning the Sami population, given their status as an indigenous people that have lived in Scandinavia from prehistoric times. The fact that in the north, Sami, Norwegians and immigrants of Finnish and Russian heritage have lived in multicultural communities for hundreds of years, and the recent recognition of the Sami as a people with specific cultural and political rights, led to the formulation of a hypothesis stating that the common history of Norwegians and Sami in northern Norway would give rise to a media coverage of the Sami based on routine and everyday experience.

The results show, however, that the hypothesis was only partially supported by our data. In our sample, the results from six newspapers support the hypothesis. Five of these are local newspapers in Finnmark, and the sixth is the largest regional newspaper in northern Norway. The number of articles in these newspapers (257) made up 85 per cent of the total number (302) in the research period. One political issue dominated news coverage, making up 35 per cent of the total number of articles, namely the debate following the presentation of the last report from the Commission on Sami Rights (NOU 1997, p.4) that contained proposals for new territorial management of land and water in the province of Finnmark that delegated more rights to the Sami Parliament.

Again, the overwhelming majority of articles were published in newspapers in Finnmark, as the question of territorial rights was, so far, restricted to Finnmark. The models of management were controversial and the subsequent public hearings and public debates reinforced existing and historical conflicts. However, these six newspapers and NRK's regional television news for northern Norway were the only news media that routinely covered Sami society in broad terms, that is, these media covered all kinds of issues concerned with Sami politics, culture, economy and other subject matters.

Outside Finnmark, the picture was bleak. Although Samis make up 20-40 per cent of the population in certain municipalities and are well-known inhabitants in the whole region, newspaper coverage of issues related to Sami culture or history were marginal in the period monitored during the project. None of the remaining 13 newspapers had more than sporadic coverage, although there were some indications that one issue generated a series of news articles that dealt with conflicts, either between the Norwegian and Sami society, or within Sami society. An example of the first was coverage of conflicts between reindeer herders and 'tourism' concerning how land and nature resources should be used.

An example of the second type which was extensively covered in a local newspaper in mid-Norway was a debate on boarding schools for Sami children. This area is home to the southern Sami population, which is small and scattered over an enormous area. The only chance for children to get education in Sami languages and culture is by attending a boarding school. This means that the children must stay away from their parents for long periods, and may suffer from this loss. In this case, there were conflicts within Sami society concerning whether it was morally justifiable for parents to prioritise education in Sami culture at the expense of daily contact with their children. In general, conflicts seemed to generate a majority of the articles in our study.

On national television, *one* news slot that included an interview with the President of the Sami Parliament made up the entire coverage on the two different national channels that were analysed in two different weeks. There were no indications in any of these that the Sami Parliament was in session during that period.

To conclude this discussion, the hypothesis that Norwegian news media would routinely cover Sami issues was not supported except for the six newspapers mentioned above. In all other news media, marginalisation is the general picture. When Sami issues were covered at any length, these were, not surprisingly, on conflict themes. There are probably a number of reasons for this finding, ranging from the fact that the Samis are a very small proportion of the Norwegian population, to the suggestion that racism, denial and the invisibility of minorities have been part of the Norwegian nation-building processes and these mechanisms still seem to be working in Norwegian media. According to the media coverage, Samis were just as invisible in the Norwegian public sphere at the turn of the millennium as they have been in Norwegian history books for the past 100 years.

Conclusion

Several conclusions can be drawn from this project. The media situation for Sami communities in Norway is in many ways better than elsewhere as there is a public policy that keeps broadcasting and newspapers alive. However, what the analysis shows quite clearly is that just as in other societies, political and cultural inequalities create conflict and controversies tied to the construction of identities and that the media are in the midst of these issues wherever they are located.

Results from this project to some extent support findings from other countries which argue that media coverage of minorities and indigenous peoples is marginal, stereotypical and discriminating. More importantly, from the perspective used here, is the fact that the Norwegian media reinforce the shortcomings of the Sami media described above. Samis who belong to 'minorities within the minority', that is, who live outside the central Sami areas in Finnmark and/or, as with the southern Sami, speak another language, are invisible not only in Norwegian media, but are also, to some extent marginalised by their own media. One explanation for this is lack of resources, another is probably conflict over identity.

Notes

1   The data were collected by a number of different methods: content analyses of Sami and Norwegian news media, surveys among Sami audiences, interviews with media actors and workers as well as document analyses to map the economic and political frameworks of the different media.
2   Finnmark is the northernmost province in Norway, and the name literally means the 'land of the Sami'.
3   NOU 1997: 4 *Naturgrunnlaget for samisk kultur.*
4   Our sample is not representative of the Sami population in terms of age and education. The young and the well educated are over-represented but we do not know what kind of impact this has on language. No statistics exist which give information about how many of the total Sami population speak the language, as there are no statistics that refer to the correct number of people of Sami heritage.
5   The main reason why frequencies are shared between *Sámi Radio* and *P2*, is, according to NRK, the difficult topographical and geographical conditions in northern Norway, which makes it impossible or very costly to set up an extra channel for Sami Radio.
6   In English 'Embers.'
7   In English approx. 'Our Times.'
8   In English 'News.'
9   In English approx. 'Sami Times.'
10   By 'central Sami areas' I refer to the constituencies of Kautokeino and Karasjok in Finnmark. The survey uses the constituencies of the Sami Parliamentary elections as geographical classification units. The constituencies must be distinguished from administrative units such as municipalities (in Norwegian: 'kommuner') and provinces (in Norwegian: 'fylker'). Only in the cases of Kautokeino and Karasjok, are constituencies identical with municipalities, and no constituency follows the borders of the provinces. There are two reasons why constituencies were chosen as the geographical point of reference: first, linguistic and cultural cleavages in the Sami population do not follow the borders of Norwegian provinces but rather cross both these administrative borders within Norway and national borders. The constituencies catch more of these cleavages than other alternatives. Second, the Sami register is based in municipalities, but municipalities could not be used for methodological and ethical reasons. It would be too easy to identify respondents since some municipalities have very few registered Sami voters, nor would it be possible to run statistical analyses on categories with such low numbers.

References

Dahl, H.F. and Bastiansen, H.G. (1999), *Over til Oslo· NRK som monopol 1945-1981* (*Over to Oslo; NRK as a monopoly institution 1945-1981*), Cappelen, Oslo.

Føllesdal, A. (1998), 'Indigenous minorities and the shadow of injustice past', Working Paper 98/7, ARENA, Oslo.

Hætta, O. M. (1984), 'NRKs samiske sendinger: 1946-1984', ('NRK's programmes in Sami: 1946-1984') MA thesis, University of Tromsø, Tromsø.

Husband, C. (1994), *A Richer Vision: the development of ethnic minority media in Western democracies*, John Libbey, London.

Kymlicka, W. (ed.) (1995), *The Rights of Minority Cultures*, Oxford University Press, Oxford.

Lindstad, M. and Fjellstad, Ø. (1999), *Pressen og de fremmede* (*The press and the foreigners*), IJ-forlaget, Kristiansand.

NOU (1997) *Naturgrunnlaget for samisk kultur* (Norwegian Official Reports Series: On the territorial foundations of Sami culture), Justisdepartementet, Oslo.

Oskal, N. (1999), 'Kultur og rettigheter' ('Culture and rights'), in H. Eidheim (ed.) *Samer og nordmenn: Temaer i jus, historie og sosialantropologi*, Cappelen, Oslo, pp. 141-163.

Rawls, J. (1973), *A Theory of Justice*, Oxford University Press, Oxford.

Skogerbø, E. (2000), 'Samiske medier: Innhold, bruk og rammevilkår' ('Sami media: contents, usage and conditions'), Department of Media and Communication, University of Oslo, Oslo.

11 Diasporic Media and Public 'Sphericules'

STUART CUNNINGHAM and JOHN SINCLAIR

Introduction

The research team which authored *Floating Lives: The Media and Asian Diasporas* (Cunningham & Sinclair, 2000) mapped the mediascapes of Asian diasporic communities against the background of the theoretical and policy territory of understanding media use in contemporary, culturally plural societies such as Australia. In this chapter, we will explore, to a greater degree than was possible in *Floating Lives,* the nature of the public 'sphericules' formed around diasporic media as a specific form of public communication, by engaging with public sphere debates and assessing the contribution that the research conducted for *Floating Lives* might make to those debates.

The public sphere, advanced in its classic sense through the work of Jürgen Habermas (1989), is a space of open debate standing over and against the state as a special subset of civil society in which the logic of 'democratic equivalence' is cultivated. The concept has been regularly used in the fields of media, cultural and communications studies to theorise the media's articulation between the state/government and civil society. Indeed, Nicholas Garnham claimed in the mid-1990s that the public sphere had replaced the concept of hegemony as the central motivating idea in media and cultural studies (Garnham, 1995). This is clearly an overstatement, but it is equally certain that, almost forty years since Jurgen Habermas first published his public sphere argument, and almost thirty since it was first published in outline in English (Habermas, 1974), the debate continues over how progressive elements of civil societies are constructed, and how media might support, inhibit or, indeed, be more than coterminous with, such self-determining public communication. The debate is marked out at either end of the spectrum by those for whom, on the one hand, the contemporary Western public sphere has been tarnished or even fatally compromised by the encroachment of media, particularly commercial media and communications (Schiller, 1989). On the other, there are those for whom the media have become the main if not the only vehicle for whatever can be held to exist of the public sphere in such societies. Such 'media-centric'

177

theorists within these fields can hold that the media actually *envelop* the public sphere:

> The 'mediasphere' is the whole universe of media...in all languages in all countries. It therefore completely encloses and contains as a differentiated part of itself the (Habermasiàn) public sphere (or the many public spheres), and it is itself contained by the much larger semiosphere...which is the whole universe of sense-making by whatever means, including speech....it is clear that television is a crucial site of the mediasphere and a crucial mediator between general cultural sense-making systems (the semiosphere) and specialist components of social sense-making like the public sphere. Hence the public sphere can be rethought not as a category binarily contrasted with its implied opposite, the private sphere, but as a 'Russian doll' enclosed within a larger mediasphere, itself enclosed within the semiosphere. And within 'the' public sphere, there may equally be found, Russian-doll style, further counter-cultural, oppositional or minoritarian public spheres. (Hartley, 1999, pp. 217-8)

Hartley's topography has the virtue of clarity, scope and heuristic utility, even while it remains provocatively media-centric. This is mostly due to Hartley's commitment to the strictly textual provenance of public communication, and to his interest in Lotman's (1990) notion of the semiosphere more so than Habermas' modernist understanding of the public sphere standing outside of, and even over against, its 'mediatisation'.

We will complicate that topography by suggesting that minoritarian public spheres are rarely sub-sets of classic nationally-bound public spheres, but are nonetheless vibrant, globalised but very specific spaces of self- and community-making and identity (see Husband, 1998). We strongly agree with Hartley, however, in his iconoclastic insistence that the commercial realm must be factored into the debate more centrally and positively than it has to date. There is typically no role assumed by the state in diasporic media, or at best, only marginal involvement, in part because the intellectual property and copyright status of much of the audio-visual entertainment product is dubious.

We will also stress another neglected aspect of the public sphere debate developed by Jim McGuigan (1998, p. 92) - the 'affective' as much as 'effective' dimension of public communication, which allows for an adequate grasp of entertainment in a debate dominated by ratiocinative and informational activity. McGuigan speaks of a 'rather softer' conception of the public sphere than is found in the work of Habermas and others (1998, p. 98) and develops these ideas around the significance of affective popular politics expressed through media mobilisation of western responses to poverty and aid campaigns. Underdeveloped, though, and tantalisingly so, is

178

the role played by the entertainment content of the media in the formation and reproduction of public communication (McGuigan, 1998, p. 98, quoting Garnham, 1992, p. 274).

Todd Gitlin has posed the question as to whether we can continue to speak of the ideal of *a* public sphere/culture as an increasingly complex, polyethnic, communications-saturated series of societies develop around the world. Rather, what might be emerging are numerous public 'sphericules': 'does it not look as though the public sphere, in falling, has shattered into a scatter of globules, like mercury?'(1998, p. 173). Gitlin's answer is the deeply pessimistic one of seeing the future as the irretrievable loss of elements of a modernist public commonality.

The spatial metaphor of fragmentation, dissolution, of the centre not holding, relies on the singular nation state to anchor it. Thinking of public sphericules as constituted beyond the singular nation state, as global narrowcasting of polity and culture, assists in restoring them to a place – not necessarily counter-hegemonic but certainly culturally plural and dynamically contending with western forms for recognition – of undeniable importance for contemporary, culturally plural societies and any media, cultural and communication studies claiming similar contemporaneity.

There are now several claims for such public sphericules. One can speak of a feminist public sphere and international public sphericules constituted around environmental or human rights issues. They may take the form of 'subaltern counterpublics', as Nancy Fraser (1992) calls them, or they may be termed 'taste cultures', such as those formed around gay style (which doesn't of course exclude them from acting as 'counterpublics'). As John Hartley and Allen McKee put it in *The Indigenous Public Sphere* (2000, p. 3), these are possibly peculiar examples of public spheres, since they precede any nation that a public sphere normally expresses – they are the 'civil societies' of nations without borders, without state institutions and without citizens.

These authors go on to suggest that such public spheres might stand as a model for developments in late modern culture generally, with a 'do-it-yourself' citizenship based on culture, identity and voluntary belonging rather than one based on rights granted by, and obligations to, a state. The present argument is in part a contribution to the elaboration of just such a project. However, there are still undeniably relations of dominance, still 'mainstreams' and 'peripheries'; there is not simply a series of sphericules, overlapping to a greater or lesser extent. While such an explanatory model goes some distance in explaining the complexity of overlapping taste cultures, identity formations, social commitments and specialist understandings which constitute the horizon of many, if not most, citizens-consumers in post-industrial societies, there are broad consensuses and agenda-setting capabilities which cannot be gainsaid in enthusiasm for embracing *tout court* a capillary model of power. As Hartley and McKee themselves identify, the key is the degree of control over the meanings created about and within the sphericule, and by whom this control is exercised (2000, pp. 3, 7).

In contrast to Gitlin then, we argue that the emergence of ethno-specific global mediatised communities suggests that elements we would expect to find in 'the' public sphere are to be found in microcosm in these public sphericules. Such activities may constitute valid and indeed dynamic counter-examples to a discourse of decline and fragmentation, while taking full account of contemporary vectors of communication in a globalising, commercialising and pluralising world.

Ongoing public sphere debates in the field continue to be structured around dualisms which are arguably less aids than inhibitors to analysis: dualisms like public/private, information/entertainment, cognition/affect or emotion, public versus commercial culture, and the 'master' dualism – is there *a* public sphere or many public sphericules? What follows is no pretence at an Hegelian *Aufhebung,* catching up these dualisms in a grand synthesis, but rather a contribution to a more positive account of the operations of media-based sphericules – in this case, ethno-specific diasporic sphericules – which place a different slant on highly generalised debates about globalisation, commercialisation, and the fate of public communication in these contexts.

The Ethno-Specific Mediatised Sphericule

First, we use the diminutive 'sphericules' because these micro cultural worlds are social fragments that do not have critical mass. Nevertheless, they share many of the characteristics of the classically-conceived public sphere – they provide a central site for public communication within globally-dispersed communities, stage communal difference and discord productively, and work to articulate insider ethno-specific identities - which are by definition 'multi-national', even global - to the wider 'host' environments.

The audience research for *Floating Lives* was conducted in communities in Australia. While Australia is, in proportional terms, the world's second-largest immigrant nation next to Israel, the relatively low numbers of any individual group (at present, over 150 ethnic groups speaking over 100 different languages) has meant that a critical mass of a few dominant Non-English Speaking Background (NESB) groupings has not made the impact that Hispanic peoples, for example, have made in the

United States. No one non-Anglo-Celtic ethnic group has, therefore, reached 'critical mass' in terms of being able to operate significantly as a self-contained community within the nation. For this reason, Australia offers a useful laboratory for testing notions of diasporic communities which need to be 'de-essentialised', adapted to conditions where ethnicities and sub-ethnicities jostle in ways that would have been unlikely or impossible in their respective homeland settings, or where long and sustained patterns of immigration have produced a critical mass of singular ethnicities.

Sinclair et.al.'s (2000) study of the Chinese in *Floating Lives* posits that the sources, socio-economic backgrounds and circumstances of Chinese immigrant arrivals in Australia have been much more diverse than that of Chinese communities in the other great contemporary immigrant-receiving countries such as the United States, Canada, Britain, and New Zealand, or earlier immigrant-receiving countries in Southeast Asia, South America, Europe, and Africa. To make sense of 'the' Chinese community is to break it down into a series of complex and often interrelated sub-groupings based on geographical origin – Mainland (People's Republic of China); Southeast Asia (Malaysia and Singapore); Taiwan; Indochina (Vietnam, Laos, Cambodia); and Hong Kong. Even then, geographical origin is a cipher for other variables of difference, notably length of residence in Australia, socio-economic status, education and language use.

Similarly, Cunningham and Nguyen's (2000) Vietnamese study demonstrates that there are significant differences along axes of generation, ethnicity, region of the home country, education and class, and recency of arrival and conditions under which arrival took place amongst a quite small population. For the Fiji Indians in Manas Ray's work (2000), if it was legislated racial discrimination that compelled them to leave Fiji, in Australia they find themselves 'othered' by, and othering, the mainland Indian groupings who contest the authenticity of the Fiji Indian claims to rootedness in Indian popular culture.

The formats for diasporic popular media owe much to their inscription within 'narrowcast' cultural spaces and share significant attributes: karaoke, with its performative, communal and de-aestheticised performative and communal space (Wong, 1994), the Vietnamese variety music video and 'Paris/Sydney/Toronto by Night' live show formats; and the typical 'modular' Bollywood film and accompanying live and playback music culture.

Against the locus of examination of the 'diasporic imagination' as one of aesthetically transgressive hybridity produced out of the 'ontological condition' occupied by the migrant subject, these forms are not aesthetically progressive or transgressive texts; their politics cannot be read off their texts. Much diasporic cultural expression is a struggle for survival, identity and assertion, and can be a struggle enforced by the necessities of coming to terms with the dominant culture. And the results may not be pretty. The instability of cultural maintenance and negotiation can lead, at one extreme, to being locked into a time warp with the fetishised homeland grasped as it once might have been but no longer is or can be; and, at the other, to assimilation to the dominant host culture and a loss of place within one's originary culture. It can involve insistent reactionary politics and extreme over commercialisation due to the necessity to fund expensive forms of media for a narrowcast audience. For example, Naficy (1993, p. 71) cites a situation in 1987 when Iranian television in Los Angeles was scheduling over 40 minutes advertising per hour; Naficy (1993) and Kolar-Panov (1997) recount textual material of excoriating tragedy, fictional self-immolation and actual atrocity scenarios played out in some Iranian and Croatian video.

Second, there is explanatory payoff in pursuing the specificity of the ethno-specific public sphericule in comparison to other emergent public spheres. Like the classic Habermasian bourgeois public sphere of the café society in 18th and 19th century France and Britain, they are constituted as elements of civil society. However, our understanding of civil society is formulated out of its dualistic relationship to formal apparatuses of political and juridical power. Ethno-specific sphericules constitute themselves as potentially global civil societies which intersect with state apparatuses at various points (immigration law, multicultural public policy, and for the irredentist and the exilic, against the regimes which control homeland societies). It follows that ethno-specific public sphericules are not congruent with international taste cultures borne by a homogenising global media culture. For diasporic groupings *were* parts of states, nations and polities and much of the diasporic polity is about the process of remembering, positioning and, by no means least, constructing business opportunities around these pre-diasporic states.

It is out of these realities that the assumption grows that ethnic minoritarian publics contribute to the further fragmentation of the majoritarian public sphere, breaking the 'social compact', subsuming nation and ethnicity into state, which has been foundational for the modern nation state. Irredentist politics and 'long-distance' nationalism, where the prime allegiance continues to be an often defunct state or regime, are deemed non-progressive by most academic and social commentators. However, a focus on the popular culture of diasporas and its place in the construction of public sphericules complicates these assumptions, as it shows that a variety of voices contend for recognition and influence within the micro-polity, and great generational renewal arises from the vibrancy of such popular culture.

Sophisticated cosmopolitanism and successful international business dealing sits alongside long-distance nationalism – the diasporic subject is typically a citizen of a western country, who is not stateless and is not seeking the recognition of their national status within their 'new' country, like the prototypical 'fourth world' instances in the European context like the Basques, the Scots, or the Welsh. These sphericules are definitively transnational, even global, in their constitution but equally identify as ethnic-national, unlike the usually commented-upon emerging transnational polities and cultures of global corporate culture, world-spanning NGOs and international bodies of governments.

Perhaps the most consistent relation, or non-relation, that diasporic media has with the various states into which they are introduced is around issues of piracy. This gives another layer to the notion of civil cultures standing over and against the state. Indeed, given that significant amounts of cultural production exists in a para-legal penumbra of copyright breach and piracy, there is a strong desire on the part of the entrepreneurs who disseminate such product to keep their distance from organs of the state. It is apparent that routinised piracy makes of much diasporic media a 'shadow system', as Kolar-Panov (1997, p. 31) dubs ethnic minority video circuits, operating in parallel to the majoritarian system with few industry linkages.

Third, they reconfigure essentialist notions of community and reflex anti-commercialism. These sphericules are communities in a sense which goes beyond the bland homogenising that the term 'community' usually connotes in policy discourse. On the one hand the ethno-specific community assumes an importance greater by far than the term usually means in mainstream, as the community *constitutes* the markets and audiences for the media services – there is almost no cross-over or recognition outside the specific community, in many cases, of the cultural production produced within and for the community. The 'community' therefore becomes an economic calculus, not only a multicultural demographic instance. The community is to an important extent constituted through media (Hartley & McKee 2000, p. 84), in so far as media performance is one of the main reasons to meet together, and there is very little else available as a mediator of information and entertainment. These media and their entrepreneurs and audiences work within a de-essentialised community and its differences as a condition of their practice and engagement.

Diasporic media are largely commercially-driven (with significant exceptions like *Worldwatch* on Australia's national public multicultural channel, SBS) - but are not fully fledged markets. They are largely constituted in and through a commercial culture but this is not the globalising, homogenising commercialism that has been posed by the neo-Marxist political economists as threatening cultural pluralism, authenticity and agency at the local level. With notable exceptions, like global Chinese popular cultural forms such as Canto-pop and Hong Kong cinema, which have experienced significant cross-over into both dominant and other emerging contemporary cultural formations, and the Indian popular music and cinema (Bollywood) which is still more singularly based in Indian homeland and diasporic audiences, this is small business commercialism which deals with the practical specificities of cultural difference at the local level as an absolute precondition of business viability.

Fourthly, the spaces for ethno-specific public communication are mediacentric, and this affords new configurations of the information-entertainment dualism. Given the sometimes extreme marginalisation of many diasporic groupings in public space, and their lack of representation within leaderships of influence and persuasion in the dominant forums of the host country, ethno-specific media become, by default, the main organs of communication outside of certain circumscribed and defined social spaces, such as the Chinatowns, Koreatowns, the little Saigons, the churches and temples, or the local video, spice and herb parlours.

It is a mediacentric space but, unlike the way that mediacentricity can give rise to functionalist thinking (the idea that media are the cement that forms and gives identity to the community), it should be thought of as rather 'staging' difference and dissension in ways that the community *itself* can manage. There are severe constraints on public political discourse amongst refugee-based communities like the Vietnamese. The 'compulsive memoralisation' (Thomas, 1999, p. 149) of Vietnam's pre-Communist past and the compulsory anti-Communism of the community leadership is internalised as unsavoury to mainstream society. As part of the pressure to be the perfect citizen in the host society (Hage, 1998, p. 10), there is considerable self-censorship in the public expression of critical opinion. This filtering of political partisanship for external consumption is also turned back on itself in the community, with attempts by members of the community to have the rigorous anti-Communist refugee stance softened (by the mid 1990s, only 30 per cent of the Vietnamese community in Australia were originally refugees) being met with harsh rebuke. In this situation, Vietnamese entertainment formats, discussed below, operate to create a space where political and cultural identities can be processed in a self-determining way, where voices other than the official, but constitutive of community sentiment, can speak.

Mediacentricity also means, in this context, a constant blurring of the information-entertainment distinction, giving rise to a positive sense of a 'tabloidised' sphericule wherein McGuigan's *a*ffective as well as *e*ffective communication takes on another meaning. The information-entertainment distinction - usually maintained in the abundance of available media in the dominant culture - is blurred in the diasporic setting. As there is typically such a small diet of ethno-specific media available to these communities, they are mined deeply for social (including fashion, language use, and so on) cues, personal gossip, public information as well as singing along to the song or following the fictional narrative. Within this concentrated and contracted informational and libidinal economy, 'contemporary popular media as guides to choice, or guides to the attitudes that inform choices' (Hartley, 1999, p. 143) take on a thoroughly continuous and central role in information and entertainment for creating a negotiated *habitus*.

Vietnamese Communities

The Vietnamese are by far the largest refugee community in Australia. For most, 'home' is a denigrated category while 'the regime' continues in power, and so media networks, especially music video, operate to connect the dispersed exilic Vietnamese communities. As Cunningham and Nguyen (2000) argue in *Floating Lives*, there are obviously other media in play (community newspapers, Hong Kong film and video product) but music video carries special significance and allows a focus on the affective dimension of public communication. Small business entrepreneurs produce low budget music video mostly out of southern California (but also Paris), which are taken up within the fan circuits of America, Australia, Canada, France and elsewhere. The internal cultural conflicts within the communities centre on the felt need to (1) maintain pre-revolutionary Vietnamese heritage and traditions; (2) find a negotiated place within a more mainstreamed culture; or (3) engage in the formation of distinct hybrid identities around the appropriation of dominant Western popular cultural forms. These three cultural positions or stances are dynamic and mutable; but the main debates are constructed around them, and are played out principally within variety music video formats.

Whilst by no means exhausting the media diet of the Vietnamese diaspora, live variety shows and music video are undeniably unique to it, as audio-visual media made specifically by and for the diaspora. These media forms bear many similarities to the commercial and variety-based cultural production of Iranian television in Los Angeles studied by Naficy in his benchmark *The Making of Exile Cultures* (1993), not least because Vietnamese variety show and music video production is also centred on the Los Angeles conurbation. The Vietnamese grouped there are not as numerous or rich as Naficy's Iranians and so have not developed the business infrastructure to the extent where it could support the range and depth of media activity recounted by Naficy. The business infrastructure of

Vietnamese audio-visual production is structured around a small number of small businesses operating on very low margins.

To be exilic means not, or at least not 'officially', being able to draw on the contemporary cultural production of the home country. Indeed it means actively denying its existence in a dialectical process of mutual disauthentification (Carruthers, 1999). The Vietnamese government proposes that the *Viet Kieu* (the appellation for Vietnamese overseas which carries a pejorative connotation) are fatally Westernised. Ironically, the diasporic population makes a similar counter-charge against the regime, proposing that the homeland population has lost its moral integrity through the wholesale compulsory adoption of an alien western ideology – Marxist-Leninism.

Together, the dispersed geography and the demography of a small series of communities frame the conditions for 'global narrowcasting': that is, ethnically-specific cultural production for widely dispersed population fragments centripetally organised around their disavowed state of origin. This makes the media, and the media use, of the Vietnamese diaspora fundamentally different from that of the Indian or Chinese diasporas. The latter revolve around massive cinema and television production centres in the 'home' countries that enjoy international cachet. By contrast, the fact that the media uses of the Vietnamese diaspora are globally oriented but commercially marginal ensures that they flourish outside the purview of state and major commercial vectors of subvention and trade.

These conditions also determine the small business character of the production companies. These small enterprises run at low margins and are constantly undercut by piracy and copying of their video product. They have clustered around the only Vietnamese population base that offers critical mass and is geographically adjacent to the much larger ECI (entertainment-communications-information) complex in southern California. There is evidence of internal migration within the diaspora from the rest of the US, Canada and France to southern California to take advantage of the largest overseas Vietnamese population concentration and the world's major ECI complex.

Over the course of the twenty and more years since the fall of Saigon and the establishment of the diaspora through flight and migration, a substantial amount of music video material has been produced. Thuy Nga Productions, by far the largest and most successful company, organises major live shows in the US and franchises appearance schedules for its high profile performers at shows around the global diaspora. It has produced over sixty two-to-three hour videotapes since the early 1980s, as well as a constant flow of CDs, audio-cassettes and karaoke discs in addition to documentary specials and re-releases of classic Vietnamese movies. The other companies, between them, have also produced hundreds of hours of variety music video.

Virtually every overseas Vietnamese household views this music video material, most regularly attend the live variety performances on which the video material are based, and a significant proportion have developed comprehensive home libraries. The popularity of this material is exemplary, cutting across the several axes of difference in the community: ethnicity, age, gender, length of time since arrival, educational level, refugee or immigrant status, and home region. It is also widely available in pirated form in Vietnam itself, as the economic and cultural 'thaw' that has proceeded since Doi Moi policies of greater openness has resulted in extensive penetration of the homeland by this most international of Vietnamese forms of expression. As the only popular culture produced by and specifically for the Vietnamese diaspora, these texts attract an emotive investment within the overseas communities which is as deep as it is varied. The social text that surrounds, indeed engulfs, these productions is intense, multi-layered and makes its address across the differences within the community.

The key point linking attention to the textual dynamics of the music videos and media use within the communities is that each style cannot exist without the others, because of the marginal size of the audience base. From the point of view of *business* logic, each style cannot exist without the others. Thus, at the level both of the individual show/video and company outputs as a whole, the organisational structure of the shows and the videos reflects the heterogeneity required to maximise audience within a strictly narrowcast range. This is a programming philosophy congruent with 'broadcasting' to a globally spread, narrowcast demographic: 'the variety show form has been a mainstay of overseas Vietnamese anti-communist culture from the mid-seventies onwards' (Carruthers, 1999).

In any given live show or video production, the musical styles might range from pre-colonial traditionalism to French colonial era high modernist classicism, to crooners adapting Vietnamese folksongs to the Sinatra era and to bilingual cover versions of *Grease* or Madonna. Stringing this concatenation of taste cultures together are comperes, typically well known political and cultural figures in their own right, who perform a rhetorical unifying function:

> Audience members are constantly recouped via the show's diegesis, and the anchoring role of the comperes and their commentaries, into an overarching conception of shared overseas Vietnamese identity. This is centred on the appeal to...core cultural values, common tradition, linguistic unity and an anti-communist homeland politics. (Carruthers, 1999)

187

Within this overall political trajectory, however, there are major differences to be managed. The stances evidenced in the video and live material range on a continuum from 'pure' heritage maintenance and ideological monitoring, to mainstream cultural negotiation, through to assertive hybridity. Most performers and productions seek to situate themselves within the mainstream of cultural negotiation between Vietnamese and Western traditions. However, at one end of the continuum there are strong attempts both to keep the original folkloric music traditions alive and to keep the integrity of the originary anti-Communist stance foundational to the diaspora, through very public criticism of any lapse from that stance. At the other end, Vietnamese-American youth culture is exploring the limits of hybrid identities through the radical intermixing of musical styles.

Fiji Indian Communities

In a remarkably short time, essentially since the coups of the late 1980s which pushed thousands of Fiji Indians out of Fiji and into diaspora around the Pacific Rim in cities like Vancouver, Auckland and Sydney, the community in Sydney has fashioned a vibrant popular culture based on consumption and celebration of Hindi filmdom and its associated music, dance and fashion cultures. It is a particular irony that a people 'extracted' from mainland Indian polity and culture a century or more ago – for whom the relationship with the world of Hindi film is a purely imaginary one – should embrace and appropriate such a culture with far greater strength than those with a much more recent connection.

Manas Ray's analysis of the Fiji Indian public sphericule in *Floating Lives* (2000) is structured around a comparison with the expatriate Bengalis. The two groups are contrasted on a caste, class and cultural consumption basis, and Ray stresses that, given that there is no critical mass of sub-ethnicities within the Indian diaspora in Australia, cultural difference is definitional. The Bengalis are seen as locked into their history as bearers of the Indian project of modernity which they assumed centrally under the British Raj. The once unassailed centrality of the educated, Hindu Bengali gentry, the *bradralok*, in the political and civic institutions of India has been challenged in the decades since independence by the subaltern classes: 'It is from this challenge that the *bradralok* flees, either to relatively prosperous parts of India or, if possible, abroad – to the affluent west, taking with them the dream of a nation that they were once so passionate about and the cultural baggage which had expressed that dream.' The Bengali diaspora, argues Ray, frames its cultural life around the high culture of the past, which has become a 'fossilised' taste culture (2000, p. 143).

In startling contrast to the Fiji Indian community, which is by far the highest consumer of Hindi films, for the Indian Bengalis, Indian-sourced film and video is of little interest and is even the subject of active disparagement. Their literature and other high cultural forms, which once had 'organic links to the independence movement and to early post-independence hardship and hope', have fossilised into a predictable and ageing taste culture remarkably similar whether the Bengali community is in Philadelphia, Boston, London, Dusseldorf, Dubai or Sydney (Ray, 2000, p. 143). The issues of inter-generational deficit, as the young turn to western youth culture, are evident.

The politics of popular culture are fought out across the communal fractions and across the generations. The inter-communal discord between mainland Indians and Fiji-Indians, which are neither new nor restricted only to Australia – where many mainland Indians continue to exhibit deeply entrenched casteist attitudes and Fiji-Indians often characterise mainland Indian's with the same kind of negativity they were wont to use for ethnic Fijians – are often played out around media and film culture. There are elements of a fully-blown popular culture debate being played out. At the time of a particularly vitriolic controversy in 1997, the editor of the mainland *Indian Post* argued that while the Fiji-Indians are 'good Hindus' and 'they are the people who spend', on the other hand their 'westernised ways' and 'excessive attachment to filmy culture' bring disrepute to the Indian community as a whole (Dello, 1997). The resolution to these kinds of issues are often found in the commercial realities that Fiji Indians are the main consumers of the products and services advertised in mainland Indian shops!

Despite virtual slavery in the extraction period and uprootedness in the contemporary period, the affective dimension of the Fiji Indian public sphericule is deeply rooted in Hindu belief and folklore. The *Ramayan* thus was used to heal the wounds of indenture and provide a cultural and moral texture in the new settlement. A strong emotional identification to the *Ramayan* and other expressions of the Bhakti movement – a constrained cultural environment, continued degradation at the hands of the racist white regime, a disdain for the culture of the ethnic Fijians, a less hard–pressed post-indenture life and, finally, a deep-rooted need of a dynamic, discursive site for the imaginative reconstruction of motherland – were all factors which, together, ensured the popularity of Hindi films once they started reaching the shores of Fiji. This was because Hindi film deployed the *Ramayan* extensively, providing the right pragmatics for 'continual mythification' of home (Ray, 2000, p. 156).

As a result, second generation Fiji-Indians in their twice-displaced settings of Sydney, Auckland or Vancouver have developed a cultural platform that, though not counter-hegemonic, is markedly different from their western host cultures. In contrast, 'the emphasis of the first generation Indian Bengali diaspora on aestheticised cultural forms of the past offers the second generation very little in terms of a home country popular youth culture with which they can identify' (Ray, 2000, p. 145).

Chinese-Origin Communities

Chinese groups in Australia present a microcosm of the differences within the Chinese diaspora: differences in countries or regions of birth, languages, dialects, religions, and degree of 'de-Sinicisation' of values and behaviour. As such, they provide an excellent opportunity for the study of diasporic cultural identities, specifically of the factors which shape the identities of people of Chinese descent on a more universal scale. The research reported in Sinclair et. al. (2000) provides data from household and ethnographic studies of a range of Chinese-origin groups in Melbourne, a city which has attracted Chinese settlers since the 1850s.

Of the several factors which divide these Chinese-origin communities, one of the most consequential in terms of media use is political alignment, fundamentally between the PRC and Taiwan, complicated by the fact that both these countries are also fertile sources of current migration. This political division is recognised in the *Worldwatch* program, a daily feed of foreign-language news services on SBS, the national free-to-air multicultural network. *Worldwatch* offers Chinese services from both CCTV4, the international channel of the PRC national network, and from Asia Television Limited, a privately-provided international service from Hong Kong. Originally, the CCTV service was the only one on offer, but SBS added the ATV service in response to demand from lobby groups. The CCTV service is in Mandarin, and the ATV one in Cantonese, but politics, not language is the issue.

The study showed that several respondents, and not only those from Taiwan and the Mainland, complained of the pro-Communist Party character of the CCTV Mandarin news. On the other hand, the Cantonese news was thought to be rather tame and insubstantial, however necessary the service was seen to be as an alternative to that of the PRC. The respondents' comments reflect a continued close engagement with the unfolding of events in East Asia, and their 'epistephilic desire', as Naficy (1993) calls it: the need to have news from one's actual or putative 'home' nation and/or world region. While the Chinese-origin population is not

190

alone in pressing these kinds of demands on SBS, it provides a clear case of how such desire has to be satisfied in political as well as linguistic terms, how fundamental are the divisions within ethno-specific 'communities', and how the quest for specificity results in ever more differentiated, 'niche' audiences. What is unusual about this case is the institution of SBS itself, with its charter to provide minority services and to respond to the media needs of minority groups.

As minority groups go in Australia, the Chinese-origin population is quite substantial, with an estimated 400,000 people of Chinese ancestry. For this reason, and because of the relative affluence of some of the several sections within it, as well as access to abundant content, there are subscriber cable channels available commercially. At the time of the *Floating Lives* research, during 1996-98, this was the New World channel, a tiered continuous service of programming from diverse sources, but mainly Hong Kong and Taiwan, in both Mandarin and Cantonese. At the time of writing now, two channels are available as an additional tier to the Optus Vision subscriber cable service, one being the full Mandarin CCTV international service, and the other, in Cantonese, incorporating the ATV stream of programming. As noted, the news services of both of these are already available free-to-air on SBS. The only other available foreign-language channels on cable in Australia are in Arabic, Japanese, Greek and Italian. The odd one out here is Japanese, as all the others have populations of some proportion, but it seems to be availability of material as much as potential subscribers which determines the services to be put on offer.

In the realm of entertainment, and film in particular, Chinese material is less removed from the public media realm than is news. Although there are scores of video rental stores distributing Chinese-language material (mainly films and series) exclusively to Chinese-origin customers, Chinese films are available to non-Chinese audiences, both on national, free-to-air television via SBS, or in 'arthouse' cinemas. Chinese genre movies are also available, subtitled in English, in mainstream video store chains like Blockbuster. Again, availability of material is a key factor, in this case clearly attributable to the size of the Chinese population on a global basis, and the massive production and widespread distribution of all forms of popular culture for them.

The recent success of certain Chinese films with mainstream audiences, both cult/arthouse as well as popular, and the advent of Chinese videos in mainstream stores would seem to demonstrate that appreciation of Chinese culture is not restricted to the Chinese and their descendants. Rather, it becomes diffused into the host society, and appears particularly attractive to those whom we could call, without prejudice, 'cosmopolitan'. That is, Chinese media goods, if made accessible to non-Chinese-speakers via dubbing or subtitling, can appeal not just to 'communities of difference', but also 'communities of taste' (Hawkins, 1996). This makes the consumption of Chinese cultural products rather exceptional when compared to the Vietnamese or Indian, which are much more marginalised.

Second generation Chinese, for their part, respond to these products in the context of whatever assimilation they might have received into the mainstream culture, so their media experience is hybrid, or 'cross-cultural' in the best sense. It is worth remembering that it is media-oriented cosmopolitans such as these people who form at least part of the audience for SBS and other more specialized services. Several Chinese-origin respondents were as worldly in their tastes as educated and travelled members of the Anglo-Australian mainstream. By contrast, first generation Chinese surveyed indicated an ambivalent relation to Chinese films, whether on SBS or in video stores and cinemas: they were pleased to be able to see films they had not been able to see in their countries of origin, but were anxious about the impression these films might be giving the host society, in terms of the cultural stereotypes they carried. Thus, 'assimilation' as seen in media choices is not so much a function of a transition from one culture to another, as it is a fusion in which individual subjects are very much the agents of their own cultural consumption.

Conclusion

This chapter reports on a major project of grounded research that addresses a central issue not only in media and communications theory but also in public debate and policy in contemporary, culturally plural societies. Is the increased cultural and communicational diversity that is a remarkable feature of such societies an index of fragmentation and the decline of a previously more coherent and unified public life? Or, rather, don't the 'public sphericules' that are composed of the cultures and polities of minority ethnic communities exhibit in microcosm features of the (mainstreamed) public sphere?

The politics and practices of these popular cultures may constitute valid and indeed dynamic counter-examples to a discourse of decline and fragmentation. They also pose challenges for reflex postures against globalisation and commercialisation. While not necessarily counter-hegemonic or aesthetically progressive, ethnic minority popular cultures certainly create a dynamic space for public communication within marginalised communities and contend with dominant western forms, particularly for young people's identification and empowerment.

References

Chambers, I. (1996), *Migrancy, Culture, Identity*, Routledge, London and New York.

Carruthers, A. (1999), 'National Identity, Diasporic Anxiety and Music Video Culture in Vietnam', in Y. Souchou, (ed.), *House of Glass: Culture, Representation and the State in Southeast Asia*, Institute of Southeast Asian Studies (ISEAS), Singapore.

Cunningham, S. and Sinclair, J. (eds) (2000), *Floating Lives: The Media and Asian Diasporas*, University of Queensland Press, St Lucia.

Cunningham, S. and Nguyen, T. (2000), 'Popular Media of the Vietnamese Diaspora,' in S. Cunningham and J. Sinclair (eds) (2000), *Floating Lives: The Media and Asian Diasporas*, University of Queensland Press, St. Lucia, pp. 91-135.

Dello, S. (1997), Interview with Manas Ray, Sydney, May.

Fraser, N. (1992), 'Rethinking the Public Sphere: A Contribution to the Critique of Actually Existing Democracy', in C. Calhoun (ed.), *Habermas and the Public Sphere*, MIT Press, Cambridge, MA, pp. 109-142.

Garnham, N. (1992), 'The media and the public sphere', in C. Calhoun (ed.) *Habermas and the Public Sphere*, MIT Press, Cambridge, MA, pp. 359-376.

-- (1995), 'The media and narratives of the intellectual', *Media, Culture & Society*, vol. 17, pp. 359-384.

Gitlin, T. (1998), 'Public sphere or public sphericules?', in T. Liebes and J. Curran (eds), *Media, Ritual and Identity*, Routledge, London.

Habermas, J. (1974), 'The public sphere', *New German Critique*, vol. 1, no. 3, pp. 49-55.

-- (1989), *The Structural Transformation of the Public Sphere: An Inquiry in a Category of Bourgeois Society*, Polity Press, Cambridge.

Hage, G. (1998), *White Nation: Fantasies of White supremacy in a multicultural society* Pluto Press, Annandale and Comerford and Miller Publishers, West Wickham.

Hartley, J. (1999), *Uses of Television*, Routledge, London.

Hartley, J. and McKee, A. (2000), *The Indigenous Public Sphere*, Oxford University Press, Oxford.

Hawkins, G. (1996), 'SBS: Minority Television', *Culture and Policy*, vol. 7, no. 1, pp. 45-63.

Husband C. (1998), 'Differentiated Citizenship and the multi-ethnic public sphere', *Journal of International Communication*, vol. 5, nos. 1&2, pp. 134-148.

Kolar-Panov, D. (1997), *Video, war and the diasporic imagination*, Routledge, London.

Lotman, Y. M. (1990), *Universe of the mind: a semiotic theory of culture*, translated by Ann Shukman, Indiana University Press, Bloomington.

McGuigan, J. (1998), 'What price the public sphere?' in D. Thussu (ed.) *Electronic Empires: Global Media and Local Resistance*, Arnold, London.

Naficy, H. (1993), *The Making of Exile Cultures: Iranian Television in Los Angeles*, University of Minnesota Press, Minneapolis.

Ray, M. (2000), 'Bollywood Down Under: Fiji Indian Cultural History and Popular Assertion', in S. Cunningham and J. Sinclair (eds) (2000), *Floating Lives: The Media and Asian Diasporas*, University of Queensland Press, St. Lucia, pp. 136-184.

Schiller, H. (1989), *Culture Inc: The corporate takeover of public expression*, Oxford University Press, New York.

Sinclair, J., Yue, A., Hawkins, Gay, K. P. and Fox, J. (2000), 'Chinese Cosmopolitanism and media use', in S. Cunningham and J. Sinclair (eds) (2000), *Floating Lives. The media and Asian Diasporas*, University of Queensland Press, St. Lucia, pp. 35-90.

Thomas, M. (1999), *Dreams in the Shadows: Vietnamese-Australian Lives in Transition*, Allen & Unwin, St. Leonards.

Wong, D. (1994), '"I Want the Microphone": Mass Mediation and Agency in Asian-American Popular Music', *TDR (The Drama Review)* 38, no. 3, fall, pp. 152-167.

12 Australian Dreamings: Cultural Diversity and Audience Desire in a Multinational and Polyethnic State

ANDREW JAKUBOWICZ

A Few Words about White and Black in Australia

Every society has its own discursive trajectories, histories of ideas and relations embedded in the particular circumstances of their development. So it is with Australia, where white and Black can switch meanings as situations move. Thus one of the first acts after the Federation of Australia in 1901, was the Immigration Restriction Act - known thereafter as the 'White Australia Act'. That Federation also restricted the Commonwealth from making laws that would affect the Aboriginal people - this was left to the States and their variable paternalism and mendacity. It was not until the late 1960s that either of these circumstances would change substantially.

Under 'White Australia', the national government could control immigration and prohibit the entry of people deemed to be of unassimilable race - yet the powers granted to enforce control were never racial - they were linguistic (a test for literacy in a European language). It had been the British government that had insisted that there be no discrimination in law against the various peoples of the Empire, or against the Japanese, whose alliance was then being sought. Non-white was more likely to be yellow or brown, rather than black (except for the Melanesians and Afro-Americans). So 'White' actually meant capacity to speak a European tongue. Non-white was everyone who was thus to be excluded, and all those indigenous people who could not pass as white.

For many Aboriginal communities the world was also divided into two categories, our people – 'Blackfellas' - and everyone else – 'Whitefellas'. Within this world it was indigeneity that was the crucial boundary, not colour per se. In contemporary Australia very fair skinned people of indigenous descent can be Blackfellas, while very dark skinned immigrants can be classified as Whitefellas (with a laugh).

The point of this opening is to suggest that ideas of Black and white are context-dependent, and therefore the language used to describe cultural relations between groups will differ from place to place. In Australia the major dichotomies are those of Indigeneity and Settler, and Anglo(Celtic) and Migrant. These are uncomfortable dualities, as many indigenous people have non-indigenous forebears (rape being a common practice, while frontiersmen often took Aboriginal concubines since usually marriage was prohibited or unthinkable for the men). Many Irish Australians resent their allocation to the super-ordinate category Anglo-Celtic, remembering Irish history on the one hand, and anti-Irish and anti-Catholic bigotry in Australia on the other. Inter-generational conflicts between Australian-born children of non-Anglo immigrant parents also dissolve the simple assumptions of common interests and expectations. This leaves apart the cultural distinctiveness of the 200 plus national origins and 150 plus languages that make up the 'ethnic communities'. White as the political opposite of Black has come into some use in Australia recently, especially through the work of Gassan Hage (Hage, 1998; Hage and Couch, 1999). This usage reflects the influence of white theory in North America and Europe, and it is, I suggest, less useful in the Australian context.

Cultural Diversity in Australia

While multiculturalism has been a critical point of debate and contention, it has at the same time provided a forum for analyses of Australian media and their responses to cultural difference. In the Australian context the distinction is usually made between indigenous issues, which have Aboriginal and Settler communities as the critical groups, and ethnic or multicultural issues, where the tensions explored reflect cultural differences within the Settler society. Will Kymlicka has referred to a similar distinction in Canada, which he clarifies by using the terms 'multinational' (as a result of colonisation, conquest and confederation) and 'polyethnic' (as a result of immigration). 'Multicultural' he suggests is confusing 'precisely because it is ambiguous between multinational and polyethnic' (Kymlicka, 1996, p. 155).

If we then consider Australia as a multinational state with a polyethnic population, the questions of how the media relate to this diversity in audience can be encapsulated thus: in what ways and to what extent is the multinational nature of Australia reflected in the structure and content of the media? How do national minorities gain purchase on the media agendas? What is the relationship between the representation of cultural diversity in the media and the use by audiences of the media? What role does the media play for diasporic communities in integrating them into the Australian national imagery and the wider global diasporas of which they remain a part?

Audience Studies in Australia

A leading scholar of mass media audiences in Australia, Virginia Nightingale, has argued that audiences, as far as the media industry is concerned, are essentially participants 'in the world of consumption' (Nightingale, 1997, p. 353). Ratings play a crucial role in discussions about radio and television content, and dominate most of the analysis of audience and media relations. In public policy the issue of ratings remains paramount, particularly in an environment of digital convergence, expanding cable programming, and cross-media ownership legislation which restricts major players from monopolising all media forms in major city markets. With globalisation and the internationalisation of communication on an unprecedented scale across a rapidly evolving range of media, the very idea of audience is being transformed.

To meet consumption demand, Australia has a plethora of electronic media outlets, though newspapers are controlled by two major groups – News Ltd. and the Fairfax group, with the media empire of Kerry Packer looking to move in on Fairfax. There are some 48 commercial TV licences, organised into three networks. There are two national broadcasters – the Australian Broadcasting Corporation (ABC), with one national television network and a variety of national, state and local radio and on-line services, and the Special Broadcasting Service offering multicultural television and two multilingual radio networks. Pay-TV operates through three providers, while there are 220 commercial AM and FM radio licences, and 280 community radio licences (of which 80 are committed to Broadcasting to Remote Aboriginal Communities - BRACS). Community television broadcasts in some cities and regions. In addition local radio narrowcasting services operate for ethnic minorities, education, tourism and special interest. In addition, Internet sites are exploding; all the major media players have their own sites, while technologies such as video cassettes, laser discs, VCDs and DVDs have very high degrees of penetration. Australia has one of the highest take-up rates for new media technologies in the OECD.

The more theorised studies of audience behaviour have tended to focus on media effects questions, such as those regarding censorship and the categorisation of programmes by age and suitability. Probably the best-known early Australian contributions to audience analysis have been those associated with the work of Bob Hodge, Gunther Kress, David Tripp and

Theo van Leeuwen linked to social semiotics (Hodge and Tripp, 1986; Hodge and Kress, 1988; Kress and van Leeuwen, 1990; Hodge and Mishra, 1991) and of John Tulloch in the context of text and audience in popular narrative television (Tulloch and Moran, 1986; Tulloch and Turner, 1989; Tulloch, 1990). For the first group, effects emerge through a process of subjective interaction with media, where dominant and oppositional meanings are created by the audience. One case used by the second group was the study of the television soap *A Country Practice*, which explored the crucial role that the producers' ideas of the audience and actual audience feedback played in the production of television drama (Tulloch and Moran, 1986). The study used ethnographic techniques to explore how the narratives on television were incorporated into the daily lives of young people.

In addition there has been a string of research, often triggered by media trade unions, arguing that the media's under-portrayal of ethnic diversity and Indigenous people seriously distorts the understanding Australians have of their own society, while at the same time ensuring minority media workers have difficulty finding employment. Implicitly and explicitly the media are argued to be implicated in wider social relations, not simply as mirrors of that reality, but active contributors to meaning–making and the hierarchies of ethnic and race power (Communications Law Centre, 1992; Coupe, Jakubowicz et. al., 1993; Nugent, Loncar et. al., 1993; Appleton, 1995; May, Flew et. al., 2000).

Ethnicity, Identity and Australian Media

Australia is a colonial settler society, experiencing both its post-colonial development, and the pressures of globalisation. These dynamics have given rise to two rather different trajectories of media use and frame rather different questions of cultural diversity. In this section I deal only with that cultural diversity associated with the settler society, as Indigenous issues require separate and detailed examination.

Taking globalisation as a broad label for trans-border flows of capital, people and culture, we can identify tensions for immigrant communities in relation to their societies of settlement and their societies of birth. For the most part the Australian media have tended to dismiss as irrelevant the links diasporic communities may have to their countries of origin or to other fragments of the diaspora. Other than in news and current affairs 'hot spot' stories, usually addressed to the assumed Anglo-Australian viewer, mainstream media reflect a view of the world predicated on Australo-centric concerns. The 'in-comers' for the most part have little influence on how

198

audiences are addressed, what cultural knowledges are built into media accounts, or what listening/viewing position the audiences are expected to assume.

Most diasporic communities have maintained their links to their cultures of origin through the Special Broadcasting Service (especially language programs on radio), community (sponsored and volunteer run) radio, commercial ethnic radio, commercial community newspapers, through video cassettes (and now laser discs, VCDs and DVDs) available through networks of ethnic outlets, or through cable and satellite, and most recently, through the Internet.

A second dimension focuses more on the local than the global. Here we see the processes through which the media tell the stories of the society to itself. The organisation of production in what we can refer to as the mainstream media (popular or English language), is effectively controlled by an English-speaking elite, geared either to a mass market in the commercial arena, or to a smaller, better-educated audience for the national broadcaster. Despite multicultural charters and cultural diversity guidelines for both these sectors, delivery of a culturally diverse range of narratives which might speak evocatively to the society remains an unrealised desire. A leading Australian comic and filmmaker, Nick Giannopoulos, has described the situation in terms of the link between on-screen representation and institutional media power:

Look, you only have to turn on your TV set at 6.30 or at 7.00 o'clock, and have a look at the most popular soap operas overseas, Australian soap operas overseas: *Home and Away* and *Neighbours*. Look at the representative view of Australia we are giving to people in England and Europe, and other associated countries. It's one of a predominantly blonde, surfy, blue-eyed, Anglo-Saxon background community. And that is wrong. Because the people I believe who have the power in this country in terms of television – the owners of the television stations, the owners of the media - are predominantly Anglo-Saxon. And I don't believe we'll see a change until more people from non-Anglo-Saxon backgrounds begin to find themselves in those professional positions: positions of management, people who are in control of the media. Because they are the only people who can understand the discrimination that has been faced by millions of people in this country. Because they have lived through it. And unfortunately that process in Australia has been very slow. (Jakubowicz, 1999, Disc 2)

Minority Audiences

By 2000 there were many media outlets serving the diverse cultures of the society. Most language groups have at least one regular newspaper or magazine, while in some communities up to five weekly or more regular newspapers (e.g. Chinese) battled it out for audience share.

Radio had also increased dramatically, in the wake of the liberalisation of licensing arrangements, and the emergence of new delivery systems such as subscription radio. There were 95 community stations with ethnic programming (ranging from 24 hours in one language to occasional language spots during the week) stations, of which 18 were subscription (narrow-casting). Pay radio included, in Sydney for instance, Arabic, Chinese, Greek, Turkish, Farsi, Spanish, Portuguese, Croatian, Italian and Korean. SBS broadcast in the eight major cities, and provide programmes to many community stations in other towns and centres. In Sydney it covers 66 languages, controls two stations, and has high levels of penetration - up to 80 per cent in some language groups. A 1998 Vietnamese community report concluded that SBS services 'have been able to serve the cultural artistic, social and information needs of the Vietnamese community', this despite many internal political differences within the Vietnamese community (Tran, 1998). In the realm of television, free-to-air broadcasting in languages other than English is limited to SBS, though on pay television Optus offers up to seven channels in single languages, while Foxtel has three.

Detailed research on ethnic community audiences is limited. A major study for the national government on immigrant use of media for settlement information was carried out in 1991 (Newspoll, 1991), the results making it clear that the media environment is highly segmented by ethnicity among first generation people from non-English speaking backgrounds. Pay television is beginning to reflect this situation, with the major carrier Foxtel offering a Greek and an Italian channel. Again this situation is likely to change dramatically in the wake of successful legal action in 2000, which will force the carriers to open up spare capacity to other service providers, including ethnic language programming.

More recent data from Roy Morgan Research, a commercial market research firm, has tried to unpack the television viewing patterns of ethnic groups in Australia, identified by country of birth (in a fairly idiosyncratic selection of countries, e.g. Canada gets a separate category, but Asia is pooled into one group). The key findings suggest the following situation existed over the year October 1998 to September 1999 (these figures were drawn from a cumulative set of quarterly samples totalling 54000 interviews, and were reworked for the media buying group The Media

Edge, who provided them to me). The survey offers comparative indices of propensities to consume particular types of programming, with 100 as the average. As a baseline, television viewing of any sort was about the same across different 'communities' chosen - Australia, Asia, Canada, Greece, Italy, Other Europe, New Zealand, United Kingdom, USA and Other.

The ABC, which 55 per cent of the sample had seen at least once in the past week, had its highest rate of audience support in UK (129) Canadian (110) and communities, and lowest in Greek (71), Italian (76) and Asian (85). SBS, the multicultural broadcaster, which 29 per cent of the sample had seen at least once in the past week, had its highest support in Asia (173), Other Europe (165) and also Canada (151), and its lowest among the Australian born (87). The highest viewers of pay TV were Greek-born (147) and New Zealanders (122), and the lowest were Canadians (62) and Asians (84). The most watched commercial channel - network 9 - secured strong support across the board, with the lowest rating by Canadians (87) and Asian-born (92).

While newspaper readership was fairly high for all groups (over 85 per cent up to 95 per cent), the focus of their reading differed dramatically. Thus the weekly national press (comprising two newspapers, *The Australian,* owned by News Corp, and *The Financial Review*, owned by the Fairfax group) had strongest support in the Asian community (141), and among English-speaking groups: Canada (159), New Zealand (141), the USA (146) and the UK (142), and least amongst the Italian (52) and Greek (67) groups. The most distinctively different media use lay in the area of computing magazines, where Asia (172) and USA (170) scored most interest and Greece (32) and Italy (27) scored the least, in an environment where 10 per cent of the overall sample had seen a computing magazine. Internet access figures (34 per cent of sample in the last month) are also revealing of the patterns of power that these new media support: the highest access was in the US (185) and Canadian (184) groups, the lowest on the Italian (70) and Greek (71).

While the distinctions in the Roy Morgan study are made on country of birth data, the results point up the internal differences between communities. The Greek and Italian-born audiences are likely to be older, less well educated, and more working class than the norm, with their children showing up as part of the Australian-born population. Thus the class structure of communities plays an important role in the patterns of media consumption. Yet interestingly these communities include high users of expensive options; the Greeks, for instance, have very high Pay TV useage (for the Foxtel or Optus Greek channels) but very low cinema attendance (about 11 per cent of the Greek sample had been to the cinema in the past month, compared to 30 per cent of the Australian-born, and 44 per cent of the US sample). The Greek language cinemas that used to flourish in Sydney and Melbourne have long disappeared, to be replaced by video shops and now cable television.

A recent series of studies of diasporic communities and their media use in Australia has argued that there is major cultural significance in the global flows of audiovisual media, a particularly important dimension of which lies in the power of audiences to shape meaning and use of media (Cunningham and Sinclair, 2000). SBS plays a crucial role in this globalisation, by exposing Australian audiences to a wide array of television experiences (including daily news broadcasts fed directly to the satellite from Italy, Greece, China, Indonesia, Poland and a variety of other less regular sources). Describing SBS, it is suggested that:

> SBS is a narrowcaster because it imagines the nation as a series of fragments, a multiplicity of constituencies produced through various axes of difference - often those very differences that broadcasters are unable to see in their obsession with maximising audiences... SBS also recognises its members' connection with other places, and acknowledges identities constituted through relations of movement and longing across national boundaries. (Sinclair, Yue et. al., 2000, p. 60)

The Chinese communities, for example, are said to reflect the way in which global 'ethno-specific minoritarian sphericules' (Sinclair and Cunningham, 2000, p. 28) have emerged to replace the unitary national public sphere of media studies. These sphericules are able to exist through access to re-purposed original broadcasts, pirated, web-spread or taped, retransmitted or videoed, which enable its audiences to live in part as if they share a common space, and thereby imagine that the space is only shared with members of their own language community.

Next Door Neighbours

There has only been one major systematic study of ethnic minority audiences in Australia, carried out in 1992 (Coupe, Jakubowicz et. al., 1993). This research demonstrated the critical role for new immigrants played by the media, in the process of settlement. It also showed the processes of negotiation on which the ethnic audiences embarked when they engaged with mainstream television and media. This project, which involved sixty group discussions in the languages of origin, with some 700 respondents, explored a variety of questions about audiences and their perceptions of and responses to representation in the media, particularly television. At the time, video cassettes in minority languages were circulating widely, either brought in by visitors or rented through specific language or ethnic video shops, though cable or satellite were not available.

The overwhelming responses reflected the relatively powerless position they experienced as audiences: their communities were not involved in the production of media content, so there was little reflection of their experiences in the media. Some sense of their concerns can be seen in the sorts of responses given by participants in the research in relation to specific issues: desires for relevant media content, concerns about existing media content, and the representation of immigrant women.

While most groups were mainly concerned with a lack of news from those parts of the world of particular importance to them, an overall pattern emerged. Those familiar with media concepts of 'news-worthiness' or of the relative coverage of regions by Western news-gathering networks would not be surprised with what was described. It was felt that local, Australian, British and North American stories dominated the news, even when the issues reported were of a trivial nature. From Europe, the UK and then Western Europe got the most coverage: 'first world nations' got more coverage than developing nations; news of Asian countries was not reported in the same proportion as that of Europe and the USA; from Asia, stories were usually about Japan and Hong Kong; most stories regarding the Middle East were about Israel and news of Africa was focused on South Africa. In this sense the Australian media can be said to be Anglo-centric, concentrating on news from English-speaking countries and the ex-colonies of the British Empire that remain dominated by an Anglo population (hence more news of Canada and South Africa than India).

Participants were also very 'angry' about the extent of media coverage given to the Los Angeles riots compared to the civil war in Croatia. One participant commented that 'every radio, television news and current affairs programme had continued hourly updates. What did we get? Nothing'. Another participant commented, 'They [the news] made such a big deal about the Los Angeles fatalities and didn't bother to mention the hundreds that are tragically dying in Croatia to save their country.' (Croatian man, Victoria) One participant voiced the sentiments of the group, saying that Australian newspapers have an important obligation to their readers to provide a consistent account of changes in the political, social and economic processes in South-East Asia. Others saw common sense in the notion of more Asian-Australian news; 'The Australian people are changing - there is not much left for them with Britain' (Filipina woman, Queensland).

Twenty-nine (about half) of the groups felt that news of their region of origin was mainly negative. We can assume the groups are familiar both with the general nature of events and the way in which they are reported locally as a comparison. There were also some more general comments on the reporting of 'Third world' or 'developing' nations. News of the underdeveloped countries were usually related to famine, natural disaster, violation of human rights, and domestic troubles which are greatly sensationalized. Reporting of such events was magnified for extravagant effect on the viewing public, thus distorting the facts.

> Sometimes old footage is used to focus attention and create more emotion, with the result of humiliating the people who came from that country being reported. Seldom do the media televise or print beautiful or successful happenings. (Filipino man, New South Wales)

> Both types of programmes concentrate on conflict and conflict spots and these are the prominent items broadcast. In fact many countries are never heard about until they are involved in conflict. (Polish man, Tasmania)

> Except for SBS, there is a strong bias for reporting the good news from the western world and bad news from Asian countries. Africa and Bengal are always shown where there is famine or flood and starving children are repeatedly portrayed rather than the event itself. (Sikh youth, Queensland)

Similar problems to those above were perceived in the reporting of news and current affairs of non-Anglo people and issues in Australia. From the point of view of the participants there was often substantial bias in reporting, with insufficient coverage of issues important to many Australians. Ethnic issues and populations were negatively associated, for example with violence, conflict and unemployment, and few positive stories, emphasising achievements and the contributions of ethnic groups to Australia, provided balance.

Three quarters (48) of the groups brought up examples of news stories that associated ethnic groups with bad news, conflict or social problems. Over half (35) the groups specifically mentioned unfair media treatment of Asian migrants. Interestingly this complaint was not always raised by the 'Asian' groups surveyed, that is of the seven South-East Asian and Chinese groups surveyed only four mentioned this. The Vietnamese and Cambodian groups, who might be expected to bear the brunt of this prejudice, did not. However it is not difficult to assess the reasons for this in the light of the Cambodian group's comments which indicated they didn't want to voice dissent and thus risk being deported.

There was considerable resentment about the way migrants are represented as being a burden on Australian society and the cause of economic problems and unemployment. There was a call for more positive stories about the contribution of migrants both economically and culturally to Australia and the need for accurate information on the relative proportions of migrants and unemployed people from different countries. This was seen as needed to counter misleading implications that distorted the real facts regarding the intake from different countries (such as the 'Asian invasion' detailed below) and that migrants from certain areas were all unskilled and unemployable. Media presentation of the lives of migrants, both in their country of origin and in Australia was suggested as a way of educating Anglo-Australians and diffusing racial conflict. On immigration issues migrants are seen as desperate people coming to the lucky country with an empty suitcase, filling it up. The group said that the media is promoting the idea that migrants are to be blamed for the recession in Australia (Timorese group, Northern Territories).

A number of groups felt that the media should distinguish between refugees and other migrants, indicating that refugees were seen as the problematic migrants. They agreed that most Australians look at migrants as taking jobs away from Australians. Migrants are also seen as taking advantage of the family reunion programme because they bring into Australia older family members who add to the people that the government will be giving social security benefits to (Filipina group, South Australia).

The 35 groups which asserted that Asians were discriminated against in terms of their representation in the media all referred to news reports about Asian immigration, usually in the context of the 'boat people'. The media's representation was thought to be biased in a number of ways:

- through misrepresenting the facts: giving misinformation about the nationality or questioning how genuine individual claims for refugee status were before the facts were ascertained;
- reporting news in negatively connoted language;
- by linking stories about Asian immigration with the issues of unemployment, illegal immigration and violence;
- by inappropriately grouping people, for example: all people from vastly different cultures and language groups as 'Asian'; all Asians as refugees or 'boat people' (including sixth generation Australians of Chinese ethnicity); all refugees as 'boat people'; all 'boat people' as illegal immigrants not deserving refugee status etc.;
- by privileging comments from individuals opposed to immigration;
- by not reporting relevant information, for example the reasons for migration, the conditions in the countries migrants were coming from, the hardships endured by migrants, and direct quotes or stories of the individuals referred to in stories;
- by failing to report the positive contributions made by Asian migrants and the examples of discrimination and racial violence suffered by them.

In discussions, these issues or themes arose across all the groups. Similarly, participants said that the issue of the boat people often created hostile feelings towards Asian migrants. Some said that sympathetic views towards refugees were rarely shown by the media. Often the media, in featuring the plight of the boat people, will also highlight the high rate of unemployment and the cost of caring for these people. Others said that rumours on where they come from and questions about their legitimacy as refugees were often reported by the media before the government has gathered factual information on these cases (Tongan group, New South Wales).

It was also thought that the way the media had handled the Asian immigration issue has 'encouraged racism'. One particular incident was mentioned: an attack upon four young Asian students by a group of mostly Anglo students last year was clearly 'ignored' by the media, as there was no follow-up to the report even when police arrested the victims rather than the attackers. This was despite one witness who wrote in to 'report the facts' of what really took place (Chinese group, New South Wales).

Some respondents commented that the Australian media seldom described the lives and the problems of adjustment faced by Asian immigrants in Australia. They were of the opinion that such programmes might help the Australian public better understand the feelings of the Asian immigrants living in Australia. Three quarters of the groups thought that non-Anglo Australians were represented differently and less positively than Anglo-Australians in news and current affairs programs. (Non-Anglo) migrants, they thought, were used as scapegoats for the various economic and social ills of Australia. By highlighting negative stories and failing to cover positive stories the media gave an overall negative picture of non-Anglo Australians, so that ethnicity came to be perceived as a problem. The practice of speaking for non-Anglo groups or the choice of low-status individuals as representatives of ethnic groups exacerbated negative perceptions as well as presenting a limited and often incomplete story of important issues.

The representation of women drew considerable attention, reflecting tensions between tradition and modernity, and significant differences between men and women. Within the groups areas of contradiction or division occurred because:

• men and women within the groups felt differently, for example about the desirability of female nudity and explicit sex on the screen, or the disproportionate representation of young, slim, 'sexy' women in advertisements;

- representations of women were perceived as being very different in different types of programmes or stories: women on the news generally are more likely to be older and to possess authority, women on certain soap operas were more likely to be pretty girls, career women or mothers, while women in advertising were more likely to be either sexy or mothers.

Between groups, what were considered to be good or positive representations of women varied. Where groups were predominantly of one gender a sometimes more consistent but extreme view was expressed, for example a largely male (14 males to 4 females) group concluded that women were shown to be more important than men. Women who were clearly physically distinguishable from representations of Anglo women were more likely to be critical of limited notions of beauty. Groups where the majority of women worked mainly within the home thought the traditional role of women as mother/carer tended to be undervalued whereas others claimed that women were largely seen in this traditional role which they thought was a negative and restrictive practice: for them the presentation of women as professionals and independent working women was seen as positive. Groups who felt that the media had a strong influence on individuals were likely to see unrealistic representations of women as harmful, setting an impossible ideal for many women: they expressed concerns on what effect this might have on women's and girls' self esteem. Groups who consider the media less influential (as just entertainment) might consider fantastic representations as interesting and the use of stereotypes in advertising justifiable as a sales ploy. Differences in the reading of a range of images led to different conclusions, for example some groups felt advertising's representation of women as young/ slim/ sexy/ beautiful/ glamorous were flattering and positive, while others feel that they are limited and insulting.

Twenty-seven groups felt that representations of women in the media were generally negative. Only five groups thought media representations of women were positive, of which two were referring to only some representations. The three remaining groups felt that women were treated 'pretty well equally as men' (German, Tasmania; Finnish, Queensland; Serb, Western Australia). Twenty-seven groups categorised most representations of women as unrealistic, with 11 also finding them to be negative. No group thought that representations of women were positive and unrealistic.

Women in the media, as previously mentioned, were either shown as traditional housewives or presented in glamorous and sexy images to sell products to the public. Sometimes these images tended to exaggerate and were for the most part not realistic (Spanish-speaking group, Northern

Territories). Six groups felt that representations were realistic, with two groups making advertisements an exception to this. Comments were along the lines of it being agreed by most that women are portrayed in the media both in traditional roles as nurturers and in the role of professionals and achievers in the working environment. This was seen as a realistic and accurate representation of women's role in modern society (Hungarian group, Tasmania).

Many (38) groups were concerned with the frequent portrayal of women as 'sex objects', 'bimbos' or 'sexy'. This was the dominant representation of women in advertising, music videos and some soap operas. Such women were valued only for their appearance which was conventionally young, thin, and dressed in revealing costumes. Women in such advertisements rarely spoke or said anything intelligent or important. The young woman was a body offered for consumption by the presumed male audience. It was interesting to notice that it was the male segment of the group who took the lead in commenting on the negative way some soaps portray women: 'Women are used as sex objects. They rarely have anything interesting to say' (Maltese man, Victoria).

The opinion that women were depicted in a manner that exploited their sexuality was mentioned in relation to general programming, but also in advertising that had nothing to do with women, where they were used as a sexual object to sell the product. Opinion from both sexes viewed this practice negatively and although men tended to enjoy it, they expressed the feeling that it was not correct. As a woman's appearance is crucial in the media, the characteristics accepted as positive or beautiful become very important. The participants believed that non-Anglo women are not only rarely represented but notably absent in depictions of feminine beauty.

Respondents also noted that advertisements reflecting 'beauty' were dominated by Anglo-Australians. This was especially evident where women were concerned. Shampoos, make-up, toiletries and lingerie were all advertised by women bearing the classic Anglo features. It was agreed that this also extended into magazine advertising and that Asian, Aboriginal or Mediterranean Australians were rarely, if ever, seen in ads reflecting beauty or sophistication (Macedonian group, Western Australia). The female members of the group agreed that women in soap operas were mainly Anglos because they were attractive, but they felt that black can be beautiful too (Cocos Malay women, Western Australia).

Some women expressed concern about the images of 'beautiful' women because it often made them feel bad about themselves, therefore it was considered harmful to only show one particular image of women. This was also related to the issue of why some migrants feel bad about their dark features given that these features are hardly ever portrayed as being beautiful (Spanish-speaking group, New South Wales).

When non-Anglo women were represented it was felt that it was usually in a negative way. Eight groups particularly objected to the way in which their own or other groups of women were portrayed. In addition to the distress the Filipina women reported on being stereotyped as mail-order brides and prostitutes, a number of other groups picked up on the passive but sexually available connotations routinely accompanying 'Asian' women, with the Singapore Girl airline advertisements rating a few mentions. Most were concerned with the image Asian women were given with regards to sex and sensuality. Examples such as Channel 9's report on 'Sex' with Sophie Lee were used to illustrate this concern.   On one particular episode of 'Sex' the idea of 'Fantasy Calls' was debated. The visuals that went with the commentary repeatedly came back to a scene where an Asian girl was lying on a bed taking a fantasy call. With each repeat of the scene, the Asian girl became increasingly more provocative. In this commentary, other 'Fantasy girls' who were not of Asian descent were also shown. However, the Asian girl scenes were obviously more sensational and gained dominant exposure (Macedonian group, Western Australia).

Ethnic Audiences and Indigenous Representation

Responses to the representation of indigenous Australians provide a sense of the deeply seated cultural tensions associated with Aboriginality. Thus ethnic groups discussing their media(ted) experiences of Indigenous Australians typically argued that the media only reflected the most negative and threatening (to Whitefellas) aspects of the Aboriginal experience. Thirty-seven of the groups thought that the representation was one-sided, unfair, too harsh or thought that insufficient history or background was given to explain the position of Aborigines in Australia. If the negative aspects were shown, then the (historic) reasons for their existence must be shown as well and it must be made clear that individual behaviour cannot be made representative for the behaviour of a whole group: 'There are white alcoholics, fighters and dole bludgers too, but no station presents all whites as such' (Dutch group, South Australia). Some of the groups (12) felt that such negative representations contributed to racism and/or was damaging to the self esteem of the Aboriginal community.   Others (14) recommended that positive images should be shown to balance the negative stereotype. The view of the majority of groups could be represented by the following response: 'We never see Aborigines. We never have contact with them. I

209

find it difficult to comment.' Respondents agreed that in film they were either represented as the aloof bushman or the drunk civilian assimilated into Anglo culture. Respondents also felt that the only image they have of Aborigines is associated with crime, booze, unemployment or Land Rights disputes. Beyond this, and perhaps their special form of art, there was very little to comment about (Macedonian group, Western Australia).

Half of the members of the group were of the opinion that there was a negative stereotyping image in relation to Aborigines. They are shown as downgraded persons, who live under terrible conditions and do nothing to improve their personal and social position. Also they are associated with criminal offences. The participants did not support the attachment of negative stereotyping to Aborigines. They concluded that it is discriminating and could contribute considerably towards racism (Greek group, South Australia).

Indigenous Audiences and Cultural Production

This perspective continues as the predominant sense of Indigenous groups in the media a decade later. The tensions have probably deepened since that time, as Aboriginal communities have won some significant victories in their struggle for recognition of their rights. Two major events contributed to the increased awareness of the Indigenous/non-Indigenous relationship: the 1992 High Court Mabo decision, which destroyed the pretence of *terra nullius* (that Australia in 1770 was available for taking by settlement not conquest); and the 1996 Wik decision, which further defined the rights of Aboriginal groups to continuing native title. The Conservative government decided to seek a legislative retraction of the gains made under Wik, and Aboriginal-government relations continued to decline. In May 2000, 300,000 supporters of Aboriginal reconciliation marched across the Sydney Harbour Bridge demanding that the government apologise for past injustices, and work towards restitution of rights. Media attention to Aboriginal issues and presence has been rising, but still with limited impact outside news, current affairs, and sports programming. Discussing the critical issues for Indigenous media in Australia for a government report on broadcasting policy, Meadows has argued:

> The aim of much community-based production is to alter people's perceptions of the world and to challenge myths and stereotypes about particular cultures. The primary role of Indigenous media is to provide *a first level of service* to its communities. It is because the mainstream media have failed to serve Indigenous audience needs that much of the Indigenous

media production worldwide has emerged. Audience surveys of Native broadcast media, particularly in the Arctic, reveal that local media are the primary sources of information about Indigenous affairs for most Native people. (Meadows, 1999, p. 1)

Meadows and van Vuuren (1998) in their study of the audience for a Murri (Aboriginal) community radio station in Brisbane, Queensland, have found that apart from word of mouth, the station acted as the primary source of information about Indigenous affairs for Brisbane's Indigenous community, most of whom were regular listeners. Around 100,000 people, many non-Indigenous, tuned in to the station each week for its combination of community news, Indigenous perspectives, and music. Focus groups run as part of the survey revealed a strong sense of community 'ownership' of the station. Its country music format was identified as one of its major elements of success (Meadows, 1999).

An emphasis on community-generated media characterises Indigenous media, with a rapid increase in community radio, and the growth of a national indigenous radio network, linked by satellite. In addition, the National Indigenous Media Association of Australia (NIMAA) emerged in December 1992. By 1999 NIMAA had a membership of around 130 community media producers across all sectors - print, radio, television and video, multimedia, and film. The desire for a separate system over which Indigenous people can exert some influence and in which they can take pride of ownership reflects their exclusion from other media outlets. While there are a very few Aboriginal journalists and actors in the mainstream media - perhaps one or two with regular roles in television drama, for instance - there is an awareness in the Indigenous communities that the non-Indigenous media may speak about them, but speak neither to them nor for them.

In recognition of this problem, the Aboriginal and Torres Strait Islander Commission (ATSIC) developed a media policy that explored the interrelationships between audience and producers. The key elements of the policy included the following (Meadows, 1999):

- *Equity considerations*: Indigenous people should have the right to full access to information and entertainment available through national and regional media.
- *Cultural restoration, preservation and growth*: Broadcasting has the potential to provide communities with means to maintain languages and cultures.
- *Efficiency of communication*: Indigenous access and/or control of local radio and television can substantially improve delivery and exchange of vital information on such issues as health, child welfare, substance abuse, domestic violence, education etc.

- *Employment*: Indigenous control provides employment and training opportunities in urban and remote communities and the possibility of access to mainstream media employment.
- *Enhanced self-image*: Watching or listening to culturally and linguistically relevant programming enhances a sense of worth and community profiles.

It was clear from this interpretation of the situation that empowerment through engagement with media production would have major social benefits for Indigenous communities. The distinction between audience and producer was taken for granted in the dominant culture where producers are drawn from the culture and work within its semiotic codes and social and cultural assumptions. For Aboriginal Australians mainstream media usually represents just one more agency for their cultural extinction.

Meadows continued this perspective in his brief for ATSIC, developed in January 2000 (Meadows, 2000), where he indicated that a telephone survey revealed that 4AAA had around 60 per cent of Brisbane's Indigenous community as regular listeners who identified the station as theirs, and who used it as their primary *media* source of information about Indigenous affairs. While Indigenous people interviewed identified television as their main source of general news, 'word of mouth' was their major source of information about Indigenous community affairs. Mainstream television and radio were ranked near the bottom of a list of sources of Indigenous information. This suggests that mainstream media continue to fail to satisfy the information needs of the Brisbane Indigenous community.

Indigenous audiences seek news about themselves and access to their cultural spaces through media that they control; when they use mainstream media, they are entering a foreign place, where the terms of address are distinctively alienating, and the dependability of information about their own world is low.

Conclusion

Media audiences in Australia reflect the complex nature of the cultural and social diversity of this colonial settler society, a dominant culture descended from British colonial power. There is an uncertain disengagement from this allegiance, but the culture is still infused with the legacy of the colonial relationship. There is a diversity of popular cultures reflecting the range of peoples impelled to the country under the impacts of globalisation, a variety of racisms which infuse all cross-cultural relationships, and Indigenous peoples who are the vibrant remnants of pre-existing nations. For many of these audiences, particularly those who are 'subaltern' to the dominant culture, their communication rights are truncated, and their avenues for self-expression heavily constrained by the controllers of access to the means of media production.

In recent years new technologies and greater diversity have opened up the opportunities for minority audiences to find avenues for their cultural needs. In pursuing these avenues the unifying pressures of the mainly monocultural national media (and their reinforcement of a hierarchy of cultural power) have been undermined, creating two countervailing flows of communication. The increasingly diasporic nature of cultural minorities is reflected in the international orientation of communities, and their increasing capacity (though not necessarily desire) to see their primary linkages as other globally dispersed segments of their ethnic group. The potential for intra-communal communication also empowers communities in their locality to orient themselves towards local political and social issues, and recognise the value of political action across ethnic boundaries to defend the overarching interests of cultural minorities. For instance, some of the most committed supporters of Aboriginal reconciliation are immigrants from other post-colonial societies (such as India or Sri Lanka), who recognise the damage wrought by the past history of British imperialism and its White neo-colonial descendants.

The Australian dreaming may be increasingly fragmented, while the white fantasies and nightmares have become tinged with many hues. The national imaginary has been invaded by competing narratives; audiences want to see their questions and issues dealt with in the rituals of the society, and those audiences are increasingly frustrated by their exclusion or marginalisation.

References

Appleton, G. (1995), 'Television and the Multicultural Audience', conference paper, Communications Law Centre, Sydney.

Communications Law Centre (1992), *The representation of non-English Speaking Background People in Australian Television Drama*, Communications Law Centre, Sydney.

Coupe, B., Jakubowicz, A. and Randall, L. (1993), *Next Door Neighbours: a report for the Office of Multicultural Affairs on ethnic group discussions of the Australian media*, Australian Govt. Pub. Service, Canberra.

Cunningham, S. and Sinclair, J. (eds) (2000), *Floating Lives. The Media and Asian Diasporas*, University of Queensland Press, Brisbane.

Hage, G. (1998), *White Nation*, Pluto, Sydney.

Hage, G. and Couch, R. (eds) (1999), *The Future of Australian Multiculturalism*, Research Institute for Humanities and Social Sciences, University of Sydney, Sydney.

Hodge, B. and Kress, G. (1988), *Social Semiotics*, Polity Press, Cambridge.

Hodge, B. and Mishra, V. (1991), *Dark side of the dream: Australian literature and the postcolonial mind*, Allen & Unwin, Sydney.

Hodge, R. and Tripp, D. (1986), *Children and television: a semiotic approach*, Polity Press, Cambridge.

Jakubowicz, A. (1999), *Making multicultural Australia: a multimedia documentary*, Board of Studies NSW, Sydney.

Kress, G. and van Leeuwen, T. (1990), *Reading images*, Deakin University Press, Geelong, Victoria.

Kymlicka, W. (1996), 'Three Forms of Group-Differentiated Citizenship in Canada', in. S. Benhabib (ed.) *Democracy and Difference: contesting the boundaries of the political*, Princeton University Press, Princeton, pp. 153-170.

May, H., Flew, T. and Spurgeon, C. (2000), *Report on Casting in Australian Commercial Television Drama*, QUT, Brisbane.

Meadows, M. (1999), *Indigenous Media in Australia: A background paper*, Australian Key Centre for Cultural and Media Policy, Brisbane.

-- (2000), *Urban Indigenous media audiences in Australia*, Australian Key Centre for Cultural and Media Policy, Brisbane.

Meadows, M. and van Vuuren, K. (1998), 'Seeking an audience: Indigenous people, the media and cultural resource management', *Southern Review* 31(1): pp. 96-107.

Newspoll (1991), *Media and Immigrant Settlement*, Bureau of Immigration and Population Research, Melbourne.

Nightingale, V. (1997), 'Media Audiences', in S. Cunningham and G. Turner (eds) *The Media in Australia: Industries, Texts, Audiences*, Allen and Unwin, Sydney, pp. 281-295.

Nugent, S., Loncar, M. and Aisbett, K. (1993), *The People We See on TV: Cultural Diversity on Television*, Australian Broadcasting Authority, Sydney.

Perera, S. (1998), 'The level playing field: Hansonism, globalisation, racism', *Race and Class*, 40(2-3), pp. 199-208.

Productivity Commission (2000), *Inquiry into Broadcasting: Final Report*, Productivity Commission, Canberra.

Sinclair, J. and Cunningham, S. (2000), 'Diasporas and the Media', in S. Cunningham and J. Sinclair (eds) *Floating Lives: the Media and Asian Diasporas*, University of Queensland Press, Brisbane, pp. 35-90.

Sinclair, J., Yue, A., Hawkins, G., Gay, K.P. and Fox, J. (2000), 'Chinese Cosmopolitanism and Media Use', in S. Cunningham and J. Sinclair (eds) *Floating Lives: the Media and Asian Diasporas*, University of Queensland Press, Brisbane, pp. 35-90.

Tran, A. T. (1998), 'SBS-Radio & Vietnamese language program', *Integration: The Magazine for Multicultural and Vietnamese Issues* (14), pp. 88-97.

Tsiolkas, C. (1995), *Loaded*, Vintage, Sydney.

Tulloch, J. (1990), *Television drama: agency, audience, and myth*, Routledge, London.

Tulloch, J. and Moran, A. (1986), *A Country Practice: quality soap*, Currency Press, Sydney.

Tulloch, J. and Turner, G. (eds) (1989), *Australian television: programs, pleasures and politics*, Allen & Unwin, Sydney.

Index